Techno Politics in Pr[...]
Campaigning

Techno Politics in Presidential Campaigning: New Voices, New Technologies, and New Voters examines how new media and new technologies gave voice to candidates and voters in one of the most compelling presidential campaigns in recent history. The 2008 U.S. presidential campaign saw politicians utilizing all types of new media—Facebook, MySpace, YouTube, Twitter, e-mail, and cell phone texting—to reach voters of all ages, ethnicities, socio-economic backgrounds, and sexual orientations. This volume examines the use of these media and considers the effectiveness of reaching voters through these channels. It explores not only the use of new media and technologies but also the role these tactics played in attracting new voters and communicating with the electorate during the 2008 presidential debates. Chapters focus on how the technologies were used by candidates, the press, and voters.

Offering a detailed perspective on the unprecedented and influential role of media technology in political campaigning, this volume provides key insights for scholars, researchers, and students in political communication and political science.

John Allen Hendricks is Director of the Division of Communication and Contemporary Culture, and Professor of Communication at Stephen F. Austin State University. He is the co-editor of a book titled *Communicator-in-Chief* and he has published numerous journal articles and book chapters on political communication.

Lynda Lee Kaid is Professor of Telecommunication and Research Foundation Professor at the University of Florida. A Fulbright Scholar, she has also done work on political television in several European, Asian, and Latin American countries and is the author/editor of more than 25 books on political advertising and political communication.

Techno Politics in Presidential Campaigning

New Voices, New Technologies, and New Voters

Edited by

John Allen Hendricks
and
Lynda Lee Kaid

Routledge
Taylor & Francis Group

NEW YORK AND LONDON

First published 2011
by Routledge
270 Madison Avenue, New York, NY 10016

Simultaneously published in the UK
by Routledge
2 Park Square, Milton Park, Abingdon, Oxon OX14 4RN

Routledge is an imprint of the Taylor & Francis Group, an informa business

Typeset in Sabon and Gill Sans by
Florence Production Ltd, Stoodleigh, Devon
Printed and bound in the United States of America on acid-free paper by
Walsworth Publishing Company, Marceline, MO

Library of Congress Cataloging in Publication Data
Techno politics in presidential campaigning: new voices, new technologies,
and new voters/edited by John Allen Hendricks and Lynda Lee Kaid.
    p. cm.
    11. Presidents – United States – Election – 2008. 2. Political campaigns –
Technological innovations – United States. 3. Communication in politics –
Technological innovations – United States. 4. Mass media – Political
aspects – United States. 5. Digital media – Political aspects – United
States. I. Hendricks, John Allen. II. Kaid, Lynda Lee.
JK5262008 T43 2010
324.973'0931–dc22   2010024795

ISBN13: 978–0–415–87978–1 (hbk)
ISBN13: 978–0–415–87979–8 (pbk)
ISBN13: 978–0–203–85126–5 (ebk)

As always, because of their continued love and support,
my achievements are dedicated to Stacy, Abby, and Haydyn.
J.A.H.

To Clifford A. Jones.
L.L.K.

Contents

Figures

Tables

Abbreviations

AEJMC   Association for Education in Journalism and Mass Communication
ANOVA   Analysis of variance
APSE   American Political Science Association
BEA   Broadcast Education Association
CIRCLE   Centre for Information and Research on Civic Learning and Engagement
GLM   General Linear Model
OBEA   Oklahoma Broadcast Education Association
OLS   Ordinary least squares
PIE   Political information efficacy
SSCA   Southern States Communication Association

Preface

Techno Politics in Presidential Campaigning: New Voices, New Technologies, and New Voters examines how new media and new technologies gave voice to new candidates and new voters in one of the most important presidential elections in U.S. history. The precedent-setting 2008 election established a model for how future contenders for the White House must communicate with the electorate to remain competitive. Presidential campaigns must now effectively use new media technologies encompassing not only the interface of television, video, and computers but also Web sites, blogs, Twitter, social networking sites like *Facebook* and *MySpace*, *YouTube* channels, Twitter accounts, e-mail, podcasting, RSS feeds, and cell phone texting. During the 2008 campaign, politicians utilized every available new media technology to reach voters of all ages, ethnicities, socio-economic backgrounds, and sexual orientations, inspiring and motivating Americans to participate in the democratic process.

The twenty-first century is a particularly challenging era for politicians to communicate effectively with voters and constituents. A shift *away from* usage of traditional media such as terrestrial television, radio, and newspapers is occurring. This shift is accompanied by migration *toward* new technological advancements that allow for immediate access to information. Traditional television conduits have been supplanted by 24-hour cable news channels, and printed newspapers are now frequently accessed electronically. The twenty-first century audience is no longer a passive audience but active consumers who deliberately seek out specific information and interact directly with it and with those who sponsor and produce it. Of course, the Internet, or the World Wide Web, has spurred the development of an impressive array of technologies that allow and encourage twenty-first century voters to post thoughts on political issues, invite feedback through blogs, make and distribute their own political videos on *YouTube*, or connect with friends and associates through social networking sites like *Facebook* and *MySpace*. Barack Obama and his presidential campaign team were particularly adept at using these new technologies, and his victory in November has been attributed to their impressive skills with these technologies.

Communication in 2008 was also affected by the historic emergence of new voices, represented by notable candidacies of female and minority presidential contenders. For the first time, American voters had the opportunity to consider a diverse assortment of candidates from both political parties. Hillary Rodham Clinton became the first former First Lady to seek her own place behind the desk in the Oval Office. Hispanic voters saw their interests visibly represented by the candidacy of New Mexico governor Bill Richardson. The voices of African-Americans were certainly magnified by the success of Barack Obama in obtaining, first, the Democratic Party nomination and then in winning the ultimate prize, the presidency. Republicans gave voice to the substantial older American population when they nominated war hero John McCain. Republicans also chose their first female vice-presidential candidate, Alaska governor Sarah Palin, a new voice that has continued to resonate with many segments of the American population.

New voters, particularly young voters, were energized in 2008 by these new voices and by the new technologies that encouraged their active participation in politics. These new voters represent the largest and most ethnically diverse generation in American history, a seismic generational shift that is likely to impact American politics longitudinally for quite some time. Referred to as the Millennial Generation, the 18-to-29 year olds were born between the years of 1982 and 2003. Not only are "Millennials" addicted to all of the new media technologies that cell phones and the Internet offer, but they have proven to be a civically engaged generation that actually votes and participates in the political process. In the 2008 presidential election, more than 50 percent of this demographic voted. This emerging generation of new voters and multicultural voices is indeed likely to change the American political landscape.

This book capitalizes on what the convergence of these factors produced, examining the effects of the convergence of these new voices, new technologies, and new voters in the 2008 campaign. Through an analysis of these factors, this book considers (1) voter learning during presidential campaigns; (2) specific types of campaign messages distributed via new media technologies; (3) the interaction of the electorate both among peers and also between the candidates and the electorate; (4) representations of the candidates distributed through new media technologies; as well as (5) the emergence of a new type of voter that expects and requires a very different communication strategy than traditional voters have required of candidates in the past.

Some of the research in this book was presented at the Broadcast Education Association's 2009 convention in Las Vegas. It was the topic of BEA's Research Symposium, titled *Techno Politics: New Voices, New Technologies, New Voters.*

This book will have wide appeal to students and scholars in communication, information technology, and political science. Politicians, media professionals, political observers, and new technology consumers will also find useful clues for understanding the role of new technologies in communicating with new voters. Every reader will gain insight into the election of the first African-American president in one of the most remarkable presidential campaigns in U.S. history.

Acknowledgments

The editors wish to thank each contributor to this book. Without their diligent work and enthusiasm for better understanding political communication, this book would not have come to fruition. Each editor is fortunate to have the support and understanding of academic institutions that value and promote the importance of scholarly and intellectual pursuits such as this project. Thus, the editors wish to express appreciation to Stephen F. Austin State University and the University of Florida. Some of the research in this book was presented at the Broadcast Education Association's 2009 convention in Las Vegas. It was the topic of BEA's Research Symposium, titled: *Techno Politics: New Technologies, New Voices, New Voters.* The editors wish to thank Linda Bathgate, acquisitions editor at Routledge/Taylor & Francis, for her support of this project. Finally, the editors wish to express appreciation for the continued support of their spouses, Dr. Stacy Nason Hendricks and Dr. Clifford A. Jones.

About the Editors

John Allen Hendricks (Ph.D., University of Southern Mississippi) is Director of the Division of Communication and Contemporary Culture, and Professor of Communication at Stephen F. Austin State University in Nacogdoches, Texas. Dr. Hendricks edited the books *Communicator-in-Chief: How Barack Obama Used New Media Technology to Win the White House* (Lexington Books, 2010) and *The Twenty-First-Century Media Industry: Economic and Managerial Implications in the Age of New Media*. His research has been published as scholarly articles and chapters in *21st Century Communication: A Reference Handbook; The Business of Entertainment: Movies, Music, and Television; American Journalism: History, Principles, Practices; Feedback; Journal of Radio and Audio Media; Southwestern Mass Communication Journal; Communications and the Law*; and, numerous other publication outlets. He is editor of "Studies in New Media" for Lexington Books in Lanham, Maryland.

Dr. Hendricks currently serves as a member of the Board of Directors of the Broadcast Education Association (BEA) representing District 5. He is past President of the Oklahoma Broadcast Education Association (OBEA) and is a former *ex-officio* member of the Board of Directors of the Oklahoma Association of Broadcasters (OAB). He is a former Chair of both the Southern States Communication Association's (SSCA) Political Communication and Mass Communication divisions.

Lynda Lee Kaid (Ph.D., Southern Illinois University) is Professor of Telecommunication and Research Foundation Professor at the University of Florida where she specializes in political communication. A three-time Fulbright Scholar, she has also done work on political television in several European, Asian, and Latin American countries.

Dr. Kaid is the author/editor of more than 25 books, including *The Encyclopedia of Political Communication, The Handbook of Political Communication Research, Videostyle in Presidential Campaigns,* and *Political Advertising in Western Democracies*. She has written over 150 journal articles and book chapters on various aspects of political communication and received over $2 million in external grant funds for her research efforts, including support from the U.S. Department of Commerce, the U.S. Department of Education, the National Endowment for the Humanities, the Election Assistance Commission, and the National Science Foundation.

Dr. Kaid is a former Chair of the Political Communication Divisions of the International Communication Association and the National Communication Association and has served in leadership roles the American Political Science Association (APSE) and the Association for Education in Journalism and Mass Communication (AEJMC).

About the Contributors

Eisa Al Nashmi (M.A., University of Florida) is a Doctoral Student at the University of Florida's College of Journalism and Communication. His research interests include new media and political communication in the Middle East. He is currently a sponsored student from Kuwait University where he is expected to teach at the university's journalism department upon his completion of his doctorate. His study, "Internet Political Discussions in the Arab World: A Look at Online Forums from Kuwait, Saudi Arabia, Egypt and Jordan," recently got accepted by the *International Communication Gazette*.

Monica Ancu (Ph.D., University of Florida) is a Social Science Researcher investigating the role and use of the Internet in political campaigns. Primarily, her research focuses on how political candidates use online social networks, blogs, and Web sites for political campaigning. She also studies online political advertising, and how Internet communication affects voters' political attitudes, behavior, and perceptions of candidates. Dr. Ancu's research on the 2004 and 2008 U.S. presidential elections was published in *Journalism Studies*, *American Behavioral Scientist*, *Journal of Broadcast and Electronic Media*, as well as in several books. Dr. Ancu teaches visual communication, Web design, online journalism and new media classes in the Journalism and Media Studies Department at University of South Florida, St. Petersburg.

Mary C. Banwart (Ph.D., University of Oklahoma) is an Associate Professor in the Department of Communication Studies at the University of Kansas. Her research focuses on political campaign communication and the influence of gender in political campaigns. Dr. Banwart has authored book chapters and journal articles examining the strategic use of advertising in political campaigns, gendered uses of communication on campaign Web sites, the gender gap, and news coverage in mixed-gender races. She co-authored the book, *Gender and Political Candidate Communication: VideoStyle, WebStyle, and NewsStyle*. Dr. Banwart coordinates the Leadership Studies Minor at the University of Kansas, and teaches undergraduate and graduate courses in political communication as well as leadership and communication.

Pamela Jo Brubaker (M.A., Brigham Young University) is a Doctoral Student in the College of Communications at The Pennsylvania State University. Her research interests focus on strategic communications and media effects. Specifically, she examines how new media technologies are being used to facilitate political discourse, public relations campaigns, and social relationships. She has seven years of professional public relations experience in the high-tech industry. She has taught a variety of public relations and public-speaking courses at Brigham Young University, Utah Valley University, and The Pennsylvania State University.

Sindy Chapa (M.B.A., University of Saint Thomas) is Assistant Professor of Advertising and the Associate Director of the Center for the Study of Latino Media and Markets at the School of Journalism and Mass Communication at Texas State University, San Marcos. Chapa has been conducting research in several countries since 2001. Her interest in cross-cultural research has grown out of her experience in Mexico, China, Cuba, Peru, and Chile where she has conducted several studies on advertising, online and video-game consumption, and consumer decision-making. Her work has been published in several journals, including the *Journal of International Consumer Marketing*; *Consumption, Markets and Culture*; *Journal of Customer Behaviour*; *Journal of Interactive Advertising*; and *International Journal of Business Disciplines*. Chapa has also co-authored book chapters in several textbooks.

David A. Dulio (Ph.D., American University) is Associate Professor of Political Science at Oakland University where he teaches courses on campaigns and elections, Congress, political parties, interest groups, and other areas of American politics generally. Dulio has published seven books, including *Cases in Congressional Campaigns: Incumbents Playing Defense in 2008* (with Randall E. Adkins, Routledge 2010), *Vital Signs: Perspectives on the Health of American Campaigning* (with Candice J. Nelson, Brookings Institution Press 2005), and *For Better or Worse? How Professional Political Consultants are Changing Elections in the United States* (SUNY Press 2004). He has written several articles and book chapters on subjects ranging from the role of professional consultants in U.S. elections to campaign finance. During 2001–2002, Dulio served as an American Political Science Congressional Fellow on Capitol Hill working in the U.S. House of Representatives Republican Conference for former U.S. Rep. J.C. Watts, Jr. (R-OK).

Juliana Fernandes (M.A., University of Florida) is a Doctoral Candidate in the College of Journalism and Mass Communications at the University of Florida. Her research interests include affective impact of advertising, effects of time perspective on voting behavior, and international political communication. She has published several book chapters, as well as an article in the *American Behavioral Scientist*.

Timothy K. F. Fung (M.Phil., Hong Kong Baptist University) is a Doctoral Candidate in the School of Journalism and Mass Communication at the University of Wisconsin, Madison. His research interests include social impact of new media, political communication and risk communication. His work has appeared in *Mass Communication & Society*, *New Media & Society*, *Journal of Electronic Commerce Research*, and *Journal of Educational Computing Research*.

Gary Hanson (M.A., Kent State University) is an Associate Professor in the School of Journalism and Mass Communication at Kent State University. His research and publishing interests include the impact of changes in the media delivery system and journalism accuracy. Prior to joining the academy, Hanson spent 25 years as a local television news executive. He is a past national chairman of the Radio Television News Directors Association.

Paul Haridakis (Ph.D., Kent State University) is Associate Professor of Communication Studies at Kent State University. Dr. Haridakis' research is cross-disciplinary, appearing in various journals and books published in the fields of law, mass communication, political science, psychology, and justice studies (e.g., *Communication Yearbook*; *Free Speech Yearbook*; and *Media Psychology*; *Mass Communication & Society*; *Communication Law & Policy*; *Temple Political & Civil Rights Law Review*; *Saint Louis University Public Law Review*; *Journal of Broadcasting & Electronic Media*; *Newspaper Research Journal*; *Communication Quarterly*; *Journal of Mass Media Ethics*). He is a co-author of *Research Methods: Strategies and Sources* (7th ed.). He is a co-editor of *War and the Media: Essays on News Reporting, Propaganda and Popular Culture* (McFarland & Co.) and *Sports Mania: Essays on Fandom and the Media in the 21st Century* (McFarland & Co.).

Amy E. Jasperson (Ph.D., University of Minnesota) is Associate Professor of Political Science at the University of Texas at San Antonio. Dr. Jasperson's research interests center on American politics and political communication and her research has been published in a range of journals including *Political Communication*; *Polity*; *International Journal of Public Opinion Research*; *Journal of Advertising*; *American Behavioral Scientist*; *American University Journal of Gender, Social*

Policy and the Law; and the *Journal of Political Marketing.* Her work also appears in *Campaigns and Political Marketing; Lights, Camera, Campaign!; Media, Politics, and Political Advertising; Framing Terrorism: The News Media, the Government and the Public;* and *Congressional Quarterly's Guide to Political Campaigns in America.* During the 109th Congress, Dr. Jasperson served as an APSA Congressional Fellow working on media and telecommunications issues.

Ji Young Kim (M.S., Syracuse University) is a Doctoral Student at the University of Florida majoring in Public Relations. Prior to joining the University of Florida, she earned her Master's degree in New Media from Syracuse University and she was enrolled in the Public Diplomacy program between 2007 and 2008 at the same university. She received her undergraduate degree in Business Administration (second major in Mass Communications) from Sogang University in Korea. Kim's research interest includes international and government public relations, and the use of interactive media in the public relations practice.

Rita Kirk (Ph.D., University of Missouri) is Professor of Public Affairs at Southern Methodist University. Dr. Kirk is an Althsuler Distinguished Teaching Professor, and is a Meadows Distinguished Professor. Dr. Kirk is the author of three award-winning books and articles, including *Political Empiricism: Communications Strategies in State and Regional Elections; Hate Speech,* a book analyzing implications for hate discourse in public communication, with co-editor David Slayden; and *Solo Acts: The Death of Discourse in a Wired World.* Dr. Kirk has published numerous articles, many of them focusing on the use and impact of emerging technology on campaign communication. Her 2005 article on blogs in campaign communication for *American Behavioral Scientist* was one of the journal's most widely read pieces. Specializing in communication strategy, she has more than 25 years of experience as a strategist for city council, mayoral, state, U.S. Representative, and gubernatorial races. In addition to her political consulting, Dr. Kirk serves as a communications consultant to several national and multinational corporations on public policy matters.

Mitchell S. McKinney (Ph.D., University of Kansas) is Associate Professor in the Department of Communication at the University of Missouri. His research interests include presidential debates, political campaigns, media and politics, and presidential rhetoric.
Dr. McKinney is the co-author/editor of four books, including *The 1992 Presidential Debates in Focus* (with Diana B. Carlin); *Civic Dialogue in the 1996 Presidential Campaign* (with Lynda Lee Kaid & John C. Tedesco); and two edited volumes of political communication studies, including *The Millennium Election: Communication in the 2000 Campaign,* and *Communicating Politics: Engaging the Public in*

Democratic Life. His research appears in major communication, journalism, and political science journals, including *Journal of Communication*; *Communication Monographs*; *Communication Studies*; *Journalism Studies*; and *American Behavioral Scientist*.

Dr. McKinney has served as a staff member in the U.S. Senate and at the White House. He has served as a consultant/adviser to C-SPAN, the U.S. Commission on Presidential Debates, and the Korean government. Dr. McKinney has provided expert political commentary for such national media as the *New York Times*, *USA Today*, CNN, and NPR.

Maridith Dunton Miles (M.A., University of Florida) is a Doctoral Student in Mass Communication at the University of Florida. Her research interests include public diplomacy, political campaigning, gender roles in political communication, and media political bias.

David L. Painter (M.A., University of West Florida) is a Telecommunications Instructor and Doctoral Student in the College of Journalism and Mass Communications at the University of Florida. His research interest is Political Communication. His research has been published in the *American Behavioral Scientist* and the *Encyclopedia of Journalism*. He has also presented research papers at the American Political Science Association and Broadcast Education Association national conferences.

Dan Schill (Ph.D., University of Kansas) is an Assistant Professor in Corporate Communication and Public Affairs at Southern Methodist University. His research examines the strategies and tactics political figures use to manage the news media and how voters respond. Dr. Schill is the author of the book, *Stagecraft and Statecraft: Advance and Media Events in Political Communication*. He has received top-paper awards from the Political Communication Divisions of the International Communication Association, National Communication Association, and the Central States Communication Association. Dr. Schill is a sought-after expert on political communication and his research and analysis has appeared in the *Wall Street Journal*, *Chicago Tribune*, CNN, ABC News, *Dallas Morning News*, *Fort Worth Star Telegram*, *The American Prospect*, and other local and regional media outlets.

Evan Serge (M.A., Virginia Tech) is a Doctoral Student at the University of Florida. His research interests include new communication technology, advertising, and political communication.

Kendall Sharp (B.A., University of Florida) will complete her Master's degree in publishing from Pace University in 2010. Her research interests include political communications and campaigning, educational book publishing, children's book publishing, electronic publishing, and a wide variety of marketing and public relations research. Her writing has appeared in the *Independent Florida Alligator* and *The Gainesville Sun*. Currently, Sharp works as a Marketing and Editorial Assistant at Maupin House Publishing, Inc. in Gainesville, Florida.

Jesper Strömbäck (Ph.D., Stockholm University) is Lubbe Nordström Professor and Chair in Journalism as well as Professor in Media and Communication at Mid Sweden University, Sundsvall, Sweden. He is also Research Director at the Centre for Political Communication Research at Mid Sweden University. Dr. Strömbäck's research focuses on comparative political communication, election news coverage, political public relations, marketing and campaigning, and the mediatization of politics. He has published more than 25 scholarly articles on political communication, in addition to about 15 books on the same subjects. Dr. Strömbäck's most recent books are: *The Handbook of Election News Coverage Around the World* (co-edited with Lynda Lee Kaid, 2008); *Communicating Politics: Political Communication in the Nordic Countries* (co-edited with Toril Aalberg and Mark Ørsten, 2008); and *Global Political Marketing* (co-edited with Jennifer Lees-Marshment and Chris Rudd, 2009).

Kjerstin Thorson (M.A., University of Missouri) is a Doctoral Student at the University of Wisconsin-Madison. Her research explores the effects of the changing media environment on political engagement and the formation and maintenance of political identity. She also explores the impact of new media on evaluations of traditional news media. Recent research projects have investigated the effects of blog commentary on the credibility of online journalism; the contributions of media use in shifting conceptions of citizenship among young adults; the role of pro-social news media messages in activating citizen conceptions of self; and the effects of exposure to uncivil political communication on emotions, partisan social identity, and political participation. Her work has been published in *Mass Communication and Society*, *Journal of Computer Mediated Communication*, and *Journal of Interactive Advertising*. Thorson worked for several years in public relations and corporate communications.

Terri L. Towner (Ph.D., Purdue University) is an Assistant Professor in the Department of Political Science at Oakland University in Michigan. Towner's teaching and research focus is on American politics. Specifically, Dr. Towner is interested in public opinion, media coverage of elections and political institutions, the politics of race and class, and quantitative methods. Dr. Towner's research has been published as chapters and journal articles in outlets such as the *Routledge Handbook of Political Management*, *Government and Politics in Florida*, and the *Judicature*. She is currently involved in research on the link between the economy and Iraq War attitudes, and trust in elected officials and the political system. Towner is also presently engaged in research examining the pedagogical value of social networks.

Emily Vraga (M.A., University of Wisconsin-Madison) is a Doctoral Student in the School of Journalism and Mass Communication at the University of Wisconsin-Madison. Her research focuses on how individual predispositions and motivations influence the processing of news and political content, particularly in the realm of new media content. Specifically, she studies how individuals respond to messages that are incongruent with or attack their party identification. Research projects have included the effects of refutations on political identification on political information processing, the influence of motivations on source identification for intermingled new media messages, and whether the effects of frames are centered in the change in perspective or in the attendant facts. Her research has been published in *Political Communication* and *Mass Communication and Society*.

Andrew Paul Williams (Ph.D., University of Florida) is an Independent Researcher who taught communications classes at Virginia Tech, University of Florida, and Flagler College. His research focuses on political communication and new and emerging technologies, which is primarily guided by framing theory and the concept of interactivity. Dr. Williams has been recognized for his outstanding teaching by the International Communication Association (ICA) and has received top-paper awards at the annual conferences of the Broadcast Education Association (BEA) and the International Communication Association (ICA). His work has been published in journals such as *American Behavior Scientist, Harvard International Journal of Press/Politics, Journalism Studies, Mass Communication and Society*, and *Journal of International Business Disciplines* and as book chapters. He is the co-editor of the book, *The Internet Election: Perspectives of the Web in Campaign 2004*. Dr. Williams has worked as a print news reporter, in public relations and marketing, and as a communication consultant.

Zheng Xiang (M.S., Iowa State University) is a Doctoral Student in the College of Journalism and Communication at the University of Florida with specialization in political communication and international communication. Her research interests center on new media in China, risk communication, public diplomacy and political communication. Xiang has presented papers at the Association for Education in Journalism and Mass Communication (AEJMC) and the Broadcast Education Association (BEA).

Hyun Jung Yun (Ph.D., University of Florida) is an Assistant Professor in the Department of Political Science at Texas State University. She earned two doctoral degrees in two different disciplines, one in Political

Science and the other in Journalism and Communication, from the University of Florida. Dr. Yun's research is dedicated to interdisciplinary approaches across mass communication, public opinion, media effects, geopolitics and applied methodology, utilizing theory-oriented political science at the macro level of state, nation, and media as well as application-oriented communication studies at the micro level of the individual focusing on persuasion, media advocacy, political perception, political communication process, and policy attitudes. Dr. Yun's publications appear in several leading journals, such as *American Behavioral Scientist*, *Journalism Studies*, and *The American Review of Politics*.

Section I

New Technologies

Chapter 1

Shaping the New Presidential Campaign

John Allen Hendricks and Lynda Lee Kaid

The 2008 presidential campaign was one of the most remarkable in this nation's history due to a confluence of several intriguing precedents that occurred during the battle for the White House. First, the 2008 campaign offered the electorate the most diverse slate of candidates ever fielded in U.S. history, an impressive array of new voices. These new voices included an African-American candidate who obtained the Democratic Party's nomination and eventually the presidency; a former First Lady; the oldest individual ever to vie for the presidency; and a female governor who became the Republican vice presidential candidate. These new voices embraced enthusiastically the new technologies that have gained traction in the interconnected nation the U.S. has become. From e-mail and Web sites to blogs and computerized message response systems, 2008 campaigns welcomed the plethora of new technologies that broadened the means of communicating and interacting with voters and helped candidates raise staggering amounts of money to fund their race for the ultimate prize. These new voices, armed with new technologies, attracted and persuaded a precedent-setting number of new voters to participate in the electoral process. The chapters in this volume explore the impact of these new voices, new technologies, and new voters in 2008.

New Voices and New Technologies in 2008

Barack Obama was not the first African-American to run for president of the United States, but he was the first to gain his party's nomination and to achieve electoral success. Obama was not the first presidential candidate to use the Internet and related forms of new technologies, but his campaign adopted a wide array of technologies and used them effectively to communicate with both traditional and new voters. Effective political communication is important because, as Denton and Kuypers (2008) noted, ". . . politics and communication go hand in hand because they are parts of human nature" (p. xi). On a basic level, the new media technologies and the Internet were used in 2008 to communicate candidate policy positions and for fundraising purposes. However, it was also used much more extensively and strategically than in any prior presidential campaign.

The Internet gained popularity among the American population during the mid-1990s. In 1992, it was the Bill Clinton presidential campaign that first used the Internet to communicate with the electorate. The Clinton campaign created a Web site that was used to post candidate biographies, candidate positions on policies, and the full text of speeches. However, as Davis (1999) notes, ". . . Internet use was far smaller then, and there was little notice from journalists or the public, few of whom would have been connected at the time" (p. 87). In 1996, the Clinton campaign raised approximately $10,000 through the Internet, a pittance when compared to the $2.7 million raised by Al Gore's campaign in 2000 or the $20 million garnered by Howard Dean's campaign in 2004 (Trent & Friedenberg, 2008). Remarkably, the Obama campaign used the Internet to raise a staggering half a billion dollars. Vargas (2008) suggests that the Obama campaign's use of the Internet ushered ". . . in a new digital era in presidential fundraising" (para. 1). Moreover, Trent and Friedenberg (2008) assert, "clearly, the Internet has become a key weapon in the arsenal of political fundraisers" (p. 406). In Chapter 4 of this volume, Williams and Serge elaborate on the types and functions of messages used by both Obama and McCain in their e-mail communications with voters, and they identify requests for financial contributions as a major theme of these messages.

Television remained an important avenue for candidate – voter communication in 2008. When new voice Sarah Palin was chosen as the Republican vice-presidential nominee, both CNN and Fox News quickly produced featured documentaries on the Alaska governor. In Chapter 11 Miles, Kaid, and Sharp provide evidence that viewing both documentaries had identifiable, positive effects on evaluations of Palin. However, CNN viewers learned more about Palin's issue positions, but viewers of both cable channels learned more about her personal qualities than about issues. In Chapter 10 Mitchell McKinney and Mary Banwart illustrate that Palin was also successful in affirming her issue competency when she and Democratic nominee Joe Biden faced off in the vice-presidential debate. Palin used the televised debate to improve confidence in her understanding of military and economic issues, succeeding in raising her evaluation levels among independent voters.

Although television remained the primary source for election news and information during the 2008 election, a Pew Research Center study (2008) found that 33 percent of Americans used the Internet to get their election news, compared to only 10 percent in 2004. The study also determined that 18 to 29 year olds are three times more likely to use the Internet as their primary source for campaign information than are older Americans, confirming that "Among the youngest cohort (age 18–29), TV has lost significant ground to the internet" (para. 3).

Post-election surveys confirmed that more than half of the nation's adult population were online users of political information (Smith, 2009). Interestingly, McCain supporters were more likely to be Internet users than Obama supporters, perhaps due to their higher education levels (Smith, 2009). However, the Pew Research Center found that Obama supporters were more likely to use the Internet in an active manner such as exchanging political information by posting comments on blogs or social networking sites such as Facebook or MySpace and sending/receiving e-mails and text messages with political content than McCain supporters (Smith, 2009). For example, only 38 percent of McCain supporters received e-mails from the candidate compared to 48 percent of Obama supporters (Smith, 2009). Seventeen percent of Obama supporters got text messages from the candidate or Democratic Party compared to only 7 percent of McCain supporters (Smith, 2009). In Chapter 2, Monica Ancu illustrates that Obama also used Twitter more frequently than McCain, but he used this technology as a one-way communication channel and engaged in no interactive encounters with supporters.

In the Pew Research Center study, it was verified that the Internet played a dominant role for young voters engaged in the 2008 presidential campaign. More than half of online users under the age of 35 engaged in "participatory" online activities that included ". . . the use of social media platforms such as online social networks, video sharing sites, blogs and status update services such as Twitter" (Smith, 2009, p. 13). Further, the study found that e-mail was the preferred means of communicating political information followed by text messaging and instant messaging. Smith (2009) found that "40% of all adults engaged in some type of e-mail-based political communication in 2008, with one in ten doing so on a daily basis" (p. 28). In the 2008 campaign, peer-to-peer Internet technologies were the preferred means of distributing and receiving political information. In Chapter 5, Paul Haridakis and Gary Hanson compare older and younger voters' use of social networking technologies for political information seeking. In Chapter 6, Timothy Fung, Emily Vraga, and Kjerstin Thorson examine attack strategies used in blogs, concluding that the use of incivility when making political attacks may mean that "greater citizen participation in the debate may ultimately prove detrimental to a more deliberative public sphere online." In their study, citizens exposed to attacking statements on blogs that used incivility were more likely to react with anger and other negative emotions.

Although television remains a major player in distribution of political information and advertising, the electorate relies on the Internet for video-packaged information. Young adults are the dominant users of online videos with political messages. In the 18–29-year-old demographic,

57 percent viewed online videos from a campaign or a traditional news organization while 54 percent watched online videos from sources other than campaigns (Smith, 2009). Furthermore, it was found that 25 percent of African-Americans and Hispanics who were online political users were active participants in obtaining political messages via e-mail alerts and customized Web pages. Smith (2009) noted, "In each case minorities are significantly more likely to do these activities than whites" (p. 34).

New Voters and New Technologies

The 18 to 29 year olds, or the Millennial Generation, includes those individuals born between 1982 and 2003 and is the largest and most ethnically diverse generation of any prior generation in this nation's history (Winograd & Hais, 2008). By the 2008 campaign, there were more than 50 million Millennials eligible to vote. Fifty-three percent of the youth eligible to vote did so in 2008 which was a five percent increase from the 2004 presidential election (Mellow, 2009), making them one of the largest groups of new voters in the 2008 election cycle. Obama garnered 66 percent of the votes in this demographic, which was 12 percent higher than the youth vote the Democratic presidential nominee received in 2004 (Mellow, 2009). Forty-five percent of voters between the ages of 18–29 years of age identified themselves as Democrats compared to 26 percent as Republicans and 29 percent as Independent (Tufts University, 2008). In Chapter 3, Towner and Dulio demonstrate that young citizens who paid attention to candidate Web sites during the 2008 campaign exhibited significantly higher levels of candidate issue stance knowledge, whereas those who paid attention to video-sharing and social networking sites were less informed about factual or candidate issues. However, heavy viewing of video-sharing and social networking sites increased feelings of likeability toward Obama.

Obama's effective use of new media technologies may explain why he garnered such an impressive amount of the youth vote. Hershey (2010) explains, "Although both campaigns had sophisticated Web sites and made extensive use of the Internet in other ways, Obama was light years ahead of McCain in exploiting new applications" (p. 139). Mellow (2009) suggests that Obama may have received such a significant majority of the youth vote as a result of his ". . . campaign's well-organized use of new technologies" (p. 158). Barack Obama was able to garner more than just the youth vote in the 2008 campaign. He garnered 95 percent of the African-American vote and 67 percent of the Hispanic vote (Mellow, 2009). Nearly 40 percent of the Millennial Generation can be identified as a member of a minority group (Leyden, Teixeira, & Greenberg, 2007). In Chapter 7, Yun, Jasperson, and Chapa show that ethnicity seems to be "the most consistent and reliable indicator for candidate evaluations."

In 2008 this led, of course, to a strong preference for Barack Obama among ethnic minority voters.

This Millennial Generation is, of course, quite technologically savvy (Winograd & Hais, 2008). Leyden, Teixeira, and Greenberg (2007) assert, ". . . the Millennials are the generation that came of age completely at home with the new technologies and new media that are reshaping politics. No one gets these new tools better than they do" (para. 26). To reach this demographic in 2008, both presidential campaigns utilized new media technologies including Internet advertising (Kaye, 2009).

In April 2006, a survey revealed that 18 to 25 year olds spend an average of 21.3 hours per week online checking e-mail and using instant messaging (Leyden, Teixeira, & Greenberg, 2007). Regarding the online habits of the Millennial generation, the same survey indicated 86 percent of this demographic checked e-mail daily, 56 percent read news online daily, 41 percent used social networking sites like Facebook and MySpace daily, and more than 52 percent indicated they had a personal profile page on either Facebook or MySpace (Leyden, Teixeira, & Greenberg, 2007). Liedtke (2009) reported that one in five people with Internet access between the ages of 18 to 34 have accessed Twitter to update their profiles at least once. Similarly, Winograd and Hais (2008) found that nearly 80 percent of Millennials use social networking sites. Unquestionably, the Millennial Generation is technologically sophisticated and relies heavily on the Internet and new media, especially social networking sites such as Facebook, MySpace, and Twitter. Peer-to-peer online and mobile communication is a primary trait of this new generation.

Thus, during the 2008 campaign, both Barack Obama and John McCain offered young supporters new media offerings, especially opportunities to participate in social networking sites. The John McCain campaign team established "McCainSpace" and the Obama campaign team, or Triple O as the Obama Internet strategy team was known as, created "MyBarackObama." Both sites were very similar to Facebook and allowed users to customize the page by posting profiles and links to blogs and/or to create networks of friends. Interestingly, as late as August of 2008, the "McCainSpace" was inactive and noted it was "under construction" (Project for Excellence in Journalism, n.d.). The social networking Web sites of both candidates also permitted supporters to volunteer for the campaign and donate money (Project for Excellence in Journalism, n.d.).

The Obama campaign amassed more than 13 million e-mail addresses and, in total, sent more than a billion e-mails (Vargas, 2008). Obama's text messaging program had a million subscribers, and "MyBarackObama" had 2 million profiles (Vargas, 2008). The John McCain campaign team was unable to compete with these numbers and this strategy. Vargas (2008) remarked, "No other major campaign this cycle put technology and the Internet at the heart of its operation at this scale. Inevitably, the scope of the operation was the envy, if not outright obsession, of other campaigns" (para. 11). In Chapter 4 Williams and Serge show that, while most of these e-mail messages were not substantive or issue oriented, they did encourage interactivity and provided hyperlinks to expand the viewers' participation.

Both McCain and Obama posted campaign videos on YouTube during the 2008 presidential campaign. YouTube is an online video portal where candidates posted advertisements and other campaign propaganda for political enthusiasts to watch free of charge. YouTube, like all new media technologies, unleashes the power of the Internet and allows not only the candidates to create and post videos, but also ordinary citizens can create and post videos to the Web portal. YouTube is one of the most popular Web sites visited on the Internet; in fact, it is the third-busiest site on the Internet as ranked by Alexa.com. It was started in 2005 and sold to Google, Inc. for $1.65 billion, and was named TIME magazine's "Invention of the Year" in 2006.

The videos posted, or uploaded to YouTube are not only watched, but also forwarded to friends who in turn watch the videos and then continue forwarding the videos. The videos that are continuously forwarded are called viral videos. CNN partnered with YouTube to allow average citizens to submit videos with questions that would be shown to the candidates and then the question would be answered during a presidential primary debate. In Chapter 9, Brubaker discusses the role of new technologies in the presidential debates, arguing that new technology approaches like the CNN/YouTube debate offer new opportunities for voter involvement and participation.

The television networks incorporated another technology element in their coverage of presidential debates. In Chapter 8, Rita Kirk and Dan Schill explain how CNN used automated response dials to register audience reactions to the debates on a moment-by-moment basis. Summary evaluations of these responses were then shown to the television audience simultaneously as the debate progressed. Such response systems have been used to register evaluations of debates for decades, but CNN's decision to share the outcome with the larger viewing audience as the live debate was shown was somewhat controversial.

The Millennials who supported Obama are a very diverse group, and the voting patterns from the 2008 presidential election reflect that diversity. Among young voters between the ages of 19 to 29 years of age who supported Obama, 11 percent were Hispanic, 19 percent were African American, and 6 percent identified themselves as gay, lesbian, or bisexual (Tufts University, 2008). Although the ethnic diversity of Obama's supporters was impressive, for the Millennial Generation, race is not an issue. Millennials have "... relatively colorblind attitudes on racial issues" (Winograd & Hais, 2008, p. 95). Young voters delayed making a decision on who to vote for in the 2008 election until after September, but once the decision was made the young voters did indeed participate in the democratic process.

By the 2016 presidential campaign, this group of relatively new voters will make up more than one-third of the eligible voting population in America and will play a significant role in future presidential campaigns (Leyden, Teixeira, & Greenberg, 2007). In fact, "Signs indicate that Millennials are civic-minded, politically engaged, and hold values long associated with progressives, such as concern about economic inequalities, desire for a more multilateral foreign policy, and a strong belief in government" (Leyden, Teixeira, & Greenberg, 2007, para. 4). With a strong group and community orientation, this generation will sustain current usage and even encourage more usage and innovative applications of new media technologies in future political campaigns. Winograd and Hais (2008) state it most clearly, "The candidate who combines the newest in online campaign technology with the message that attracts Millennial voters will not only win the technology arms race, but also the presidency of the United States—and partisan dominance in the civic era that is just around the corner" (p. 188).

Finally, the Internet has made it possible to access more easily the attitudes of the international community toward American politics and political leaders. In Chapter 12 David Painter and his colleagues used online databases to locate newspaper coverage of the 2008 U.S. campaign in six countries (Brazil, China, Egypt, Saudi Arabia, South Korea, and the United Kingdom). Although they did conclude that "Obamamania" was characteristic around the world, they did discover some differences among countries in how positive their coverage of Obama was. This analysis provides valuable information about other voices that may impact the United States as it pursues its goals in a global society.

References

Davis, R. (1999). *The web of politics: The internet's impact on the American political system*. New York: Oxford University Press.

Denton, R. E., Jr. & Kuypers, J. A. (2008). *Politics and communication in America: Campaigns, media, and governing in the 21st century*. Long Grove, IL: Waveland Press.

Hershey, M. R. (2010). The media: Coloring the news. In M. Nelson (Ed.), *The elections of 2008*. Washington, DC: CQ Press, pp. 122–44.

Kaye, K. (2009, January 6). *Google grabbed most of Obama's $16 million in 2008*. Clickz.com. Retrieved June 10, 2009, from www.clickz.com/3632263.

Leyden, P., Teixeira, R., & Greenberg, E. (2007, June 20). *The progressive politics of the millennial generation*. New Politics Institute: A Think Tank for Politics. Retrieved June 10, 2009, from www.newpolitics.net/node/360?full_report=1.

Liedtke, M. (2009, February 15). Can all that Twitters turn to gold amid the gloom? *Herald Democrat*, p. B1.

Mellow, N. (2009). Voting behavior: A blue nation? In M. Nelson (Ed.), *The elections of 2008*. Washington, DC: CQ Press, pp. 145–62.

Pew Research Center for the People & the Press. (2008, October 31). *Internet now major source of campaign news: Continuing partisan divide in cable TV news audiences*. Retrieved June 10, 2009, from http://pewresearch.org/pubs/1017/internet-now-major-source-of-campaign-news.

Project for Excellence in Journalism: Understanding News in the Information Age. (n.d.). *Engagement and participation*. Retrieved June 10, 2009, from http://journalism.org/print/12773.

Smith, A. (2009). *The internet's role in campaign 2008*. Washington, DC: Pew Internet & American Life Project. Retrieved June 10, 2009, from www.pewinternet.org/Reports/2009/6-The-Internets-Role-in-Campaign-2008.aspx.

Trent, J. S., & Friedenberg, R. V. (2008). *Political campaign communication: Principles & practices* (6th Ed.). Lanham, MD: Rowman & Littlefield.

Tufts University, Medford, MA, Jonathan M. Tisch College of Citizenship and Public Service. (2008, December 19). *Young voters in the 2008 presidential election*. Retrieved June 10, 2009, from www.civicyouth.org/PopUps/FactSheets/FS_08_exit_polls.pdf.

Vargas, J. A. (2008, November 20). Obama raised half a billion online. *The Washington Post*. Retrieved June 10, 2009, from http://voices.washingtonpost.com/44/2008/11/20/obama_raised_half_a_billion_on.html.

Winograd, M., & Hais, M. D. (2008). *Millennial makeover: MySpace, YouTube, and the future of American politics*. New Brunswick, NJ: Rutgers University Press.

Chapter 2

From Soundbite to Textbite
Election 2008 Comments on Twitter

Monica Ancu

What do President Obama, Ashton Kutcher, a graduate student of New York University, and a koala bear named Bundaleer at the Tampa Zoo all have in common? If you guessed Twitter accounts, you are correct.

Barack Obama was one of the first American politicians to embrace this mobile-based social network by debuting his account in April 2007 in the preliminary stages of the presidential campaign primaries. Ashton Kutcher joined Twitter in January 2009 and quickly became one of the most famous *tweeples* (Twitter jargon meaning one who tweets or twitters) after entering, and winning, a race to gain a million Twitter friends (called followers) against CNN. The New York University graduate student Corey Menscher created his Twitter account in fall 2008 to display messages from a sensor worn by his pregnant wife recording every time the baby kicked. Messages recorded the date and time of the event and read: "I kicked Mommy at 08:33 p.m. on Thu, Dec 18!" (Cain Miller, 2009). Last but not least, Bundaleer, the koala bear, joined Twitter when he made the journey from Australia to his new home in Florida. He tweeted throughout the flight about courteous flight attendants and plane food until safely landing in Tampa (Lake, 2009).

Along with these four users mentioned above, Twitter subscribers include the most diverse entities, such as several NASA astronauts and the two Mars rovers, Congress and White House members, major commercial companies alongside small businesses and individual entrepreneurs, journalists and media organizations, and tens of millions of regular individuals who draw on this social network for information, promotion, entertainment, and countless other social needs. As of June 2009, Twitter had become one of the 50 most popular Web sites worldwide (Alexa.com, 2009). And reports from market-research companies place Twitter in third place as the most popular social network Web site, after Facebook and MySpace, in the U.S. (Kazeniac, 2009). From February 2008 to February 2009, Twitter's membership recorded an astonishing 1,382 percent growth rate (Nielsen Online, 2009a).

Apart from being at the top of the list in online social networking, Twitter has also become a place for breaking news and the commentary that follows. Almost every major event taking place after summer 2008 has found an outlet on Twitter. Twitter was the first social network Web site to post and distribute first-hand eye-witness reports about major events such as a U.S. Airways emergency plane landing in the Hudson River in January 2009, Michael Jackson's death, and the disputed 2009 Iranian election. With its quick, fast-paced, and mobile ability, Twitter seems to be an ideal channel for real-time information sharing.

During the 2008 U.S. presidential campaign, Twitter hosted a special page entitled "Election 2008" to aggregate and display users' tweets about election events. Election-related comments from any Twitter user including the two presidential candidates, the major political parties, and a plethora of political groups were posted every second on the Twitter election page in a continuously scrolling, continuously refreshed ticker-like stream of tweets. Twitter's "Election 2008" page functioned from September 25 to

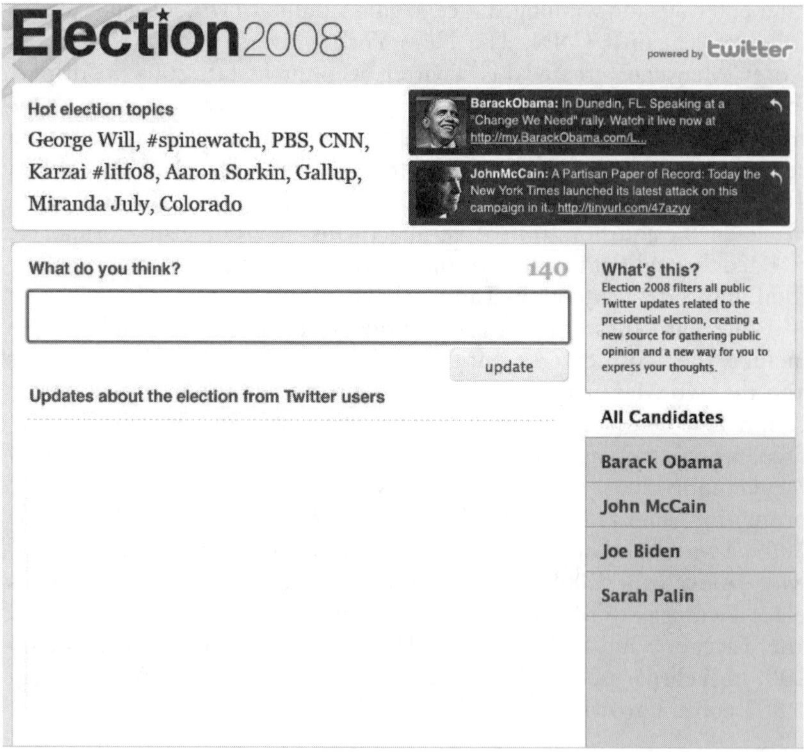

Election2008   powered by **twitter**

Hot election topics
George Will, #spinewatch, PBS, CNN,
Karzai #litfo8, Aaron Sorkin, Gallup,
Miranda July, Colorado

BarackObama: In Dunedin, FL. Speaking at a
"Change We Need" rally. Watch it live now at
http://my.BarackObama.com/L...

JohnMcCain: A Partisan Paper of Record: Today the
New York Times launched its latest attack on this
campaign in it. http://tinyurl.com/47azyy

What do you think?   140   **What's this?**
                                                              Election 2008 filters all public
                                                              Twitter updates related to the
                                                              presidential election, creating a
                                                              new source for gathering public
                                                              opinion and a new way for you to
                                              update   express your thoughts.

Updates about the election from Twitter users

All Candidates

Barack Obama

John McCain

Joe Biden

Sarah Palin

Figure 2.1 Screenshot of the Twitter Election 2008 page

a few days after Election Day (November 4, 2008), and this chapter is dedicated to studying its content.

Specifically, this study analyzed all tweets posted by Barack Obama ($n = 261$) and John McCain ($n = 26$), and 1,664 randomly selected tweets written by average users and streamed through the Twitter election page. The two vice-presidential candidates, Democrat Joe Biden and Republican Sarah Palin, did not have separate Twitter accounts. Combined, candidate and user tweets amounted to a final sample of $N = 1,951$.

The user comments were overwhelming in number and therefore impossible to analyze, even collect, in their entirety. Throughout the campaign period, the researcher accessed the election page three times a day at random times and collected the most recent comments on the screen. During the later analysis stage, comments from users outside the United States, and from users that seemed under 18 of age (judging by their profile pictures or other information publicly available) were eliminated from the sample, reducing the number of valid user tweets to 1,664. The researcher analyzed tweets from valid U.S. voters, based in the United States and over 18 years of age. However, Twitter profiles do not disclose demographic information such as verified geographic location, gender, age, or party affiliation. At the time of the 2008 campaign, demographic reports point to Twitter users being predominantly males (63 percent of all Twitterers), 35–44 years old (26 percent of all users), and living in California (57 percent of all Twitter visitors) (Tancer, 2008).

A Short History of Twitter

What exactly is Twitter and how does it work? Twitter started in March 2006 by asking its users the question: "What are you doing now?" Any Twitter subscriber could reply by either typing the answer in a form on Twitter.com or by submitting a text message from a cell phone. The answers, called tweets, are limited to 140 characters making Twitter a cross-breed medium between instant messaging and blogging. The 140-character limit also explains why Twitter is sometimes referred to as a micro-blogging service. In a way, Twitter is the Morse code of social media Web sites, allowing information transmission in small 140-character bursts. Message shortness and mobile access are the two features that set Twitter apart from all other social network Web sites and cause people to either love its chatty nature or hate its hasty, unpolished shallowness.

Either loved or hated, overall Twitter has been embraced by Internet users. Around the time of the 2008 presidential campaign, about 11 percent of all online U.S. users said they used this Web site. Similar to all other social network Web sites, Generation X and Generation Y constitute the bulk of Twitter audience, with about 20 percent (or one in five) online adults aged 18 to 34 having used Twitter. In contrast, Twitter adoption by Americans over the age of 35 drops significantly to under 10 percent of the population (Pew Internet, 2009).

Political candidates' adoption of Twitter and similar social network Web sites recognizes changing media consumption patterns of the American electorate, especially young voters. Television is still the number one source of information for the majority of U.S. citizens. However, the Internet has steadily climbed to number two at the expense of other mainstream media like newspapers, radio, and even television itself. Once online, the average Internet user spends the most time on search engines and search portals, PC software Web sites, e-mail, and social media sites. Web metrics data seem to indicate that the three major social network Web sites, Facebook, MySpace and Twitter, have become the primary channels to communicate online causing the decline of other online tools like instant messaging (Nielsen Online, 2009b). As of early 2009, Internet users were spending more time on social networking Web sites than on e-mail (Nielsen Online, 2009c).

The 2008 U.S. presidential campaign marked the first adoption of Twitter by major political candidates. Studying how this new tool and new type of social network was used is important in keeping current with the continuously evolving practices in online political campaigning. Scholars of technology adoption argue that early adopters and early uses of each new technology shape its future uses and norms (Bijker, Hughes, & Pinch, 1987; MacKenzie & Wajcman, 2002; Rogers, 1995). That happens because the first individuals to adopt a technology are usually opinion leaders who influence how the rest of the adopters will use the technology (Rogers, 1995). Therefore, studying the first visible use of Twitter in political campaigning is more than an academic exercise, and constitutes a mandatory step in understanding and predicting the future political uses of Twitter.

Presidential Candidates on Twitter

Barack Obama

Barack Obama's first tweet in April 2007 in the very beginning of the Democratic primaries read: "Heading to the first presidential debate. Hope you watch tonight at 7 p.m. EST on MSNBC." Throughout the campaign, Obama posted 261 tweets and gained 115,000 followers, a modest number compared to the millions on his Facebook account and also the millions of Twitter users who became followers after he won the presidency. Obama's last campaign tweet appeared on November 5, 2008, and said: "We just made history. All of this happened because you gave your time, talent and passion. All of this happened because of you. Thanks."

Content analysis of all Obama's tweets reveals that he aimed almost exclusively at disseminating campaign information to supporters. Obama's most frequent type of tweet was stereotypically phrased to announce imminent or past public appearances for him and his major spokespersons such as his spouse, Michelle: "In Asheville, NC at a 'Change We Need' rally. Watch it live at http://my.barackobama.com/l..." (1:28 p.m. October 5, 2008) or "Held a town hall event at Earl Wooster High School in Reno, NV earlier today. Watch it at: http://tinyurl.com/6dn543..." (5:32 p.m. August 17, 2008).

Occasionally, Obama attempted supporter mobilization: "Encouraging everyone to register & vote. Visit http://VoteForChange.com for registration, absentee & early vote info" (6:26 p.m. September 23, 2008); and fundraising: "Reminding everyone to donate by midnight tonight and you could be chosen to dine with me and a few supporters. http://barackobama.com/dine" (3:05 p.m. March 31, 2008). However, mobilizing and fundraising messages were very minimal and accounted for less than five percent of all Obama's tweets.

Equally important is the question about what was missing from Obama's Twitter feed, namely discussion of policy issues, political attacks, and interactive dialogue with his Twitter followers. Only about 10 out of the 261 tweets referenced the candidate's position on a policy issue. Here are some examples:

- Just spoke at Cooper Union in NYC, called for immediate relief for the housing crisis & an additional $30 billion to jumpstart the economy (11:10 a.m. March 27, 2008).

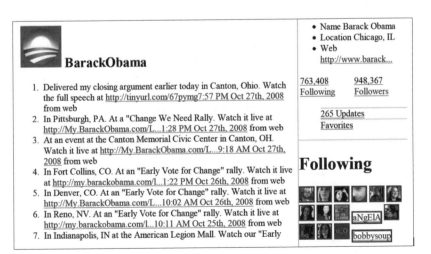

Figure 2.2 Screenshot of Barack Obama's Twitter page

- At the University of Iowa envisioning affordable universal healthcare by end of first term (10:32 a.m. May 29, 2007).
- Thinking we can cut oil consumption by 2.5 million barrels of oil per day and take 50 million cars' worth of pollution off the road by 2020 ... (4:01 p.m. May 8, 2007).

On the negative campaigning front, Obama waived political attacks against the opposing team. Only one of his tweets references John McCain: "Troubled by today's unemployment figures, the latest indicator of how badly America needs fundamental change from Bush–McCain policies" (12:48 p.m. April 3, 2008). The only other negative tweet is directed at President Bush: "Wondering why four years after President Bush landed on an aircraft carrier and declared 'Mission Accomplished,' we are still at war?" (1:12 p.m. May 1, 2007).

Perhaps the most surprising feature of Obama's Twitter account is the total lack of interaction with the Twitter community. Similar to all other social networks, Twitter users can connect to each other and exchange both private and public messages. The Obama campaign did not produce interactive content, did not reply to any followers, and used the account strictly as a one-way information push. Only a few rare tweets such as the following timidly invited feedback from supporters: "Going to be on The Daily Show with Jon Stewart tonight. 11:00 p.m. ET on Comedy Central. Hope you watch & reply with your thoughts after" (9:25 p.m. April 21, 2008). Despite violating interactivity norms on a social media Web site, the campaign gained a large audience and was the most popular Twitter account in terms of followers during the fall months prior to Election Day.

John McCain

McCain's 2008 campaign was routinely criticized for lacking adoption of the newest online technology tools. Twitter and all other social media Web sites were peripheral to the Republican's candidate campaign mix. McCain debuted his Twitter account in September 2008, only two months prior to Election Day, and posted a meager 28 tweets until Election Day. His account numbered only about 3,000 followers, about 40 times less than Obama's.

Content analysis of McCain's tweets shows that he used Twitter mainly for announcing the release of campaign ads and linking back to his campaign Web site. A few of McCain's tweets attacked the Obama and Biden campaign, like the following tweet posted on October 20, 2008: "Biden: 'Gird Your Loins' for International Crisis: Joe Biden tells it like it is: Mark my words, http://tinyurl.com/6yfuej," or like this one: "Obama Surrogate Unable To Cite One Obama Bipartisan Accomplishment: http://tinyurl.com/3q7hck" (8:00 p.m. October 15, 2008).

McCain's Twitter also attacked media outlets not supportive of his

JohnMcCain

Follow

1. Start following me on my Senate Twitter: https://twitter.com /SenJohn...1:30 PM Feb 27th from web

2. Chris Matthews, Not A Constitutional Scholar: Earlier this week Chris Matthews exhibited such a stunni.. http://tinyurl.com/6qyjoy4:30 PM Oct 24th, 2008 from twitterfeed

3. Junk: Just after the New York Times ended months of intense speculation by announcing its endorsement .. http://tinyurl.com /64raka4:30 PM Oct 24th, 2008 from twitterfeed

- Name John McCain
- Location Arlington, VA
- Web http://www.johnmc...
- Bio John McCain has a remarkable record of leadership and experience that embodies his unwavering lifetime commitment to service.

6,370   9,737
Following   Followers

26 Updates
Favorites

Figure 2.3 Screenshot of John McCain's Twitter page

campaign, such as *The New York Times*: "Another Trash 'Report' from the New York Times: Today the New York Times launched yet another in a series of vicious attacks on Senator John McCain, this time targeting not the candidate, but his wife Cindy http://tinyurl.com/5t7hj8" (8:00 a.m. October 18, 2008).

A few months after the election, the senator rejoined Twitter, updating his account on a regular basis and quickly attracting over one million supporters. In a press interview in summer 2009, he called Twitter "a phenomenal way of communicating" and claimed being "flooded" with responses from his Twitter followers (Stewart, 2009).

Voters on Twitter

The bulk of Twitter messages about the 2008 general election came from individual users. An analysis revealed that the majority (60 percent) of these tweets were very close to trivial rants, personal, and random thoughts about the election or the candidates. Here are some of these types of comments, posted by users from a desire for self-expression:

- User *danielholter*: "Alec Baldwin just called Palin 'Bible Spice' on Letterman. I like him more now" (October 29).
- User *westjb*: "If Obama wins, I'm prepared to take residence in Australia" (October 29).
- User *jeremyvaught*: "On this Halloween, I'm thinking the most scary thing most of you peeps will hear is, 'I'm voting for John McCain' boo!" (October 31).

However, the election-related political dialogue on Twitter was not all insignificant. Some tweets (8 percent) talked about policy issues, usually mentioning a certain candidate's position or voting record on a certain issue. Although the tweets had minimal issue information, readers could still acquire some knowledge about candidates, such as "A 1998 tax filing 4 the McCain-led group shows $448,873 grant to Khalidis Center 4 Palestine Research and Studies for work in the West Bank" (user *ConchitaKitty*, October 29), or "House Democrats Contemplate Abolishing 401(k) Tax Breaks" (user *IndyEnigma*, October 28).

Some users did use Twitter for specific purposeful political action, such as dissemination of information about candidates. About 42 percent of all user tweets contained hyperlinks to another Web page with content related to one of the candidates. Of all the hyperlinks, about 31 percent went to media and news Web sites, about 6 percent linked to McCain's and Obama's campaign Web sites, about 4 percent went to YouTube, 2 percent went to other Twitter profiles, and 5 percent linked to miscellaneous Web sites. "Some kind of wonderful? Think again. Five myths about John McCain, ... shattered! http://tinyurl.com/4rh96q," wrote user *TonyXavier* with a link to a feature on John McCain by the *Rolling Stone* magazine (October 31), while user *deaconDaniel* was "Munching celery. Reading an Obama article: http://tinyurl.com/5lpnc7" (October 29).

Twitter users also used the medium to exchange alerts about campaign info and events, with 27 percent of user tweets announcing a future campaign event or advertising participation in one:

- User *lapilofu*: "@jwisser I'm sitting across from Sarah Palin!" (October 31).
- User *addicuss*: "On a huge line at the jmu Obama rally I hope I get in" (October 28).
- User *USATODAYlife:* "McCain appears on TV's Saturday Night Live" (November 1).

About 20 percent of user tweets urged followers to take political action, and about eight percent of users mentioned they performed, or will perform, a political action such as volunteering, donating, or attending a campaign event. For instance, user *dphamilton* urged readers to "Sign up for the online McCain phone bank here: http://tinyurl.com/4sjem2," (October 31), and user *knscott* posted "started my 4 day volunteerism with the Obama camp. Today next to a woman, pro-life, 70s, and republican making calls for Obama" (October 30).

On Election Day, Twitter was inundated with get-out-and-vote requests. Messages like the following could be read every minute throughout the day: "Justicar has voted. Get out there and vote! (Unless you're voting for Sarah Palin ... in which case, stay home, please.)" (posted by user

Justicar, November 4). Or: "forsberg_chris's neighbors have a homemade McCain/Palin sign, another has a "nobama" poster. I thought I flew back from Indiana? Regardless, go vote." (user *forsberg_chris*, November 4).

In tone, user tweets tended to be neutral toward the candidates (55 percent), although there were both negative (31 percent) and positive (14 percent) tendencies. Interestingly enough, about 85 percent of all negative tweets pointed to Sarah Palin, while 89 percent of all positive comments were made in reference to Barack Obama. This pattern might be connected to the audience demographics explained earlier. Although the researcher does not have verified demographics for the sampled user comments, market studies of Twitter membership show them as predominantly California-based males between the ages of 25 to 44, a predominantly Democratic electoral group. Also, since the McCain campaign was not active on Twitter, it seems reasonable to assume that Republican supporters were not particularly active on the Web site either.

Overall, Twitter users had various possibilities for generating and participating in political discussion: they expressed personal opinions, praised and criticized the candidates, obtained and disseminated information and online content about them, advertised their own involvement and promoted opportunities for others to become involved, and commented in real-time about campaign events. All major campaign events broadcasted live on television, such as the debates, *Saturday Night Live* and other late-night talk-show appearances, interviews and press conferences, were paralleled on Twitter by hundreds of tweets per minute.

Absent from users' tweets was, however, real interaction with other Twitter users. Only about 5 percent of all tweets were addressed directly to fellow twitterers, with most tweets being posted to a general, unspecified audience. This lack of direct address toward other Twitter users is somewhat unusual since social networking sites thrive on the need for connecting, interacting, collaborating, and grooming relationships with other users. However, user tweets analyzed in this study showed that most were produced out of a desire for self-expression (user wanted to express a one-way personal opinion) rather than interaction or dialogue with peer users. This finding matches a study of uses and gratifications of Twitter, that showed that this Web site is "a network of people scanning, reading and occasionally posting written messages" (Crawford, 2009, p. 528).

Conclusion

This study looked at the first time Twitter was used for political discussion during a major U.S. election. Despite the shallowness of political dialogue on Twitter in 2008, this communication mode has plenty of potential for important consequences on political life. The Web site has a massive audience, and users can post tweets and disseminate information within seconds. Out of all social networking Web sites, Twitter is perhaps the most flexible and responsive to its users. The home page of the Web site, as well as each profile page, displays the top "trending topics" of the moment, a list of keywords most frequently mentioned by the users. If a few Twitter users start a conversation on, let's say, the Iraq war, and if enough Twitter users join that conversation, their tweets will become a trending topic, displayed for the entire Twitter community to see and open to all to participate. Such heightened potential for viral messages makes Twitter a powerful communication tool for candidates who can use it to inform, mobilize, and respond to attacks and for users who can use it to engage and participate.

Despite the shallowness, Twitter creates "an awareness of group activity" (Levy, 2008) and gives individuals diverse opportunities, from a passive assessment of public opinion to active expression of self-opinion. Even individuals who chose not to contribute actively to public dialogue, but to read and listen privately instead, might be influenced in their behavior and beliefs by the community opinion. Such individuals, usually referred to as "lurkers," contribute to an online community by functioning as an audience and encouraging others to make public contributions (Crawford, 2009). While consuming the public discussion, such users are exposed to information and opinion about campaigns and candidates, information that might affect their original beliefs. For the mere fact that it increases the number of voices that can be heard in a political debate, Twitter should get good ratings as a channel for political dialogue.

Twitter offers political candidates access to millions of users who follow their messages in real-time. Obama used Twitter to update around a million supporters about his campaign appearances. McCain, only an occasional user of Twitter, posted links to the latest campaign ads to lure Twitter followers to his campaign Web site. Despite the fact that neither candidate replied to supporters, twitterers responded to them, sending inquiries, criticism and praise, and overall creating a publicly visible political dialogue. Even a one-sided conversation between candidates and supporters, research shows, has the potential to build a sense of community and increase campaign interest on the part of constituencies (Stromer-Galley & Baker, 2006). Despite lack of interaction, social media create parasocial relationships between communicator and audience and the illusion of a 'friendship' between politicians and voters. This bond, despite its illusory nature, still creates engagement, scholars argue (Rafaeli, 1990, p. 136).

References

Alexa.com (2009, June 28). *Traffic report on Twitter.com*. Retrieved December 30, 2009, from: www.alexa.com/siteinfo/twitter.com.

Bijker, W. E., Hughes, T. P., & Pinch, T. J. (Eds.) (1987). *The social construction of technological systems: New directions in the sociology and history of technology*. Cambridge, MA: MIT Press.

Cain Miller, C. (2009, April 13). Putting Twitter's world to use. *The New York Times*. Retrieved December 30, 2009, from: www.nytimes.com/2009/04/14/technology/internet/14twitter.html.

Crawford, K. (2009). Following you: Disciplines of listening in social media. *Continuum: Journal of Media & Cultural Studies, 23*(4), 525–535.

Kazeniac, A. (2009, February 9). *Social networks: Facebook takes over top spot, Twitter climbs*. Compete.com. Retrieved December 30, 2009, from: http://blog.compete.com/2009/02/09/facebook-myspace-twitter-social-network/.

Lake, L. (2009, June 24). Jet-setting koala 'tweets' his way to Tampa zoo. *Tampa Bay Online News*. Retrieved December 30, 2009, from: www2.tbo.com/content/2009/jun/24/na-jet-setting-koalatweets-his-way-to-tampa-zoo/news-metro/.

Levy, J. (2008, Summer). Beyond boxers or briefs? New media brings youth to politics like never before. *Phi Kappa Phi Forum, 14–16.*

MacKenzie, D., & Wajcman, J. (2002). *The social shaping of technology* (2nd Ed.). Buckingham: Open University Press.

Nielsen Online (2009a, February). *NetView. U.S., home and work*. Retrieved December 30, 2009, from: http://en-us.nielsen.com/rankings/insights/rankings/internet.

Nielsen Online (2009b, March). *By the numbers*. Retrieved December 30, 2009, from: http://en-us.nielsen.com/etc/medialib/nielsen_dotcom/en_us/documents/pdf/newsletters/by_the_numbers.Par.49243.File.dat/BTN_0903.pdf.

Nielsen Online (2009c). *Global faces and networked places: A Nielsen report on social networking's new global footprint*. Retrieved December 30, 2009, from: www.nielsen-online.com.

Pew Internet (2009, February 12). *Twitter and status updating*. Retrieved December 30, 2009, from: www.pewinternet.org/Reports/2009/Twitter-and-status-updating.aspx.

Rafaeli, S. (1990). Interacting with media: para-social interaction and real interaction. In L. A. Lievrouw (Ed.), *Mediation, information and communication* (Vol. 3). New Brunswick, NJ: Transaction.

Rogers, E. (1995). *Diffusion of innovations* (4th Ed.). New York: The Free Press.

Stewart, M. (2009, August 2). *McCain: Twitter is 'a phenomenal way of communicating.'* CNN Political Ticker. Retrieved August 10, 2009 from: http://politicalticker.blogs.cnn.com/2009/08/02/mccain-twitter-is-a-phenomenal-way-of-communicating/.

Stromer-Galley, J., & Baker, A. B. (2006). Joy and sorrow of interactivity on the campaign trail: Blogs in the primary campaign of Howard Dean. In A. P. Williams & J. C. Tedesco (Eds.), *The Internet election: Perspectives on the Web in campaign 2004*. Lanham, MD: Rowman & Littlefield, pp. 111–32.

Tancer, B. (2008, August 20). Even Gen X is a Twitter. *Time*. The Science of Search. Retrieved December 30, 2009, from: www.time.com/time/business/article/0,8599,1834131,00.html.

Chapter 3

The Web 2.0 Election
Voter Learning in the 2008 Presidential Campaign[1]

Terri L. Towner and David A. Dulio

One of the most consistent findings in political science is that the American public possesses very little political information. Classics such as Berelson, Lazarsfeld, and McPhee's (1954) *Voting* and Campbell, Converse, Miller, and Stokes's (1960) *The American Voter* illustrated citizens' lack of knowledge and information, even during highly salient events such as election campaigns. Others have come to the same conclusion in more recent work (Delli Carpini & Keeter, 1996; Price & Zaller, 1993). Moreover, even the most recent studies of citizens' knowledge of politics and government illustrate that the public does not have a great wealth of knowledge and has roughly the same levels as Americans two decades ago (Pew Research Center, 2007). There are great divides in political knowledge among the American people. While some (those who are older, white, more educated, and wealthy) are better informed; others lack even the most basic information. Young Americans are an important category of the least informed; they are also less likely to vote and engage in other campaign activities, and are more disconnected from the political system than others (Bauerlein, 2008; Wattenberg, 2007).

It has been argued that the Internet may help change this. The Internet's informational benefits have been lauded as a possible remedy for what plagues the public in terms of political activity. The Web has been argued to be a tool that can improve the democratic process by renewing citizens' enthusiasm for political involvement (Corrado & Firestone, 1996; Grossman, 1995); others have found that the Internet has a positive influence on civic participation, mobilization, and engagement (Castells, 2001; Shah, Kwak, & Holbert, 2001). More importantly for this study, Sweetser and Kaid (2008) argue, "web-based political information appears to stimulate citizens to seek additional political information on the internet, and to engage in other forms of political participation and activity" (p. 70). Given their proclivity to use the Web and their lack of political knowledge, the Internet's role in conveying information could be most critical for younger Americans.

The 2008 election cycle was the latest campaign to illustrate that candidates also believe that the Web has the potential to make a difference in politics. Candidates running for offices from President of the United States to mayor of a small town employed various Web tools to try to add value to their campaigns. From YouTube to Facebook, candidates were using the Web to attract donors, volunteers, and voters. But the question remains: Does the use of online sources influence political attitudes and behaviors? Candidates and their campaigns must think so, since they employ these tactics. But how, specifically, does attention to online sources influence political knowledge, interest, and participation?

In this chapter, we examine one aspect of this question by focusing on the public's information levels. We focus on some of the most information-starved individuals—young Americans. In particular, we are interested in whether or not the use of specific types of Internet information sources influences young Americans' knowledge of politics and government. An important contribution of this work is that we examine different types of information sources and test the differences among them. Others have studied informational effects, but many have done so by focusing on only one type of source—either online or offline. We include measures of both. More importantly, we also differentiate between sources of online information. Many early studies that investigate "the Internet" did so without separating the types of information available. This approach, however, does not do justice to the many types of sources available to the information consumer. As noted above, this was clearly seen in the 2008 presidential election when we consider the various political sources on the Web including video-sharing Web sites, social networking Web sites, online newspapers, television network Web sites, and candidate Web sites. These shortcomings provide a starting point for our work, as we investigate the relationship between specific online sources and various types of political knowledge.

Political Knowledge

Measurement of political knowledge by scholars has evolved since the first studies that examined only individuals' ability to recall factual political information. Scholars moved away from these early measures because they lacked the power to illustrate the extent to which individuals could integrate different events and issues in politics (Delli Carpini & Keeter, 1996; Eveland, Cortese, Park, & Dunwoody, 2004; Eveland, Marton, & Seo, 2004; Eveland & Scheufele, 2000). More recent studies have tested knowledge by examining integration of political information rather than simple recall of disjointed facts or figures. These new studies moved beyond an individual's ability to recall bits of information to examining their base of knowledge (Graber, 1996; Neuman, Just, & Crigler, 1992). Others have examined knowledge on a single dimension including personal knowledge about candidates (Chaffee, Zhao, & Leshner, 1994), knowledge of current events (Price & Zaller, 1993), and issue knowledge about candidates (Patterson, 1980).

Neuman (1981) argued that political knowledge is comprised of two categories: differentiated and integrated knowledge. Differentiated knowledge, according to Neuman, is linked to the aforementioned factual recall of names, issues and events; integrated knowledge is the individual's ability to link the differentiated items together. Eveland et al. (2004) built on Neuman (1981) with the idea of "knowledge structure density" which also combines factual and integrated knowledge.

As we noted above, regardless of the measure of knowledge, the clear conclusion in the literature is that the American public is not well informed about politics. This holds for those classic studies mentioned earlier as well as more recent and advanced studies (Delli Carpini & Keeter, 1996). This lack of sophisticated knowledge is persistent today even in the face of a large increase in the amounts and sources of information available to the public (Delli Carpini & Keeter, 1996; Gilens, Vavreck, & Cohen, 2007) which would predict greater levels of knowledge. However, the lack of knowledge is not universal in the American electorate. Rather, some segments of the population are more informed than others. Those of higher socioeconomic status (Tichenor, Donahue, & Olien, 1970) as well as those who are more educated (Delli Carpini & Keeter, 1996) are more likely to be informed than other groups. Prior (2005) has also found informational content preference (news vs. entertainment) to be an important difference in the knowledge level.

Knowledge has an influence on political participation as well. Included here are important effects on campaign interest and voter turnout. In the former, Bartels and Rahn (2000) tie exposure to political information on cable news programs and political Web sites to an increase in political interest. Moreover, many scholars have illustrated the link between political information and turnout (Delli Carpini & Keeter, 1996; Prior, 2005; Verba, Schlozman, & Brady, 1995).

Offline vs. Online Media Outlets

Offline media outlets have played an integral role in political campaigns and elections, devoting substantial amounts of time to covering candidates and their campaigns. For decades, media and politics scholars have debated the traditional media's informational and mobilizing role during election campaigns. Much of this literature focuses on the effects of television and newspaper usage, and offers a mix of conflicting findings. On one hand, scholars often find that attention to hard-copy newspapers and television is associated with higher levels of political knowledge (e.g., Bybee et al., 1981; McLeod, Scheufele, & Moy, 1999; Robinson & Davis, 1999; Robinson & Levy, 1986; Scheufele & Nisbet, 2002; Scheufele, Nisbet, & Brossard, 2003; Weaver & Drew, 1993), whereas others have cast doubt on hard-copy newspapers and television usage and learning (e.g., Becker & Whitney, 1980; Mondak, 1995; Neuman, Just, & Crigler, 1992; Patterson & McClure, 1976; Price & Zaller, 1993).

Several methodological factors may explain these inconsistent findings, such as the type of information or knowledge examined as the dependent variable (Druckman, 2005). As Chaffee and Frank (1996) suggest, the structure, content, and usage of hard-copy newspapers and television have disparate effects on various types of knowledge (see also Eveland, 2003). For example, studies have shown that hard-copy newspaper reading is positively linked with factual recall knowledge (Becker & Dunwoody, 1982; Dalrymple & Scheufele, 2007; Pettey, 1988) and party issue knowledge (Chaffee, Zhao, & Leshner, 1994; Eveland & Scheufele, 2000; Patterson & McClure, 1976; Weaver & Drew, 1993). Candidate likes and dislikes and ideological knowledge, however, are not linked to newspaper usage (Dalrymple & Scheufele, 2007; Eveland & Scheufele, 2000). Television viewing often boosts knowledge of candidates and issues (Becker & Dunwoody, 1982; Chaffee, Zhao, & Leshner, 1994; Lowden et al., 1994; Weaver & Drew, 1993; Zaoh & Chaffee, 1995). In addition, television attention is linked to learning about candidate's personal information, shaping citizen's opinion about the candidate as a person (Sue, 1994).

Recently, the public has been going online for political information. The Internet played a large role in the 2008 presidential campaign, offering online sources that were unavailable or underused in previous presidential elections. According to a 2008 Pew research report (Smith, 2009), 55 percent of American adults used the Internet to connect to the political process during the campaign—a substantial increase compared to previous elections. In fact, the same data show that the Internet outpaces newspapers as a major source of election news for young adults. Young voters in particular have been gravitating toward Facebook, MySpace, and YouTube (Smith & Rainie, 2008; Winograd & Hais, 2008) and have become more than passive followers of political events (Owen, 2008).

Indeed, a number of studies examine Internet effects empirically and, similar to the influence of traditional media, offer a mix of findings. Past and recent research hails the Internet as an important medium that is positively related to political knowledge (Drew & Weaver, 2006; Kenski & Stroud, 2006; Norris, 2000; Shah, McLeod, & Yoon, 2001; Sotirovic & McLeod, 2004; Xenos & Moy, 2007). Other scholars, however, are not as optimistic. Several studies report that Internet usage and attention do not contribute to political knowledge (DiMaggio et al., 2001; Jennings

& Zeitner, 2003; Johnson, Briama, & Sothirajah, 1999; Wei & Ven-hwei, 2008). Similarly, Scheufele and Nisbet (2002) conclude that political and nonpolitical information seeking on the Internet is not associated with higher factual political knowledge. In fact, searching the Internet for entertainment purposes significantly *lowers* knowledge levels.

Several reasons may explain the missing link between Internet use and increased knowledge. Some scholars suggest that the Internet is simply not conducive to learning, particularly for people with low computer literacy. For instance, Eveland and Dunwoody (2000) demonstrate that nonlinear or hypermedia systems, such as the Web, may inhibit learning because their content and structure demand more cognitive information processing. Linear formats, such as hard-copy newspapers and television, require less effort, allowing effective information processing to occur (also see Eveland & Dunwoody, 2001, 2002). Tewksbury and Althaus (2000) find that online readers of *The New York Times* are less likely to recall and describe news topics than hard-copy readers.

Similar to analyses of offline media sources, several studies of Internet effects do not distinguish among different types of knowledge. Eveland and his colleagues, for example, found that nonlinear formats do not improve factual knowledge, yet hypermedia can increase knowledge structure density and organization (Eveland, Marton, & Seo, 2004; Eveland, Seo, & Marton, 2002; Eveland et al., 2004). Furthermore, many studies conclude that various Internet uses, such as searching for general, political, and entertainment information, have disparate effects on knowledge levels (Prior, 2005; Scheufele & Nisbet, 2002; Shah, Kwak, & Holbert, 2001).

Research Questions and Hypotheses

Given the varying features and designs of online newspapers, television network Web sites, presidential candidate Web sites, video-sharing Web sites, and online social networks, we suggest that each online source contributes differently to various knowledge structures. Below, we outline a series of research questions and hypotheses based on prior research.

Online newspapers are becoming a major source of political information relating to candidates, issues, and parties, as many outlets, such as NYTimes.com and Washingtonpost.com, devoted a section of the site exclusively to the 2008 election. These special sections often included the latest public opinion polls, exit polls, videos, staff-generated interviews with candidates, candidate profiles, in-depth information on candidate issue positions, campaign-specific blogs, and information on voter registration and polling locations. Much of this material offered hyperlinks to online archives, past and recent stories, related articles and videos, and readers' forums, blogs, and commentary. This nonlinear format gives online readers more choice and control regarding how they receive the news and what information they read (see Eveland, Marton, & Seo, 2004; Tewksbury & Althaus, 2000). As discussed previously, linear and nonlinear newspaper formats have different implications for audience recall and learning (Eveland, Marton, & Seo, 2004; Eveland, Seo, & Marton, 2002). Hard-copy rather than online newspaper usage is often associated with higher levels of factual knowledge (Tewksbury & Althaus, 2000). Dalrymple and Scheufele (2007), however, establish that both hard-copy and online newspapers significantly increase factual political knowledge whereas only online newspaper usage increases candidate issue stance knowledge and candidate likes and dislikes. In general, the effects of online newspapers on political knowledge are fairly mixed. Hence, we investigate the following research question:

RQ1:   Does attention to online newspapers increase levels of political factual recall knowledge, candidate issue-stance knowledge, and candidate likes and dislikes among young adults?

Similar to online newspapers, television network Web sites, such as MSNBC, CNN, and ABC, offer mainstream news often reported on their affiliated television channels. These sites include numerous articles, video clips, photos, blogs, advertisements, and links to other Web pages, archives, and related content. Many television news sites also had special sections dedicated to comprehensive election 2008 coverage. These sections featured interactive electoral maps, live streaming video of candidate debates and speeches, public opinion polls, exit poll results, candidate profiles, in-depth analysis of candidates and political issues, and online chats with guest commentators and readers. Despite the frequent use of television network sites during recent elections (see Owen, 2010; Schonfeld, 2008; Smith, 2009), the influence of these sources on political attitudes and behaviors has been unexamined by scholars. Thus, we investigate the following research question:

RQ2:   Does attention to television network Web sites increase levels of political factual recall knowledge, candidate issue-stance knowledge, and candidate likes and dislikes among young adults?

In 2008, all presidential candidates had regularly-updated Web sites that were visited frequently by online consumers (Smith, 2009). Thus, candidate Web sites are an increasingly important source of information for voters, particularly for young adults (Carlin, 2008). In general, content on candidate Web sites includes biographical sketches, contact information, family photos, links to speeches, issue and policy positions, complementary news stories, and opportunities to donate money, volunteer, plan events, and register to vote (e.g., Bimber & Davis, 2003; Davis, 1999, 2005; Selnow, 1998; Tedesco, Miller, & Spiker, 1999). Despite these features, some scholars suggest that candidate Web sites simply mirror traditional campaign tactics used in offline politics (Bimber & Davis, 2003; Margolis & Resnick, 2000). However, others argue that these Web sites offer distinctive features not found offline (Foot & Schneider, 2002; Hughes & Hill, 1998; Pippa, 2001). An examination of candidate Web sites in 2002, for example, illustrates that issue-taking strategies are the most unique part of candidate Web sites, but many online strategies, such as the issues candidates highlight, are similar to offline campaigning (Xenos & Foot, 2005).

Information obtained from candidate Web sites can influence voters. Hansen and Benoit (2005), for instance, found that viewing presidential candidate Web sites in the 2000 general election can alter perceptions of a candidate's character, policy positions, leadership, and global feelings (see also Hansen, 2000). In an experimental study of presidential candidate Web sites in 2000, Bimber and Davis (2003) reported that subjects learned something new about the candidate's issue positions and about the candidate as a person. Yet subjects viewing these sites were more likely to learn about issue positions than about the candidate as a person. Bimber and Davis also observed that exposure to candidate Web sites does not influence how much the subject likes or dislikes the candidate. Other experimental research has determined that interactivity with candidate Web sites during the 2000 presidential primary increased candidate like-ability and learning (Ahem, Stromer-Galley, & Neuman, 2000). Therefore, we expect:

> *H1a: Attention to presidential candidate Web sites will have no influence on factual knowledge.*

> *H1b: Attention to candidate Web sites will positively influence candidate issue-stance knowledge.*

> *H1c: Attention to candidate Web sites will have no affect on candidate likes and dislikes of candidates.*

During the 2008 presidential election, YouTube was one of the most popular video-sharing Web sites for candidates and voters (Smith, 2009). Much of the content on candidates' YouTube channels was posted by the presidential campaigns themselves. Candidate channels included biographical information, updates from campaign staff, "insider" infor-mation, candidate endorsements, and other material. More traditional candidate information, such as stump speeches, rallies, interviews, and television commercials, was also posted by the campaigns. Moreover, citizens could post text or video responses to clips posted by the campaigns, creating a video Web log (or vblog). YouTube also featured videos about the presidential race created by the general public which included issue-related commentaries, videos from the campaign trail, attacks on the opponent, satirical or humorous sketches, and other information not written or created by trained journalists.

Therefore, all types of political information could be accessed on video-sharing Web sites—from a campaign's latest TV ad to satire, as well as entertainment-focused content such as the "Obama Girl" videos. That is, online videos did not always contain substantive political information. Indeed, the most-watched political videos were entertainment focused (Owen, 2010). Madden (2007) reported that young adults are more likely to watch comedy and humorous online videos than news videos. Young adults also consume more music, animation or cartoons, movies or television shows, and sports videos than older adults. During the campaign, the most-watched politically oriented video on YouTube was will.i.am's "Yes We Can" music video (over 20 million views), which featured many other celebrities. In comparison, the most-viewed purely political video was an attack on John McCain with over 8 million views. Thus, individuals may view online videos for mainly entertainment purposes.

Scholars are only beginning to examine the political implications of online videos. A study conducted during the 2008 presidential primary season found that respondents who get news from social networking sites, both YouTube and social networks, learned very little information about politics and the primary candidates (Baumgartner & Morris, 2009). Therefore, we expect that:

> *H2a: Attention to video-sharing Web sites will have no influence on factual knowledge.*

> *H2b: Attention to video-sharing Web sites will have no influence on issue-stance knowledge.*

> *H2c: Attention to video-sharing sites will positively influence candidate likes and dislikes.*

Along with candidate Web sites and online videos, social networking sites have emerged as an attractive campaign tool. In general, these sites enable candidates and supporters to post campaign events, comments, announcements, links, notes, videos, and photos. Candidates use social networking sites to mobilize voters, promote voter registration, recruit campaign volunteers, and receive exposure (Gueorguieva, 2008; Williams

& Gulati, 2007). In 2008 the content on the presidential candidates' Facebook and MySpace pages included biographical and contact information, candidate interests, family photos, photos from the campaign trail, videos of stump speeches and rallies, event listings, notes from the candidate and campaign staff, information on voter registration and polling locations, and opportunities to donate money and volunteer. In many ways, social networking sites allow users to have a virtual relationship with their favored candidate. Voters could become a candidate's "fan" or "friend," and view and post comments on videos, photos, and links. In addition, social networking sites are customizable and offer ways to engage politically. For example, users can display their political interests, add an "I support Obama" button on their profile, and create and join political groups, such as "John McCain for President."

Given the substantial increase in social networking usage since 2005 (Smith, 2009), many scholars have begun to examine the sites' features, uses, and influence, particularly in the political arena (Gueorguieva, 2008; Martin & Schmeisser, 2008; Williams, 2008; Williams & Gulati, 2007, 2009; Winograd & Hais, 2008). However, recent research is skeptical about social networks, as few social network users regularly get information about news and events (Smith, 2009). Many social networkers use their sites for sharing and communication rather than information gathering, as many of the sites' political activities are "social" or a form of "communitainment" (see Cornfield, 2010; Smith, 2009). Pasek, more, and Romer (2009), for example, discovered that online social networking significantly increases offline civic engagement but is unrelated to factual political knowledge.[2] As noted above, Baumgartner and Morris (2009) found that YouTube and social networking users learned very little information about politics and the primary candidates. Similar to the expected influence of video-sharing sites, we anticipate that:

> H3a: Attention to social networking sites will have no influence on factual knowledge.

> H3b: Attention to social networking sites will have no influence on issue-stance knowledge.

Due to the "virtual relationship" created between voters and candidates on social networks, we also expect:

> H3c: Attention to social networking sites will positively influence candidate likes and dislikes.

Last, we do not propose formal research questions or hypotheses regarding the effects of television and hard-copy newspaper attention, as previous research shows that these offline sources have little or no relationship to political knowledge.

Data and Method

Data for this study were collected on October 22, 2008, from respondents at a medium-sized public university in the Midwest.[3] A total of 228 undergraduate students recruited from introductory-level political science courses participated in an online survey in a computer laboratory. We focused on college students because national surveys show that young adults are more likely than older adults to get most of their information about the 2008 presidential election from online sources (Smith, 2009). The percentage using online sources declines as age increases. Thus, young adults are a better test of the effects of online sources. The respondents in this study are relatively representative of the typical young, Internet user. The average age of respondents was 19.67 years ($SD = 2.66$). Sixty percent were women, and 80 percent identified themselves as Caucasian. Majors in political science comprised 19 percent of the respondents, with others drawn from various majors. Forty-one percent identified themselves as either a strong Democrat or a Democrat. All respondents reported having access to the Internet.

Dependent Variables

To gauge knowledge, we examined measures of both differentiated and integrated knowledge. Specifically, we used (1) political factual recall knowledge (differentiated), (2) candidate issue-stance knowledge (integrated), and (3) candidate likes and dislikes (integrated). The items measuring factual knowledge included a battery of four true/false factual statements. These asked respondents whether Dick Cheney was the current Vice President, if it was Congress' responsibility to determine a law constitutional, if the Republican Party had the most members in the House of Representatives, and if the Republican Party was more conservative than the Democratic Party. These were subsequently recoded into an additive knowledge scale ($\alpha = .77$), coded zero for respondents who answered all four questions incorrectly, 1 for one correct answer, 2 for two correct answers, and 3 for three correct answers, and 4 if all answers were answered correctly. Three items were also selected to measure candidate issue-stance knowledge, including those on increasing the military commitment in Iraq, requiring universal health care coverage, and lifting the federal moratorium on offshore drilling. Respondents were asked to identify which of the two presidential candidates promised each of these proposals. The latter issues were selected because they were central to the campaign, as shown by media coverage. These items were recoded into an additive knowledge scale ($\alpha = .80$), ranging from 0 (all incorrect answers) to 3 (all correct answers). Next, to measure candidate likes and dislikes, respondents were asked to indicate how much they liked or disliked each presidential candidate on a scale ranging from 1 (strongly dislike) to 11 (strongly like). An overall measure of candidate likes and dislikes was also created by averaging both McCain and Obama likes/dislikes together.

Control Variables

Based on previous research (Delli Carpini & Keeter, 1996; McLeod, Scheufele, & Moy, 1999; Verba, Schlozman, & Brady, 1995), we included two categories of control measures. Key demographic variables, such as gender (1 = *male*, 0 = *female*), year in school (1 = *freshmen*, 2 = *sophomore*, 3 = *junior*, 4 = *senior*) and race (1 = *White*, 0 = *non-White*), were introduced into the analysis. Also, two predispositions, political interest and party identification, were included. For political interest, we asked "Some people don't pay much attention to political campaigns. How about you? Would you say that you have been very much interested, somewhat interested or not much interested in the political campaigns so far this year?" (1 = *not interested*, 2 = *somewhat interested*, 3 = *very interested*). To measure partisan attachment, we used two questions: (1) "Generally speaking, do you usually think of yourself as a Republican, a Democrat, an Independent, or something else?" and (2) "Would you call yourself a strong Democrat/Republican or a not-very-strong Democrat/ Republican?" Answers to both questions were combined into a five-point scale (1 = *strong Democrat*, 3 = *Independent, Don't know, No preference*, 5 = *strong Republican*).

Media Use Variables

Our key independent variables were attention to campaign information in offline and online media. For offline media, we assessed attention to television and hard-copy newspapers. Regarding online media, we evaluated attention to five specific sources on the Internet, particularly online newspapers, online social networks, video-sharing Web sites, television network Web sites, and presidential candidate Web sites. We asked respondents the following question: "How much attention did you pay to information on 'television' about the campaign for President?" (1 = *a great deal*, 2 = *quite a bit*, 3 = *some*, 4 = *very little*, 5 = *none*). In subsequent questions, the phrase "television" was replaced with the words "hard-copy newspapers," "online newspapers," "online social networks," "video-sharing Web sites," "television network Web sites," and "presidential candidate Web sites." Descriptive statistics for all variables are noted in Appendix 3.1.

Method

We tested our hypotheses using hierarchical ordinary least squares (OLS) regressions with political factual recall knowledge, candidate issue-stance knowledge, and candidate likes and dislikes as the dependent variables. We entered three blocks of predictors, beginning with demographic variables, predispositions, and attention to offline and online media variables. This method allows us to examine how much each block contributes to explaining the variance, while controlling for each previously entered set of variables.

Results and Discussion

Table 3.1 presents the results of the regression models predicting political factual recall knowledge and candidate issue-stance knowledge among young adults.[4] The results show that demographics and predispositions account for a large percent of the incremental variance in political knowledge. Specifically, the relationship between gender and factual knowledge is significant, but not for candidate issue-stance knowledge. Race and year in school were not associated with either factual or candidate issue-stance knowledge. More interested young adults were more likely to correctly answer factual and candidate issue-stance questions. Offline and online media variables added an incremental 7.6 and 6.8 percent of the variance for factual and issue-stance knowledge, respectively. Attention to campaign information on television significantly increases factual knowledge ($\beta = .206$, $p < .05$), but it is not related to candidate issue-stance knowledge. Attention to hard-copy newspaper information was not associated with either factual or candidate issue-stance knowledge. Regarding online sources, online newspapers and television Web sites were unrelated to factual and issue-stance knowledge (RQ1 and RQ2). As expected, video-sharing Web sites were also unrelated to factual and issue-stance knowledge among young people, confirming H2a and H2b. Respondents using social networks were significantly less informed about factual ($\beta = -.202$, $p < .01$) and candidate issue-stance information ($\beta = -.123$, $p < .05$), as predicted by H3a and H3b. These results are consistent with studies suggesting that online social networks are more for socializing and communicating than learning about political information (Baumgartner & Morris, 2009; Cornfield, 2010; Smith, 2009). That is, joining a political group, adding an "I support Obama" profile button, posting political content, and "friending" McCain on a social network may enhance political engagement, but it does not contribute to knowledge (see Bode, 2008; Pasek, more, & Romer, 2009).

On the other hand, this analysis shows that one online media source does boost political knowledge. Confirming prior research (Bimber & Davis, 2003) and validating H1b, attention to campaign information on

Table 3.1 Predictors of Factual Political Knowledge and Candidate Issue-Stance Knowledge

	Factual political knowledge	Candidate issue-stance knowledge
Demographics		
Male	.371**	.088
	(.158)	(.120)
Race	.230	−.030
	(.194)	(.146)
Year in school	−.067	−.072
	(.081)	(.061)
Incremental R² %	7.30***	1.50
Predispositions		
Republican	.053	−.045
	(.064)	(.048)
Interest	.317**	.303***
	(.146)	(.110)
Incremental R² %	7.90***	13.0***
Offline and Online Media		
Television	.206**	.082
	(.097)	(.073)
Hard-copy newspaper	−.035	−.026
	(.076)	(.057)
Online newspaper	.015	.017
	(.069)	(.052)
Online social networks	−.202***	−.123**
	(.069)	(.052)
Video-sharing Web sites	−.060	.084
	(.072)	(.054)
Television network Web sites	.015	.029
	(.070)	(.053)
Presidential candidate Web sites	.085	.097**
	(.060)	(.045)
Incremental R² %	7.60**	6.80**
Final R² %	22.8	21.3
N	191	191

Note: All estimates are unstandardized ordinary least squares coefficients, with standard errors in parentheses. *$p < .10$. **$p < .05$. ***$p < .01$ (one-tailed).

presidential candidate Web sites significantly increases candidate issue-stance knowledge ($\beta = .097$, $p < .05$). Given the features and content of candidate Web sites, such as issue-taking strategies and the absence of competing voices (Foot & Schneider, 2002; Hughes & Hill, 1998; Pippa, 2001; Xenos & Foot, 2005), this result suggests that candidate Web sites are unique relative to other online sources. As anticipated (H1a and H1c), candidate Web sites were unrelated to factual knowledge and candidate like and dislikes.

Table 3.2 displays ordinary least squares results when candidate likes and dislikes are regressed against the same predictors used in Table 3.1. Predispositional variables accounted for almost half of the variance in Obama and McCain likes and dislikes. In columns 1 and 2, party identification was clearly the strongest predictor of candidate likes and dislikes, with Democrats liking Obama more and Republicans favoring McCain more. Likewise, race was a strong predictor of candidate likes and dislikes. Gender, year in school, and campaign interest were not related to Obama and McCain likes and dislikes. Offline and online media variables added an incremental two percent of the variance for candidate likes and dislikes. Traditional media attention did not influence likes and dislikes for either Obama or McCain, which is entirely consistent with past research (Dalrymple & Scheufele, 2007; Eveland & Scheufele, 2000). As expected, column 1 shows that respondents paying attention to campaign information on video-sharing Web sites ($\beta = .213$, $p < .10$) and online social networks significantly increased Obama likeability ($\beta = .259, p < .05$) (H2c and H3c). However, these predictors were not significant for McCain. When the two indices are combined to create a comprehensive measure of candidate likes and dislikes (column 3), attention to online social networks had a significant positive effect ($\beta = .146, p < .10$). Attention to video-sharing Web sites, on the other hand, did not significantly influence overall candidate likes and dislikes. Based on these findings, it can be concluded that attention to campaign information on online social networks increased overall candidate likeability. We can also surmise that attention to online social networks and video-sharing Web sites for campaign information were more likely to increase likeability for those candidates who regularly used these online sources (Obama) than those who did not (McCain). Last, the remaining online sources, particularly online newspapers (RQ1), television network Web sites (RQ2), and presidential candidate Web sites (H1c), were not associated with candidate likes and dislikes.

Conclusion

The medium matters. What is clear from this research is that the type of information source an individual turns to during a campaign influences how much, if any, knowledge that person actually gains. This research makes a contribution that is important to scholars as well as practitioners. In terms of scholars, this work advances the study of the Internet's role in politics as a source of information for the public. Our work is consistent with other findings from the literature that investigates specific types of media use; however, it is more comprehensive in that it simultaneously

Table 3.2 Predictors of Candidate Likes and Dislikes

	Obama likes and dislikes	McCain likes and dislikes	Overall candidate likes and dislikes
Demographics			
Male	−.251	.193	−.029
	(.333)	(.352)	(.220)
Race	−1.31***	.889**	−.209
	(.412)	(.436)	(.272)
Year in school	−.007	−.130	−.068
	(.170)	(.180)	(.112)
Incremental R² %	13.0***	8.20***	2.10
Predispositions			
Republican	−1.87***	1.43***	−.221***
	(.135)	(.142)	(.089)
Interest	−.182	−.043	−.112
	(.307)	(.325)	(.203)
Incremental R² %	46.3***	33.8***	4.10**
Offline and Online Media			
Television	.084	−.014	.035
	(.205)	(.216)	(.135)
Hard-copy newspaper	−.214	.282	.035
	(.159)	(.168)	(.135)
Online newspaper	−.076	−.112	−.094
	(.145)	(.153)	(.096)
Online social networks	.259**	.033	.146*
	(.145)	(.153)	(.095)
Video-sharing Web sites	.213*	−.148	.032
	(.151)	(.160)	(.100)
Television network Web sites	.058	.185	.122
	(.147)	(.156)	(.097)
Presidential candidate Web sites	−.075	−.052	−.064
	(.127)	(.134)	(.083)
Incremental R² %	2.10	1.70	2.90
Final R² %	61.4	43.8	9.10
N	190	190	190

Note: All estimates are unstandardized ordinary least squares coefficients, with standard errors in parentheses. *$p < .10$. **$p < .05$. ***$p < .01$ (one-tailed).

examines the use of different types of media. Our work not only differentiates between online and offline media, it also makes a further distinction between types of online information and the different effects on knowledge. This is a more thorough investigation than those that have examined only "the Internet," or that have investigated the effects of one or two types of information.

In one respect, our findings show that television is still king. In terms of factual or differentiated political knowledge, television usage is the only medium that we found increased knowledge at a statistically significant level. In other areas, however, online information, and more importantly, specific types of online information, were important predictors of integrated knowledge. Specifically, candidate Web sites increased respondents' knowledge of candidate issue positions, and social networking and video-sharing sites increased candidate likeability. However, we also discovered that a majority of online information sources contributed little to political knowledge. In fact, social networkers have lower levels of factual and candidate issue-stance knowledge. This contrasts with some scholars and pundits who have trumpeted the claim that the Internet will be a panacea for some of the supposed ills in our system—the lack of a well-informed public and a lackluster level of participation. Our work, as well as that of others, illustrates that the Internet may not be the cure-all that it was hoped to be. But, we should be careful to note that this does not mean that it cannot have important and meaningful effects in some specific areas.

As we asked at the beginning of this research project, does the Web influence political attitudes or behavior? The results of this study help scholars begin to answer this question in important ways. Candidates have turned to these Web-based tools because they believe they can have a positive impact on their campaigns. These results help us to determine how. It is important for scholars, but possibly more important for campaign professionals, to know how the public responds to different types of information on different types of Web sites. It is important for candidates and their advisors to know, for instance, that certain sources— their own candidate Web sites versus social networking and video-sharing Web sites—contribute very different things to the campaign.

The continual repetition of the campaign Web site in stump speeches, in campaign ads, and in other outlets, can help the candidate inform voters of their positions on certain issues. Other media may help campaigns in other aspects. For instance, young Americans have more candidate likes and dislikes when they use social networking sites and video-sharing sites (for Barack Obama only). As we have noted, this is not a surprise given the entertainment-focused nature of the information contained on these sites. But this type of information can be just as important to campaigns since it can drive voters' favorability (or unfavorability) of a candidate, how comfortable someone is with the candidate, as well as name recognition, which all campaigns strive to achieve. These same sites may influence engagement with the campaign, and while they do not contribute directly to voter knowledge, they may tempt a user to go beyond Facebook or YouTube to the candidate site where actual learning does take place. In other words, voters may not learn from every type of information source available, but this does not mean that important effects do not exist.

Appendix 3.1 Descriptive Statistics

Measure	Mean	Standard deviation	Cronbach's alpha
Political factual recall knowledge	2.66	1.11	.77
Candidate issue-stance knowledge	2.35	0.829	.80
Obama likes and dislikes	7.42	3.32	
McCain likes and dislikes	4.89	2.87	
Overall candidate likes and dislikes	6.15	1.40	
Television	3.43	0.948	
Hard-copy newspaper	2.16	1.09	
Online newspaper	2.89	1.26	
Online social networks	2.31	1.16	
Video-sharing Web sites	2.35	1.13	
Television network Web sites	2.60	1.27	
Presidential candidate Web sites	2.23	1.37	
Party identification	2.76	1.25	
Political interest	1.97	0.746	
Male	0.47	0.492	
Race	0.80	0.404	
Year in school	1.90	0.948	

Notes

1. An earlier version of this paper was presented at the Southern Political Science Association conference, Atlanta, January, 2010.
2. When "social networking" was disaggregated by Web site used, Pasek, more, and Romer (2009) find that Facebook and MySpace do not operate consistently. Facebook users had higher levels of factual political knowledge whereas MySpace users had lower levels.
3. The online survey was conducted during the height of the 2008 campaign, one week after the last presidential debate between Barack Obama and John McCain and almost two weeks before Election Day. Unlike studies conducted during the primary period (see Baumgartner and Morris, 2009), we believe our survey is a better test of attention to online information sources and political knowledge among young people, as political interest and use of online information sources are likely higher during this period than during the primaries or nonelection periods.
4. Given the nature of the dependent variables in Table 3.1, ordered probit would also be an adequate method of estimation besides OLS regression. Thus, we estimated these models using both techniques and did not find significant differences. For ease of interpretation, we present the results of the OLS regressions.

References

Ahem, R. K., Stromer-Galley, J., & Neuman, W. R. (2000). *When voters can interact and compare candidates online: Experimentally investigating political web effects.* Paper presented at the International Communication Association Annual Conference, Acapulco.

Bartels, L., & Rahn, W. M. (2000). *Political attitudes in the post-network era*. Paper presented at the American Political Science Association Annual Meeting, Washington, DC.

Bauerlein, M. (2008). *The dumbest generation: How the digital age stupefies young Americans and jeopardizes our future (or, don't trust anyone under 30)*. New York: Penguin.

Baumgartner, J. C., & Morris, J. S. (2010). MyFaceTube politics: Social networking web sites and political engagement of young adults. *Social Science Computer Review, 28* (1), 24–44.

Becker, L. B., & Dunwoody, S. (1982). Media use, public affairs knowledge and voting in a local election. *Journalism Quarterly, 59*, 212–218.

Becker, L. B., & Whitney, C. D. (1980). Effects of media dependencies: Audience assessment of government. *Communication Research, 7*(1), 95–120.

Berelson, B. R., Lazarsfeld, P. F., & McPhee, W. N. (1954). *Voting*. Chicago: University of Chicago Press.

Bimber, B., & Davis, R. (2003). *Campaigning online: The Internet in U.S. elections*. New York: Oxford University Press.

Bode, L. (2008). *Don't judge a Facebook by its cover: Social networking sites, social capital, and political participation: A pilot study*. Paper presented at the Midwest Political Science Association Annual Meeting, Chicago, IL.

Bybee, C., McLeod, J. M., Leutscher, W. D., & Garramone, G. (1981). Mass communication and voter volatility. *Public Opinion Quarterly, 45*, 69–90.

Campbell, A., Converse, P. E., Miller, W. E., & Stokes, D. E. (1960). *The American voter*. Chicago: University of Chicago Press.

Carlin, C. (2008). *The young vote: Engaging America's youth in the 2008 elections and beyond*. Washington, DC: The Brookings Institution.

Castells, M. (2001). *The Internet galaxy: Reflections on the Internet, business and society*. Oxford: Oxford University Press.

Chaffee, S. H., & Frank, S. (1996). How Americans get political information: Print versus broadcast news. *Annals of the American Academy of Political and Social Science, 546*, 48–58.

Chaffee, S. H., Zhao, X., & Leshner, G. (1994). Political knowledge and the campaign media of 1992. *Communication Research, 21*(3), 305–324.

Cornfield, M. (2010). Game-changers: New technology and the 2008 presidential elections. In L. J. Sabato (Ed.), *The year of Obama: How Barack Obama won the White House*. New York: Longman, pp. 205–230.

Corrado, A., & Firestone, C. M. (1996). *Elections in cyberspace: Toward a new era in American politics*. Washington, DC: The Aspen Institute.

Dalrymple, K., & Scheufele, D. (2007). Finally informing the electorate? How the Internet got people thinking about presidential politics in 2004. *The Harvard International Journal of Press/Politics, 12*, 96–111.

Davis, R. (1999). *The web of politics: The Internet's impact on the American political system*. New York: Oxford University Press.

Davis, R. (2005). Presidential campaigns fine-tune online strategies. *Journalism Studies, 6*(2), 241–244.

Delli Carpini, M., & Keeter, S. (1996). *What Americans know about politics and why it matters*. New Haven, CT: Yale University Press.

DiMaggio, P., Hargittai, F., Neuman, W. R., & Robinson, J. P. (2001). Social implications of the Internet. *Annual Review of Sociology, 27*, 307–336.

Drew, D., & Weaver, D. (2006). Voter learning in the 2004 presidential election: Did the media matter? *Journalism & Mass Communication Quarterly*, 83, 25–42.

Druckman, J. N. (2005). Media matter: How newspapers and television news cover campaigns and influence voters. *Political Communication*, 22, 463–481.

Eveland, W. P. (2003). A "mix of attributes" approach to the study of media effects and new communication technologies. *Journal of Communication*, 53(3), 395–410.

Eveland, W. P., & Dunwoody, S. (2000). Examining information processing on the World Wide Web using think aloud protocols. *Media Pyschology*, 2(3), 219–244.

Eveland, W. P., & Dunwoody, S. (2001). User control and structural isomorphism or disorientation and cognitive load? Learning from the Web versus print. *Communication Research*, 28(1), 48–78.

Eveland, W. P., & Dunwoody, S. (2002). An investigation of elaboration and selective scanning as mediators of learning from the Web versus print. *Journal of Broadcasting & Electronic Media*, 46, 34–53.

Eveland, W. P., & Scheufele, D. A. (2000). Connecting news media use with gaps in knowledge. *Political Communication*, 17(3), 215–237.

Eveland, W. P., Marton, K., & Seo, M. (2004). Moving beyond "just the facts": The influence of online news on the content and structure of public affairs knowledge. *Communication Research*, 31(1), 82–108.

Eveland, W. P., Seo, M., & Marton, K. (2002). Learning from the news in campaign 2000: An experimental comparison of TV news, newspapers, and online news. *Media Psychology*, 4, 355–380.

Eveland, W. P., Cortese, E., Park, H., & Dunwoody, S. (2004). How Web site organization influences free recall, factual knowledge, and knowledge structure density. *Human Communication Research*, 30(2), 208–233.

Foot, K. A., & Schneider, S. M. (2002). Online action in campaign 2000: An exploratory analysis of the U.S. political Web sphere. *Journal of Broadcasting and Electronic Media*, 46(2), 222–244.

Gilens, M., Vavreck, L., & Cohen, M. (2007). The mass media and the public's assessments of presidential candidates, 1952–2000. *Journal of Politics*, 69(4): 1160–1175.

Graber, D. A. (1996). *Mass media and American politics*. Washington, DC: CQ Press.

Grossman, L. (1995). *The electronic commonwealth*. New York: Penguin.

Gueorguieva, V. (2008). Voters, MySpace, and YouTube: The impact of alternative communication channels on the 2006 election cycle and beyond. *Social Science Computer Review*, 26(3), 288–300.

Hansen, G. J. (2000). *Internet presidential campaigning: The influences of candidate internet sites on the 2008 election*. Paper presented at the Natonal Communication Association, Seattle, WA.

Hansen, G. J., & Benoit, W. L. (2005). Presidential campaigning on the Web: The influence of candidate World Wide Web sites in the 2000 general election. *Southern Communication Journal*, 70(3), 219–229.

Hughes, K. A., & Hill, J. E. (1998). *Cyberpolitics: Citizen activism in the age of the Internet*. Lanham, MD: Rowman & Littlefield.

Jennings, M. K., & Zeitner, B. (2003). Internet use and civic engagement: A longitudinal analysis. *Public Opinion Quarterly*, 67, 311–334.

Johnson, T. J., Briama, M. A., & Sothirajah, J. (1999). Doing the traditional media sidestep: Comparing the effects of the Internet and other nontraditional media with traditional media in the 1996 presidential campaign. *Journalism and Mass Communication Quarterly, 76*(1), 99–123.

Kenski, K., & Stroud, N. J. (2006). Connections between Internet use and political efficacy, knowledge, and political participation. *Journal of Broadcasting & Electronic Media, 50*(2), 173–192.

Lowden, N. B., Anderson, P. A., Dozier, D. M., & Lauzen, M. M. (1994). Media use in the primary election: A secondary medium model. *Communication Research, 21*(3), 293–304.

Madden, M. (2007). *Pew Internet & American Life Project.* Retrieved June 10, 2009 from: www.pewinternet.org/~/media//Files/Reports/2007/PIP_Online_Video_2007.pdf.pdf.

Margolis, M., & Resnick, D. (2000). *Politics as usual: The cyberspace 'revolution'.* Thousand Oaks, CA: Sage.

Martin, K. D., & Schmeisser, H. E. (2008). *The effects of social networking websites and youth voter participation.* Paper presented at the American Political Science Association Annual Meeting, Boston, MA.

McLeod, J., Scheufele, D. A., & Moy, P. (1999). Community, communication, and participation: The role of mass media and interpersonal discussion in local political participation. *Political Communication, 16,* 315–336.

Mondak, J. J. (1995). *Nothing to read: Newspapers and elections in a social experiment.* Ann Arbor, MI: University of Michigan Press.

Neuman, W. R. (1981). Differentiation and integration: Two dimensions of political thinking. *The American Journal of Sociology, 86*(6), 1236–1268.

Neuman, W. R., Just, M. R., & Crigler, A. N. (1992). *Common knowledge: News and the construction of political meaning.* Chicago: University of Chicago Press.

Norris, P. (2000). *A virtuous circle: Political communication in postindustrial societies.* Cambridge: Cambridge University Press.

Owen, D. (2008). Election Media and Youth Political Engagement. *Journal of Social Science Education, 7/8*(2/1), 14–24.

Owen, D. (2010). Media in the 2008 election: 21st century campaign, same old story. In L. J. Sabato (Ed.), *The year of Obama: How Barack Obama won the White House.* New York: Longman, pp. 167–186.

Pasek, J., more, e., & Romer, D. (2009). Realizing the social Internet? Online social networking meets offline social capital. *Journal of Information Technology and Politics, 6*(3–4), 197–215.

Patterson, T. E. (1980). *The mass media election: How Americans choose their president.* New York: Praeger Publishers.

Patterson, T. E., & McClure, R. D. (1976). *The unseeing eye: The myth of television power in national elections.* New York: Putnam.

Pettey, G. R. (1988). The interaction of the individual's social environment, attention and interest, and public affairs media use on political knowledge holding. *Communication Research, 15*(3), 265–281.

Pew Research Center. (2007). *Public knowledge of current affairs little changed by news and information revolutions: What Americans know: 1989–2007.* Retrieved August 1, 2009 from: http://people-press.org/report/319/public-knowledge-of-current-affairs-little-hanged-by-news-and-information-revolutions.

Pippa, N. (2001). *Digital divide: Civic engagement, information poverty, and the Internet worldwide.* New York: Cambridge University Press.

Price, V., & Zaller, J. (1993). Who gets the news: Alternative measures of news reception and their implications for research. *Public Opinion Quarterly, 57,* 133–164.

Prior, M. (2005). News vs. entertainment: How increasing media choice widens gaps in political knowledge and turnout. *American Journal of Political Science, 49*(3), 577–592.

Robinson, J. P., & Davis, D. K. (1999). Television news and the informed public: An information-processing approach. *Journal of Communication, 40,* 106–119.

Robinson, J. P., & Levy, M. K. (1986). *The main source: Learning from television news.* Beverly Hills, CA: Sage.

Scheufele, D. A., & Nisbet, M. C. (2002). Being a citizen online: New opportunities and dead ends. *The Harvard International Journal of Press/Politics, 7*(3), 55–75.

Scheufele, D., Nisbet, M. C., & Brossard, D. (2003). Pathways to participation? religion, communication contexts, and mass media. *International Journal of Public Opinion Research, 15*(3), 300–324.

Schonfeld, E. (2008). *News sites attract record audience on election night.* Retrieved August 1, 2009 from: www.techcrunch.com/2008/11/05/news-sites-attract-record-audience-on-election-night/.

Selnow, G. W. (1998). *Electronic whistle-stops: The impact of the Internet in American politics.* Westport, CT: Praeger.

Shah, D. V., Kwak, N., & Holbert, R. L. (2001). "Connecting" and "disconnecting" with civic life: Patterns of Internet use and the production of social capital. *Political Communication, 18,* 141–162.

Shah, D., McLeod, D., & Yoon, S. (2001). Communication, context, and community: An exploration of print, broadcast, and Internet influences. *Communication Research, 28*(4), 464–506.

Smith, A. (2009). *The Internet's role in campaign 2008.* Pew Internet & American Life Project. Retrieved June 10, 2009 from: www.pewinternet.org/~/media//Files/Reports/2009/The_Internets_Role_in_Campaign_2008.pdf.

Smith, A., & Rainie, L. (2008). *The Internet and the 2008 election.* Pew Internet & American Life Project. Online. Retrieved August 1, 2009 from: www.pewtrusts.org/uploadedFiles/wwwpewtrustsorg/Reports/Society_and_the_Internet/PIP_2008_election.pdf.

Sotirovic, M., & McLeod, J. (2004). Knowledge as understanding: The information processing approach to political learning. In L. L. Kaid (Ed.), *Handbook of Political Communication Research.* Hillsdale, NJ: Lawrence Erlbaum Associates, pp. 357–394.

Sue, V. M. (1994). *Television reliance and candidates' personal qualities in the 1992 election.* Unpublished Ph.D dissertation, Department of Communication, Stanford University, Palo Alto, CA.

Sweetser, K. D., & Kaid, L. L. (2008). Stealth soapboxes: Political information efficacy, cynicism and uses of celebrity weblogs among readers. *New Media & Society, 10*(1), 67–91.

Tedesco, J. C., Miller, J. L., & Spiker, J. A. (1999). Presidential campaigning on the information superhighway: An exploration of content and form. In

L. L. Kaid, & D. G. Bystrom (Ed.), *The Electronic Election: Perspectives on the 1996 Campaign Communication.* Mahwah, NJ: Lawrence Erlbaum, pp. 51–63.

Tewksbury, D., & Althaus, S. L. (2000). Differences in knowledge acquisition among readers of the paper and online versions of a national newspaper. *Journalism and Mass Communication Quarterly, 77*(3), 457–479.

Tichenor, P. J., Donahue, G. A., & Olien, C. N. (1970). Mass media flow and differential growth in knowledge. *Public Opinion Quarterly, 34,* 159–170.

Verba, S., Schlozman, K. L., & Brady, H. F. (1995). *Voice and equality: Civic voluntarism in American politics.* Cambridge, MA: Harvard University Press.

Wattenberg, M. (2007). *Is voting for young people?: With a postscript on citizen engagement.* New York: Longman.

Weaver, D., & Drew, D. (1993). Voter learning in the 1990 off-year election: Did the media matter? *Journalism Quarterly, 70,* 356–368.

Wei, R., & Ven-hwei, L. (2008). News media use and knowledge about the 2006 U.S. midterm elections: Why exposure matters in voter learning. *International Journal of Public Opinion Research, 20*(3), 347–362.

Williams, C. B. (2008). *What is a social network worth? Facebook and vote share in the 2008 presidential primaries.* Paper presented at the American Political Science Association Annual Meeting, Boston, MA.

Williams, C. B., & Gulati, G. J. (2007). *Social networks in political campaigns: Facebook and the 2006 midterm elections.* Paper presented at the American Political Science Association Annual Meeting, Chicago, IL.

Williams, C. B., & Gulati, G. J. (2009). *Facebook grows up: An empirical assessment of its role in the 2008 congressional elections.* Paper presented at the Midwest Political Science Association Annual Meeting, Chicago, IL.

Winograd, M., & Hais, M. D. (2008). *Millennial makeover.* New Brunswick, NJ: Rutgers University Press.

Xenos, M., & Foot, K. A. (2005). Politics as usual, or politics unusual? Position-taking and dialogue on campaign web sties in the 2002 U.S. election. *Journal of Communication, 55*(1), 169–185.

Xenos, M., & Moy, P. (2007). Direct and differential effects of the Internet on political and civic engagement. *Journal of Communication, 57,* 704–718.

Zaoh, X., & Chaffee, S. (1995). Campaign advertisements versus television news as sources of political issue information. *Public Opinion Quarterly, 58,* 41–95.

Chapter 4

Evaluating Candidate E-Mail Messages in the 2008 U.S. Presidential Campaign

Andrew Paul Williams and Evan Serge

In the 2008 presidential campaign technology appeared to advance in ways that were unimaginable only four years earlier. The impact of the Web during this campaign was indisputable. The 2008 presidential contest demonstrated that the Web had developed from what was once a new channel of communication between voters, where voters could discuss political issues during the 1996, 2000, and 2004 campaigns (Selnow, 1998), to become expected and a mainstay in political communication, as Margolis, Resnick, and Tu (1997) anticipated. According to the Pew Internet and American Life Project, the percentage of adults in the U.S. who have gone online for election information has risen from 4 percent in 1996, 18 percent in 2000, and 29 percent in 2004 to 44 percent in 2008 (Smith, 2009).

Additionally, Web offerings multiplied, and technology advanced significantly during the 2008 U.S. presidential race, providing the advantages of many more avenues for information, as well as opportunities for interactive communication between candidates and voters as predicted by Kaid (2002). Gueorguieva (2008) noted the impact YouTube and MySpace had on candidate control of messages during the 2006 elections. In the 2008 campaign, Web sites such as YouTube, Facebook, MySpace, Flickr, SecondLife, and Twitter became significant online venues for information dissemination and social networking, which provided candidates with a myriad of opportunities to diversify and increase their electronic campaigning efforts.

The Pew Internet and American Life Project reported that 59 percent of Internet users used electronic tools such as e-mail, instant messaging, text messages or Twitter to get or forward political information (Smith, 2009). The mainstreaming of the Web in the 2008 campaign, and the expectation that candidates, traditional media sources, and citizens keep up with the fast-changing technology, was exemplified by the CNN/YouTube debate that allowed an unprecedented level of civic engagement compared to traditional presidential debates (McKinney & Rill, 2009).

Both 2008 U.S. presidential candidates maintained a strong Web presence, utilizing interactive features. Democratic candidate Barack Obama and Republican candidate John McCain both established Web sites with hyperlinks to internal and external content. Discussion forums allowed site users to interact with each other. Candidates and campaign staff made regular updates to blogs. Both campaigns established accounts on newer social media Web sites, such as Facebook, MySpace, and Twitter.

Candidate Use of E-mail Messages

This chapter focuses on the McCain and Obama presidential campaigns' use of e-mail messages during the general phase of the 2008 U.S. campaign. While e-mail may seem mundane and less innovative than other Web offerings, e-mail remains an essential and popular tool of communication offered by the Internet. Jones (2009) reports that 91 percent of all U.S. citizens now use e-mail. Recognizing the size of this population, both Democratic and Republican candidates used e-mail to communicate with voters during the 2008 race.

The Pew Internet and American Life Project findings indicate that e-mail was the dominant form used to discuss the 2008 election. In fact, 40 percent of U.S. adults said that they used e-mail to engage in political communication, and 48 percent of Obama supporters and 38 percent of McCain supporters reported receiving e-mails directly from a campaign (Smith, 2009).

Stromer-Galley (2003) argued that Web and e-mail can foster users' information seeking and dissemination, but political campaigns have not utilized it well. While political officials have attempted to incorporate e-mail into their communications, many have not integrated it effectively (Scheffer, 2003). For example, Trammell and Williams (2004) found that 2002 Florida gubernatorial candidates' e-mail messages often failed to align with the message strategies of their Web sites, and interactive features were negligible in their e-mail messages.

Although improvements were made in e-mail interactive features and message congruity with other campaign communication in the 2004 presidential campaign (Wiese & Gronbeck, 2005), Williams and Trammell's (2005) findings from content analysis of campaign e-mail messages of the Bush and Kerry campaigns indicated the candidates failed to utilize many available interactive features with e-mail messages.

Williams (2005) argued that perhaps the most important development in 2008 online campaigning was the potential broad expansion of campaign communications. He suggested that viral marketing possibilities such as, "forwarding of e-mails can potentially overcome selective exposure; similar to the numerous findings about televised political ads" (p. 406). Indeed, the potential exists for campaigns to take advantage of the viral communication that forwarding e-mails may provide. Smith (2009) reported that 47 percent of e-mail users forwarded e-mail messages with political content to members of their social circle.

Cornfield (2004) suggested that campaign messages may have more impact on recipients of a forwarded e-mail message than a recipient of direct campaign e-mail and that e-mail is vital to any viral marketing strategy. Research indicates people are likely to forward an e-mail from a close, interpersonal source (Chiu, Hsieh, Kao, & Lee, 2007).

Results of studies about the effectiveness of e-mail use in political efforts are mixed. Nickerson (2007) contends that the use of e-mail by campaigns for voter registration and turnout are not cost-effective, but this may be because political campaigns are not making full use of this medium's potential. However, Bergan's (2009) research found legislators contacted via e-mail from a lobby group were more likely to vote in favor of the bill than those not contacted. Additionally, research about the 2008 U.S. campaign indicated that e-mail did matter, as 59 percent of e-mail users reported using e-mail to discuss the campaign with others at some point in the election cycle, and 17 percent of e-mail users discussed the election with another e-mail user every day (Smith, 2009).

Interactivity

Interactivity remains an integral aspect of an effective online communication strategy. Political campaigns' Web sites, while not effectively using interactivity at first, have improved in subsequent elections. Candidate Web sites in the 1996 and 1998 elections were lacking in interactive features enabling two-way communication between the candidate and the public (Stromer-Galley, 2000). Puopolo (2001) found more integration of these features, as well as more user-controlled content.

Stromer-Galley (2003) suggests that the Web offers interactivity to users, through content availability and opportunities for dissemination of information. Offering interactivity on a campaign Web site may improve evaluations of candidate attributes, including sensitivity, responsiveness, and trustworthiness. Additionally, interactivity may also increase the likelihood of user agreement with a candidate's policy positions (Sundar, Kalyanaraman, & Brown, 2003).

Focus group research revealed that e-mail, interactive chats, and discussion boards could be strong tools for candidate—public interaction (Stromer-Galley & Foot, 2002). There appears to be a relationship between the encouragement of active discussions, mobilization strategies, and interactive constructs on Usenet and other forums, such as Yahoo Groups (Stromer-Galley, 2002).

Peng, Tham, and Xiaoming (1999) argued that providing users with control of online content, by providing hyperlinks, for example, is an important form of interactivity. Stromer-Galley (2000) found presidential sites only linked to pages within their own site in the 1996 campaign. However, Foot, Schneider, Dougherty, Xenos, and Larsen (2003) analyzed candidates' use of hyperlinks on their Web sites during the 2002 U.S. campaign cycle. They concluded that candidates promoted interactivity by providing hyperlinks to external information, and this strategic use of hyperlinks may increase source credibility. Furthermore, Williams and Trammell (2005) maintain that by integrating multimedia and interactive elements, such as hyperlinks in their e-mail messages, candidates may appear to improve two-way communication with voters (Williams, & Trammell, 2005).

Williams, Trammell, Postelnicu, Landreville, and Martin (2005) found that United States 2004 presidential candidates' use of interactive elements, such as hyperlinks, multi-media, and platforms for the easy dissemination of information by forwarding e-mail messages were essential for political mobilization efforts. Additionally, they argue that hyperlinks offer users the three main types of interactivity previously noted by McMillan, (2002), user-to-system, user-to-user, and user-to-document.

Dalrymple and Scheufele's (2007) findings suggest that nonlinear connectivity and interactivity, offered through hyperlinking in online newspaper coverage of the 2004 U.S. presidential campaign, may have increased levels of integrated and differentiated political knowledge. The effective use of interactive tools on social networking sites may increase user's attitudes toward political candidates (Utz, 2009).

In addition to technical interactivity, Web sites provide textual interactivity. Content that creates a sense of textual engagement is a type of interactivity (Newhagen, Cordes, & Levy, 1995). As such, users who find content engaging may experience a perceived form of interactivity. Textual interactivity is an important technical interactivity in online political communication offerings, especially on Web sites and blogs, and that textual interactivity should be analyzed to better understand and evaluate online interactivity (Trammell, Williams, Postelnicu, & Landreville, 2006). In addition, text-based interactivity and campaign-to-user interactivity increased recall of candidate issue stances and time spent on candidate Web sites (Warnick, Xenos, Endres, & Gastil, 2005). However, their findings indicate that when textual and technical inter-activity are present, issue recall is lower. In a study of an advocacy group's blog, Moldoff and Williams (2007) suggested that the presence of self-reflexive metacommunication in posts can be a form of textual inter-activity, which encourages discussion and debate.

Kaid and Davidson (1986) developed a coding scheme called "Video-style," which measures message strategies employed in televised political ads by candidates, such as calling for change and inviting participa-tion through verbal appeals. Essentially, candidates employed textual interactivity in their ads, attempting to affect voters' engagement with the content of their ads—and obviously to influence voting choices. These message strategies from "Videostyle" were adapted and employed to analyze political Web sites and into "Webstyle" (Bystrom, Banwart, Kaid, & Robertson, 2004). Trammell, Williams, Postelnicu, and Landreville (2006) argue that the use of these message strategies identified in "Videostyle" and "Webstyle" are interactive. They argue that many of these message strategies, such as candidates' direct address to the audience, calls for action, and inviting participation inherently creates a sense of interactivity for the users' as they become engaged with the content.

Given the limited prior findings about campaign uses of e-mail messages, this study considered the following research questions:

RQ1:   Will candidates use e-mail messages to self promote at a higher rate than to attack the opponent?

RQ 2:   Will candidates speak directly to the reader more often than not in their e-mail messages?

RQ3:   Will candidates construct e-mail messages as interactive tools?

RQ4:   Will candidates use the message strategies of inviting participation or action in their e-mail messages?

RQ5:   To what extent, and for what purposes, will candidates use hyperlinks in e-mail messages?

RQ6:   What issues will candidates discuss most frequently in e-mail messages?

Method

This chapter employed a content analysis of the universe of official campaign e-mail messages sent from the McCain and Obama campaigns during the general election cycle of the 2008 U.S. presidential campaign. E-mail messages sent from Labor Day through Election Day 2004 were considered (*N* = 131), from Democratic candidate Senator Barack Obama (*n* = 68) and Republican candidate John McCain (*n* = 63).

Coding of the e-mail messages was performed by two trained coders. Intercoder reliability was established at .94 across all categories, using Holsti's formula[1] (North, Holsti, Zaninovich, and Zinnes, 1963). The e-mail was the unit of analysis, and categories included e-mail classifications, direct address, interactive tools, message strategies, hyperlinks, and issues.

Results

The first research question asked if candidates would use e-mail messages to self promote at a higher rate than to attack the opponent. In fact, self promotion was the main strategy in 82 percent of the e-mail messages. Only 18 percent of the items contained an attack on the opponent. E-mail messages sent by Obama's campaign used promotion 78 percent of the time. McCain's e-mail messages used promotion 87 percent of the time. McCain used attacks in 13 percent of his campaign's e-mail messages, and Obama used attacks in 22 percent of his e-mail messages.

The second question concerned how often the candidates spoke directly to the reader in their e-mail messages. Direct address was present in 93.9 percent of the e-mail messages. McCain used direct address in 88.9 percent of his campaign's e-mail messages, and Obama used direct address is 98.5 percent of his e-mail messages.

Interactivity was the next topic, and findings indicated that 100 percent of the e-mail messages of the McCain and Obama campaigns employed some type of technical and textual interactivity. However, these two categories of interactivity are broadly defined and included different types of interactive tools and strategies.

The most frequently used form of technical interactivity was present in the form of basic hyperlinks (i.e., stand-alone links in the form of a button or stand-alone link that was not a banner, graphic, photography, or embedded in the text of the e-mail message) in 93.1 percent of the candidate e-mail messages. The second most frequently used form of technical interactivity was embedded hyperlinks (i.e., links that were actually integrated within the body of the text of the e-mail messages) in 87.8 percent of the candidate e-mail messages. The third most frequently used form of technical interactivity was banner/image hyperlinks (i.e., links used visuals that typically appeared at the top of each e-mail message) in 89.3 percent of the candidate e-mail messages. The use of other types of technical activity were low in the e-mail messages: video (16.8 percent); search function (2.3 percent); and audio (1.5 percent). There was little variance in how McCain and Obama used technical interactivity in their e-mail messages. (Table 4.1 provides frequencies for the types of technical interactivity present in both campaign's e-mail messages.)

The most frequently used type of textual interactivity in e-mail messages of both candidates were calls to participation/action (i.e., directly asking the reader of the e-mail to do something) and metacommunication (i.e., either self-reflexive or strategy and process discourse about the candidates, campaign, or campaigning process). Both of these two types of textual interactivity appeared in 100.0 percent of the e-mail messages. The next most frequently used type of textual interactivity was direct address (i.e., content where the e-mail messages speak directly to the reader). The use of direct address was present in 88.9 percent of McCain's e-mail messages and in 98.5 percent of Obama's e-mail messages. The least frequently used type of textual interactivity was inclusive language (i.e., we . . . to the e-mail reader), present in only 34.4 percent in the e-mail messages.

Table 4.1 Technical Interactive Tools and Multimedia Present in E-Mail Messages

Technical interactivity and multimedia	Total %	McCain %	Obama %
Audio	1.5	1.6	1.5
Banner/image link	89.3	88.9	89.7
Direct link to static downloadable material	0.0	0.0	0.0
Games/quizzes	0.0	0.0	0.0
Interactive graphs	0.8	1.6	0.0
Hyperlink embedded body of e-mail text	87.8	90.5	85.3
Basic hyperlinks	93.1	87.3	98.5
Personalized downloadable material	0.0	0.0	0.0
Photo gallery	0.0	0.0	0.0
Photo-slide show	0.0	0.0	0.0
Search function	2.3	4.8	0.0
Video	16.8	11.1	16.8

Note: Percentages are of all 176 technical interactive tools and multimedia present in e-mail messages.

The fourth question addressed was whether the candidates would use the message strategies of inviting participation or action most frequently in their e-mail messages. Inviting participation or action was present in 100 percent of the candidates' e-mail messages. The second most frequently used message strategy was calling for change and was present in 26.7 percent of the e-mail messages (19.0 percent of McCain messages and 33.8 percent of Obama messages). Attacking personal qualities of a politician was present in 16.0 percent of the e-mail messages. McCain used this strategy in 7.9 percent of his e-mail messages, and Obama employed this attacking strategy in 8.8 percent of his messages. Table 4.2 identifies message strategies used by each candidate.

Another research question asked about candidate use of hyperlinks in e-mail messages. In the 131 e-mail messages analyzed, 450 hyperlinks were present. The hyperlinks were equally present in the two candidate's e-mail messages, with McCain and Obama each using 225 hyperlinks. Of these hyperlinks, the primary uses were as images (84 percent), as textually embedded referrals (70.2 percent), and as donation requests (60.3 percent). The top three uses of hyperlinks in McCain's e-mail messages were as images (89 percent), as textually embedded references (73 percent), and as volunteer requests (60.3 percent). The top three uses of hyperlinks in Obama's e-mail messages were: as donation requests (92.6 percent); as images (79.4 percent); and as textually embedded references (67.6 percent). Table 4.3 details the candidates' use of hyperlinks in their e-mail messages.

The last research question related to the issues the candidates discussed most frequently in their e-mail messages. Only 8.4 percent of the candidates' e-mail messages were classified as issue messages, compared to 87.0 percent which were about the "horse race." The main issues present in these e-mail

Table 4.2 Candidate Message Strategy Used in E-Mail Messages

Message Strategy	Prevalence %	McCain %	Obama %
Candidate as a voice for the people	9.9	6.3	13.2
Incumbency stands for legitimacy	0.0	0.0	0.0
Calling for change	26.7	19.8	33.8
Invite participation or action	100.00	100.00	100.00
Emphasizing hope for the future	13.7	19.0	8.8
Yearning for the past	2.3	1.6	2.9
Traditional values	2.3	4.8	0.0
Represent philosophical center of party	0.0	0.0	0.0
Use of statistics to support argument	3.8	1.6	5.9
Use of expert authorities to support argument	0.0	0.0	0.0
Candidate positioning himself as expert authority	5.3	6.4	4.4
Identifying with the experiences of others	5.3	3.2	7.4
Emphasizing political accomplishments	6.1	9.5	2.9
Attacking record of politician	8.4	7.9	8.8
Attacking personal qualities of politician	16.0	19.0	13.2
Attack opponent on his stands	20.6	15.9	25.0
Compare candidate stands with stands of opponent	16.0	19.0	13.2
Compare personal qualities with personal qualities of the opponent	4.6	4.8	4.4
"Above the trenches" position	5.3	7.9	2.9
Use of personal tone ("I")	44.3	39.8	48.5
Address readers as peers ("we")	33.6	11.1	54.4
Use of political experience, anecdotes to support positions	3.1	6.3	0.0
Using endorsements by party and other leaders	6.1	7.9	4.4

Note: Percentages are of all 430 message strategies present in e-mail messages.

messages were the economy (85.5 percent), war (32.8 percent), and health care (21.8 percent). The main issue content in McCain's campaign e-mail messages was the economy (80.0 percent), followed by war (32.0 percent), and defense and national security (32.0 percent). Obama's campaign e-mail messages also featured the economy (90 percent) as the foremost issue; health care and war (each at 33.3 percent) were distant contenders. Few candidate e-mail messages addressed other issues such as the environment, education, and domestic social issues.

Discussion

The candidate e-mail messages of 2008 were not as improved, or changed, as might have been expected, based on both prior research and the numerous advances in Internet and related emerging technologies. The candidate

Table 4.3 Hyperlink Presence in E-Mail Messages

Hyperlink presence	Total %	McCain %	Obama %
E-mail send to a friend, forward to a friend	22.1	31.7	13.2
Forward to local media, talk radio	0.0	0.0	0.0
Vote early, absentee ballot	4.6	7.6	4.6
Printer friendly	0.0	0.0	0.0
Donate	60.3	25.4	92.6
Respond	14.5	20.6	8.8
Sign up to volunteer, host event, etc.	42.7	60.3	26.5
General event information	13.7	20.6	7.4
Actual, embedded text	70.2	73.0	67.6
Image as a hyperlink	84.0	88.9	79.4
Link to media article	0.0	0.0	0.0
Link to candidate Web site	29.8	25.4	33.8
Link to political party Web site	0.0	0.0	0.0
Link to opponent's Web site	0.0	0.0	0.0
Link to candidates' other online presence	0.0	0.0	0.0
Other	1.5	0.0	1.5

Note: Percentages are of all 450 hyperlinks present in e-mail messages.

e-mail messages analyzed in this chapter did not demonstrate much advancement from those examined during the 2004 campaign. Overall, findings suggest only minor improvements in the e-mail messages, but there are also some indications that the candidates' use of e-mail was less advanced than the prior national U.S. election, which suggests that candidates are not harnessing the full potential that e-mail can provide with an integrated online campaign strategy.

Candidates did use their e-mail messages to self promote at a higher rate than to attack the opponent. This finding suggests this medium is being used more for reinforcement in communicating with readers, rather than focusing on the opponent. However, while the tone of most e-mail messages was positive, the majority of these promotional, candidate-controlled communications were horse-race-oriented, focusing user attention on the race itself, instead of providing substantive campaign information. These findings are similar to those of research on the use of e-mail in the 2004 campaign.

Candidates did speak directly to the reader more often than not in their e-mail messages, which suggests a commitment to engaging citizens with important parts of the campaign. When direct address was present, 100 percent of the e-mail messages requested the user to take some sort of action. Unfortunately, these calls to action were typically to attend a rally or to draw attention to a fund-raising campaign event that would do little to educate the users about the candidates' platforms and issue stances.

Candidates did construct many e-mail messages that were interactive tools. All of McCain and Obama e-mail messages contained interactive elements. However, the nature of technical interactivity was not well-developed, considering the primary form of technical interaction was hyperlinks guiding users to promotional campaign-controlled content, and the negligible amount multimedia content was inconsistent with candidates' Web sites. However, one encouraging finding was that all candidates used metacommunication as a form of textual interactivity, and the majority of both the use of self-reflexive and strategy/process metacommunication was educational. One should be cautiously optimistic about this finding, because similar to extensive use of direct address as textual activity, users' are often encouraged to interact with content that typically educated and engaged them with information about the campaign itself—and not important issues.

Candidates did use the message strategy of inviting users to participate or take some action most frequently in their e-mail messages, which can be viewed as an encouraging finding in terms of mobilization and user engagement. However, when examining the campaign e-mail messages' use of this important strategy, the majority of invitations were to visit their respective Web sites and frequently to donate money. This finding is congruent with prior U.S. campaign e-mail research and with Stanyer's (2005) research about e-mails sent by British political parties during the 2005 election cycle, in which e-mails typically were used to solicit donations.

Also disappointing was the finding that only 21.1 percent of the candidate campaign e-mail messages analyzed for this chapter invited users to forward the e-mail through the use of hyperlinks. Only 31.7 percent of McCain's and 13.2 percent of Obama's e-mail messages provided such hyperlinks. None of the candidates' e-mail messages included a technical mechanism that would make it easy for users to forward, and perhaps to personalize, e-mail messages to multiple contacts. This is currently a common, and important, online offering. The lack of an e-mail forwarding tool is a huge step backwards from the 2004 U.S. campaign when, "Nearly every Bush campaign e-mail message provided recipients with a way to forward the content simultaneously to five other people" (Williams & Trammell, 2005).

Hyperlinks were used in all e-mail messages. However, the purposes of the hyperlinks did not indicate a noteworthy advance in online political communication. The majority of hyperlinks in e-mail messages of both candidates were merely images that typically took users to their respective official campaign Web sites, requested financial donations, or asked for volunteers.

The most encouraging finding is the large amount of hyperlinks that were integrated within textual content. It was an advance to see this blending of the textual and technical functions of hyperlinks in the body of the campaign e-mail messages, which is typical in online news content. This finding should be viewed with caution, as the blending of these hyperlinks as both textual and technical forms of interactivity did not direct users to useful external information. In fact, none of the hyperlinks present directed users to media articles. Perhaps more surprisingly, none of the hyperlinks directed users to the candidates' other online presences, such as Facebook, MySpace, Flickr, or Twitter.

Candidates discussed issues infrequently in their e-mail messages. Additionally, the issue content was generally superficial, lacking in substance, and typically associated with requests for financial donations or other campaign requests. Issue content was basically present in a negligible amount of the sample of the campaign e-mail messages, and it was largely vacuous when present. Thus, as found in prior e-mail scholarship, the candidates missed opportunities to educate, engage, and motivate receivers by addressing important campaign issues.

Overall, political candidates are becoming more proficient with the use of electronic communication and are interested in finding ways to maximize their communication efforts. However, the e-mail message use as a whole during the 2008 campaign cycle was similar to the ineffective use of e-mail during the 2004 campaign (see, for example, Williams, 2006). It is surprising that there is such a disconnect from the use of e-mail compared to their other uses of the Web, which was typically much more sophisticated and provided considerable multimedia and information across a variety of Internet offering.

The fact that candidates have made only a few modest improvements in their e-mail messages indicates that the campaigns are neglecting to use e-mail as a powerful political communication tool, which has viral marketing potential and can overcome selective exposure. E-mail may be perceived as commonplace and not as innovative as the many new technological advances of recent years, but it is inexpensive, effective, and can have huge reach due to its presence on personal computers as well as on mobile devices, such as BlackBerrys and iPhones. The candidates' poor use of e-mail messages as a vital part of their electronic campaigning also means they are missing myriad opportunities to communicate with and better inform citizens about important issues that can help to further educate and activate voters.

Note

1. The formula used to compute reliability is a formula given by North, Holsti, Zaninovich, and Zinnes (1963). It is given for two coders and can be modified for any number of coders. $R = 2 (C_{1,2}) / C_1 + C_2$. $C_{1,2}$ = # of category assignments both coders agree on $C_1 + C_2$ = total category assignments made by both coders.

References

Bergan, D. E. (2009). Does grassroots lobbying work? A field experiment measuring the effects of an e-mail lobbying campaign on legislative behavior. *American Politics Research, 37*(2), 327–352.

Bystrom, D., Banwart, M., Kaid, L. L., & Robertson, T. (2004). *Gender and candidate communication: VideoStyle, WebStyle, and NewsStyle.* New York: Routledge.

Chiu, H., Hsieh, Y., Kao, Y., & Lee, M. (2007). The determinants of email receivers' disseminating behaviors on the Internet. *Journal of Advertising Research, 47*(4), 524–534.

Cornfield, M. (2004). *Politics moves online: Campaigning and the Internet.* New York: The Century Foundation Press.

Dalrymple, K. E., & Scheufele, D. A. (2007). Finally informing the electorate? How the Internet got people thinking about presidential politics in 2004. *The Harvard International Journal of Press/Politics, 12*(3), 96–111.

Davis, R. (1999). *The Web of politics: The Internet's impact on the American political system.* New York: Oxford University Press.

Foot, K., Schneider, S., Dougherty, M., Xenos, M., & Larsen, E. (2003). Analyzing linking practices: Candidate sites in the 2002 US electoral Web sphere. *Journal of Computer-Mediated Communication, 8*(3). Online. Retrieved June 15, 2010 from: http://jcmc.indiana.edu/vol8/issue4/foot.html.

Gueorguieva, V. (2008). Voters, MySpace, and YouTube: The impact of alternative communication channels on the 2006 election cycle and beyond. *Social Science Computer Review, 26*(3), 288–300.

Jones, S. (2009). *Generations online in 2009.* Pew Internet and American Life Project. Online. Retrieved August 21, 2009 from: www.pewinternet.org/Reports/2009/Generations-Online-in-2009.aspxm.

Kaid, L. L. (2002). Political advertising and information seeking: Comparing exposure via traditional and Internet channels. *Journal of Advertising, 31*(1), 27–35.

Kaid, L. L., & Davidson, D. K. (1986). Elements of videostyle: Candidate presentation through television advertising. In L. L. Kaid, D. Nimmo, & K. R. Sanders (Eds.), *New perspectives on political advertising.* Carbondale, IL: Southern Illinois University Press, pp. 184–209.

Margolis, M., Resnick, D., & Tu, C. (1997). Campaigning on the Internet: Parties and candidates on the World Wide Web in the 1996 primary season. *Harvard Journal of Press/Politics, 2*, 59–78.

McKinney, M. S., & Rill, L. A. (2009). Not your parents' presidential debates: Examining the effects of the CNN/YouTube debates on young citizens' civic engagement. *Communication Studies, 60*(4), 392–406.

McMillan, S. J. (2002). Exploring models of interactivity from multiple research traditions: Users, documents, and systems. In L. Lievrouw & S. Livingston (Eds.) *Handbook of New Media.* London: Sage, pp. 162–182.

Moldoff, J., & Williams, A. P. (2007). Metacommunication and interactivity: A content analysis of audience framing on an advocacy group's blog. *Journal of International Business Disciplines, (2)*1, 53–69.

Newhagen, J. E., Cordes, J. W., & Levy, M. R. (1995). Nightly@nbc.com: Audience scope and the perception of interactivity in viewer mail on the internet. *Journal of Communication, 45*(3), 164–175.

Nickerson, D. W. (2007). Does email boost turnout? *Quarterly Journal of Political Science, 2*(4), 369–379.

North, R. C., Holsti, O., Zaninovich, M. G., & Zinnes, D. A. (1963). *Content analysis: A handbook with applications for the study of international crisis.* Evanston, IL: Northwestern University Press.

Peng, Foo Y., Tham, N. I., & Xiaoming, H. (1999). Trends in online newspapers: A look at the U.S. web. *Newspaper Research Journal 20*(2), 52–64.

Puopolo, S. (2001). The Web and U.S. senatorial campaigns 2000. *American Behavioral Scientist, 44*(12), 2030–2047.

Selnow, G. W. (1998). *Electronic whistle-stops: The impact of the Internet on American politics.* Westport, CT: Praeger.

Sheffer, M. L. (2003). State legislators' perceptions of the use of e-mail in constituent communication. *Journal of Computer Mediated Communication, 8*(4). Online. Retrieved June 15, 2010 from: http://jcmc.indiana.edu/vol8/issue4/sheffer.html.

Smith, A. (2009). *The Internet's role in campaign 2008.* Pew Internet and American Life Project. Online. Retrieved August 21, 2009 from: www.pewinternet.org/Reports/2009/6–The-Internets-Role-in-Campaign-2008.aspx.

Stanyer, J. (2005). Political parties, the Internet and the 2005 general election: From Web presence to e-campaigning? *Journal of Marketing Management, 21*(9), 1049–1065.

Stromer-Galley, J. (2000). On-line interaction and why candidates avoid it. *Journal of Communication, 50*, 111–132.

Stromer-Galley, J. (2002). *New voices in the public sphere: Political conversation in the internet age.* Unpublished dissertation, University of Pennsylvania.

Stromer-Galley, J. (2003). Diversity of political conversation on the Internet: Users' perspectives. *Journal of Computer-Mediated Communication, 8(3).* Online. Retrieved June 15, 2010 from: http://jcmc.indiana.edu/vol8/issue3/stromergalley.html.

Stromer-Galley, J., & Foot, K. A. (2002). Citizen perceptions of online interactivity and implications for political campaign communication. *Journal of Computer Mediated Communication, 8*(1). Online. Retrieved June 15, 2010 from: http://jcmc.indiana.edu/vol8/issue1.stromerandfoot.html.

Sundar, S. S., Kalyanaraman, S., & Brown, J. (2003). Explicating Web site interactivity: Impression formation effects in political campaign sites. *Communication Research, 30*(1), 30–59.

Trammell, K. D., & Williams, A. P. (2004). Beyond direct mail: Evaluating candidate e-mail messages in the 2002 Florida gubernatorial campaign. *Journal of eGovernment, 1*(1), 105–122.

Trammell, K. D., Williams, A. P., Postelnicu, M., & Landreville, K. D. (2006). Evolution of online campaigning: Increasing interactivity in candidate web sites through text and technical features. *Mass Communication & Society, (9)*1, 21–44.

Utz, S. (2009). The (potential) benefits of campaigning via social network sites. *Journal of Computer-Mediated Communication, 14*(2), 221–243.

Warnick, B., Xenos, M., Endres, D., & Gastil, J. (2005). Effects of campaign-to-user and text-based interactivity in political candidate campaign Web sites. *Journal of Computer-Mediated Communication, 10*(3). Online. Retrieved June 15, 2010 from: http://jcmc.indiana.edu/vol10/issue3/warnick.html.

Wiese, D. R., & Gronbeck, B. E. (2005). Campaign 2004 developments in cyber-politics. In R. E. Denton (Ed.) *The 2004 presidential campaign: A communication perspective.* Lanham, MD: Rowman & Littlefield Publishers, pp. 352–388.

Williams, A. P. (2005). The main frame: Assessing the role of the Internet in the 2004 U.S. presidential contest. In R. E. Denton (Ed.) *The 2004 presidential campaign: A communication perspective.* Lanham, MD: Rowman & Littlefield Publishers, pp. 389–412.

Williams, A. P. (2006). Framing their fight: Candidate e-mail strategies in election 2004. In A. P. Williams & J. C. Tedesco (Eds.). *The Internet election: Perspectives on the Web in campaign 2004.* Lanham, MD: Rowman & Littlefield Publishers, pp. 83–98.

Williams, A. P., & Trammell, K. D (2005). Candidate campaign e-mail messages in the presidential election 2004. *American Behavior Scientist, 49*(4), 560–574.

Williams, A. P., Trammell, K. D., Postelnicu, M., Landreville, K. D., & Martin, J. D. (2005). Blogging and hyperlinking: Use of the web to enhance viability during 2004 U.S. campaign. *Journalism Studies, (6)*2, 177–186.

Section II

New Voices and New Voters

Chapter 5

Campaign 2008

Comparing YouTube, Social Networking, and Other Media Use Among Younger and Older Voters

Paul Haridakis and Gary Hanson

The 2008 presidential campaign will be remembered for a number of historic firsts. For media scholars, the most important of these may well be the increased use of social and interactive media. The media landscape changed dramatically in the four years between the 2004 and 2008 presidential election cycles with the introduction of popular social networking sites on the Internet. YouTube, the video-sharing service, Facebook, the popular social networking site, and Twitter, the micro-blogging service, were created during that period. MySpace, which was less than one year old in 2004, emerged four years later as one of the top-rated sites on the Internet in terms of user traffic.

The changes brought about by these new forms of media are pro-found. For much of our history, the mass media have been conduits for political information where information typically flowed in a single direction: from the elites (e.g., editors and commentators in terms of the news media and candidates and political operatives in terms of political advertising) outward to the general population. The rise of the Internet, specifically the social media phenomenon, provided new, albeit smaller, conduits by which information could flow in multiple directions between media professionals and the audience, and, more importantly, among members of the audience themselves. The exponential increase in the paths by which individuals with a common interest can communicate with each other has changed the media distribution model fundamentally. The personal computer has become for many the most important gateway to the larger world.

Just as important, personal computers changed the way in which media content is created. Prior to the Internet, media content and delivery systems were connected. Television companies produced and distributed their programs, as did newspapers, magazines and radio stations with their content. Now, anyone with a personal computer and even a modest amount of skill can edit photographs and videos, write blog posts and create audio messages, and deliver them through a myriad of paths.

The more social aspects of how content is produced, delivered, and shared were not lost on the voters in the 2008 campaign. Potential voters turned to social media sites in large numbers. It was reported that more than 50 percent of those who had a social networking page used it for politics and that 45 percent of Internet users watched political videos online (Hall, 2009). The candidates used social networking media to reach voters (Carr & Stelter, 2008; Cohen, 2008; Learmonth, 2008). YouTube became a widely used source for campaign video and even sponsored debates in the Democratic primary (Seelye, 2007).

By all accounts, the 2008 presidential campaign captured the attention of younger voters—perhaps because of the issues of the day (an unpopular incumbent, lingering wars in Iraq and Afghanistan), or because of the historic nature of the candidates (Barack Obama, an African-American; Hillary Clinton, a former first lady; John McCain, a former POW and war hero; and Sarah Palin, a charismatic newcomer from the Republican right). Scholars have lamented the decline in participation in politics by younger voters (Delli Carpini, 2000; Pinkleton & Austin, 2004). The 2008 campaign may have, temporarily at least, reversed that trend (Speilman, 2008). Each election cycle a new group of citizens, those who reached their eighteenth birthday since the previous presidential election, are eligible to vote for the first time. In the case of the 2008 campaign, those voters (aged 18 to 21) may be the most comfortable of all the age groups in the worlds of the Internet and social media.

Scholars study media use in every presidential cycle, but the rise of the social media phenomenon in the 2008 campaign made this a particularly interesting election to study, especially the media use among those individuals entering the electorate for the first time. The social media phenomena raise these interesting questions: did these voters use the same media as their older counterparts for political information, did they find them to be useful, and how much did first-time eligible voters engage in newer social media as compared to their older counterparts?

This chapter focuses on differences between two groups (first-time eligible voters and older voters) in terms of their media selection for political information, their perception of the usefulness of the media selected, and their motives for choosing media for political information, as well as differences in a variety of background characteristics and individual differences that have been identified in prior political communication research.

The findings suggest that despite the emergence of social media leading up to the 2008 campaign, traditional media—television, talk radio, newspapers, and magazines—were still the dominant source of political information, but the landscape was beginning to shift.

Media Choice

Historically, all new media have been used almost immediately for political information. Newspapers were a major source of political propaganda and political sentiment in the 1700s, reaching wide influence after the rise of the Penny Press in the early 1800s (Jowett & O'Donnell, 2006). Magazines also emerged as an important source of political fare in the 1800s (e.g., Wells, 2008). Radio began serious campaign coverage in the 1920s (Benjamin, 1987). Since television's coverage of the Republican National Convention in 1952, and since the presidential debates in 1960, television has been the dominant source of political information. In the 1990s, the Internet emerged as an important source of information as well (Kaid, 2002), particularly for younger users such as college students (Althaus & Tewksbury, 2000; Lee, 2006).

Today, political ads may be the most prevalent source of political information, and most people are exposed to campaign ads via television (Kaid, 2004). Television may be where young people first become exposed to politics (Chaffee & Yang, 1990). However, people who seek political information purposively may turn to media such as newspapers (Chaffee & Kanihan, 1997) and the Internet (Kaye & Johnson, 2004)—media that can provide detailed information.

Research over the years has uncovered age differences in choice of media for political fare. In recent presidential elections, Kaid, McKinney, and Tedesco (2007) found that voters over the age of 29 tended to use newspapers and TV more than did voters under the age of 29. Sweetser and Kaid (2008) suggested that younger voters were more likely than older voters to use the Internet for political information. Sweetser and Kaid also asserted that Internet blogs had become an important source of political information, and in 2006, the Pew Internet and American Life Project reported that the majority of bloggers were under the age of 30 (cited in Sweetser & Kaid, 2008, p. 72).

Blogs and other social media are used for social interaction (e.g., Haridakis & Hanson, 2009; Pempek, Yermolayeva, & Calvert, 2009; Thelwall, 2008). This is particularly relevant for the dissemination of political information because more than half a century of research has suggested that political information that originates in the media tends to be shared interpersonally (Campus, Pasquino, & Vaccari, 2008; Lazarsfeld, Berelson, & Gaudet, 1944; Yang & Stone, 2003).

Perceived Usefulness of Media for Political Information

Voters' perceptions of the usefulness of media for political campaign information is an equally important inquiry. Research has suggested that perceived usefulness of campaign media affects voter attitudes, public mood, voting behavior, and political cynicism (Leshner & Thorson, 2000). It is logical to assume that voters will turn to those media they find most useful. Questions remain whether older voters differ from younger voters in their choices of media for political information and in their perceptions of the relative usefulness of media chosen. Kaid and Postelnicu (2006) found younger readers viewed celebrity blogs to be as credible as information from political leaders. Pinkleton and Austin (2004) found that when young adults were not satisfied with TV as a source of political information they were more politically apathetic.

Individual and Media Use Differences

Motives for Using Media for Political Information

One way to understand how voters make their media choices and evaluate their usefulness is to consider motives for selecting those media and the characteristics of the voters themselves. Early researchers suggested that people use the media for functions such as surveillance (Lasswell, 1948). Later researchers identified various motives for using traditional media such as television (Rubin, 1983), newer media such as the Internet (Papacharissi & Rubin, 2000), social media such as YouTube (e.g., Haridakis & Hanson, 2009), and specific media fare such as news (Hanson & Haridakis, 2008) and political information (Kaye & Johnson, 2004; McLeod & Becker, 1974).

Salient motives identified in studies of the use of media for political information include vote guidance, information seeking, surveillance, entertainment, social utility, excitement, and reinforcement (e.g., Garramone, Harris, & Pizante, 1986; Kaye & Johnson, 2002, 2004; McLeod & Becker, 1974). Age may play a role here as well. For college students, for example, an increase in the perceived need for information (surveillance) can lead to use of a greater variety of news media (Vincent & Basil, 1997).

In addition to motives, researchers have studied other individual differences among age groups relevant to the impact of political media. This study looks at a number of them: cynicism towards politics, political self-efficacy, conservatism, elaboration and involvement with political media content, political knowledge, discussion of politics with others, and intent to vote.

Cynicism

Voter cynicism is a long-standing topic of interest among political communication scholars. Some have suggested that media exposure to negative campaign fare and political horse-race journalism leads to voter cynicism (for a review, see Sweetser & Kaid, 2008). Others have been concerned that voter cynicism adversely affects political participation (see Pinkleton & Austin, 2004).

Researchers have also examined the implications of age as it relates to political cynicism. Some research has suggested that cynicism among younger people is one of the factors related to their political disengagement and failure to vote (Bynner & Ashford, 1994; Strama, 1998). Other research suggests no age differences. Sweetser and Kaid (2008) found no differences in levels of cynicism between blog readers under the age of 30 and those over 30.

Self Efficacy

Researchers have suggested that younger voters may be less politically efficacious (feel they can make a difference politically) than older voters (Kaid, McKinney, & Tedesco, 2007). However, exposure to political media fare can enhance political self-efficacy (Sweetser & Kaid, 2008). This may be true of the Web specifically, at least for interactive users. For example, Tedesco (2006) suggested that Web interactivity can enhance younger users' political self-efficacy. One of the benefits of higher political self-efficacy is that young people who are more self-efficacious may be less politically apathetic (Pinkleton & Austin, 2004). Those who are higher in political self-efficacy are more inclined to vote or otherwise participate in political affairs (Pinkleton, Um, & Austin, 2002).

Conservatism

Winston Churchill once allegedly said, "if you aren't a liberal at 20 you have no heart and if you aren't a conservative at 40 you have no brain" (Edmonds, 2008, p. 27). Research over the years has supported the commonly held assumption that older voters are more conservative than younger voters. For example, research has suggested that college students tend to be more liberal than the general population, particularly on cultural issues (Cornelis, Van Hiel, Roets, & Kossowska, 2009; Fisher, 2008). It also has been suggested that younger voters tend to be more supportive of activist democratic candidates (Fisher, 2008).

Elaboration and Involvement

Elaboration reflects a level of involvement with media content in which audience members think about what they are consuming, what they might do with it, and what it means (Perse, 1990). Eveland (2004) suggested that older people tend to elaborate on news fare more than do younger people. Young voters tend to be less involved and interested in politics than older voters (Kaid, McKinney, & Tedesco, 2007). But interest and involvement may vary during particular campaigns. For example, Banwart (2007) found young voters' interest in the 2004 campaign was high, and Barr (2008) reported that younger voters voted in higher numbers than in 2000. At least the popular press suggested this was the case with the 2008 campaign as well.

Knowledge

Older voters tend to be more politically knowledgeable than younger voters (Eveland, 2004; Kaid et al., 2007). But media use can increase political knowledge. For example, television has been an important source of political information for both younger and older audiences (Austin & Pinkleton, 2001). People also use knowledge gained from newer media such as the Internet to make voting decisions (Farnsworth & Owen, 2004).

Political Discussion

Early research has suggested that political discussion is an important means of transmission of political information among those who attend to media and those with whom they share it interpersonally (Lazarsfeld et al., 1944; Berelson, Lazarsfeld, & McPhee, 1954). Political discussion aids political knowledge (Eveland, 2004; Scheufele, 2002) and civic participation (Wyatt, Kim, & Katz, 2000) and is positively associated with media use (Wyatt et al., 2000). Arguably, social media provide a new mechanism for discussion (Haridakis & Hanson, 2009).

Intent to Vote

Doppelt and Shearer (1999) suggested that age is a major distinguishing characteristic between voters and non-voters. However, media use predicts voting behavior (Pinkleton, Austin, & Fortman, 1998). For example, Kaye and Johnson (2002) found that Internet users are more likely to vote. If such generalizations are true, young voter turnout may increase with the growing availability of more media channels and more types of media information.

Research Questions

Our principal focus was to compare first-time eligible voters and older voters on the concepts referenced above:

> *RQ1: Did first-time eligible and older voters differ: (a) in their choice of media for acquiring political information about the campaign; or*

(b) in their perceived usefulness of various media available for political information about the campaign?

RQ2: Did first-time eligible and older voters differ in their motives for using media for political information about the campaign?

RQ3: Were first-time eligible or older voters: (a) more cynical; (b) higher in self-efficacy; (c) more involved with political content about the campaign; (d) more conservative; and/or (e) more knowledgeable about candidates' positions?

RQ4: Did first-time eligible and older voters differ in their reported: (a) cognitive elaboration on political fare; (b) number of political discussions with other people; and/or (c) likelihood to vote?

Method

Sample

The sample was comprised of two segments: college students enrolled in a communication course required as part of a large university's liberal education requirements and a non-student quota sample of adults to whom the students were trained to administer the questionnaire. The quota sample was based on the statistical abstract of the age breakdown of potential voters in the state in which the research was conducted. Data were collected the week preceding the election. A total of 462 questionnaires provided usable data. Of these, 257 were first-time eligible voters who were not old enough to vote in the 2004 presidential election (aged 18–21), and 205 were older voters (aged 22–93).

Measures

Respondents were asked to indicate how often (1 = *never*, 5 = *very often*) they used various media sources to acquire political information about the presidential campaign: television, radio, newspapers, magazines, books, the Internet and specific Internet sites such as video sharing (e.g., YouTube) and social network (e.g., Facebook, MySpace, LinkedIn) sites, and political blogs. We then asked them to assess the usefulness (1 = *not useful at all*, 5 = *very useful*) of these media for political information.

Political self-efficacy was measured with an index adapted from prior research (e.g., Morrell, 2003; Niemi, Craig, & Mattei, 1991). Respondents rated their agreement with seven items (1 = *strongly disagree*, 5 = *strongly agree*). Items reflecting low self-efficacy were reverse coded. Responses were summed and averaged (M = 3.13, SD = 0.57, α = .67).

Conservatism was measured with Mehrabian's (1996) 7-item index. Respondents rated their agreement (1 = *strongly disagree*, 5 = *strongly agree*) with each item. Responses were summed and averaged to create this index of conservatism (*M* = 3.02, *SD* = 0.72, α = .82).

Cynicism was measured with the Pinkleton and Austin (2001) 6-item political cynicism scale. Respondents rated their agreement (1 = *strongly disagree*, 5 = *strongly agree*) with each item. Responses were summed and averaged to create an index of political cynicism (*M* = 3.15, *SD* = 0.82, α = .75).

Perse's (1990) 5-item elaboration index was used to tap the respondents' level of cognitive elaboration on political content about the campaign obtained from the media they used. Participants reported how often they have thoughts referenced in the five statements (1 = *never*, 5 = *very often*). Responses to the five items were summed and averaged (*M* = 3.15, *SD* = 0.82, α = .90).

A shortened 8-item measure adapted from Zaichkowsky (1985) was used to assess involvement with political content. This 7-point semantic differential scale has been used in media research to measure involvement with media personae (Haridakis, 2006) and affinity with specific content such as fantasy sports (Spinda & Haridakis, 2008). Items were summed and averaged (*M* = 5.00, *SD* = 1.10, α = .86).

Knowledge was measured with nine items that tapped knowledge of the presidential candidates' issue positions (e.g., "which candidate is most critical of NAFTA"; "which candidate supports a timetable for with-drawing U.S. troops from Iraq"; "which candidate supports a national health care plan"). These campaign issue positions were gleaned from the candidates' Web sites. Responses to the nine questions (*correct answer* = 1, *incorrect answer* = 0) were summed and averaged to create the knowledge index (*M* = 0.57, *SD* = 0.22).

Political discussion was measured with two questions. One asked how often participants discussed politics with other people face-to-face (*M* = 2.86, *SD* = 0.78). The other question asked how often they discussed politics with others online (*M* = 1.77, *SD* = 0.91). Likelihood to vote was measured with one item that asked participants how likely (1 = *not very likely*, 5 = *very likely*) they were to vote in the election (*M* = 4.61, *SD* = 0.90).

We measured motivation for seeking information about the campaign with a 47-item scale based on past measures of interpersonal com-munication motivation and media-use motives, including those related to online media use (Hanson & Haridakis, 2008; Papacharissi & Rubin, 2000). We included an additional 12 items related specifically to motives for seeking political fare (Johnson & Kaye, 2003). Participants were asked how much each of the 59 motive statements was like their own reasons (1 = *not at all*, 5 = *exactly*) for using the media to acquire political campaign fare. Principal components factor analysis with varimax rotation identified six motive factors, accounting for 66.69 percent of the total variance. Responses to items that loaded on each factor were summed and averaged to create indices of the respective motives. Results of the factor analysis are summarized in Table 5.1.

Factor 1, *Political Evaluation,* was comprised of 11 items that reflected use of media for evaluation of issues, candidates, candidates' stands on the issues, and to reach a voting decision ($M = 3.36$, $SD = 0.86$, $\alpha = .93$). Factor 2, *Convenient Information Seeking,* included 8 items reflecting using media because they are an easy and new way to get information, they can be used anytime, they can be used for as long as one wants, they are liked, and to see what's out there ($M = 3.52$, $SD = 0.84$, $\alpha = .90$). Factor 3, *Entertaining Arousal,* consisted of four items reflecting use of media for political fare because it is amusing, thrilling, exciting, and peps one up ($M = 2.46$, $SD = 1.06$, $\alpha = .91$). Factor 4, *Gainful Companionship,* included three items reflecting using the media to connect with others, alleviate loneliness, or to get them to do something ($M = 1.71$, $SD = 0.80$, $\alpha = .82$). Factor 5, *Self Expression,* consisted of three items that reflected using the media to give one's input, to express oneself, and to answer others' questions ($M = 2.40$, $SD = 0.98$, $\alpha = .81$). Factor 6, *Pass Time,* consisted of three items pertaining to using media to occupy one's time and when there is nothing better to do ($M = 2.63$, $SD = 1.13$, $\alpha = .86$).

We conducted *t*-tests comparing first-time eligible voters and older voters on all variables. Means and standard deviations of older and younger voters on each of the above variables and results of the *t*-test analysis are reported in Table 5.2.

Results

Amount and Usefulness of Media Exposure

We asked participants to report how often they used several media for seeking political fare. Not surprisingly, first-time voters used the Internet and social networking Internet sites (e.g., YouTube, MySpace, Facebook) significantly more often than did older voters. Older voters listened to the radio, and read newspapers significantly more often than did first-time voters. There were no significant differences between the two groups in the amount of time they indicated they spent watching TV, blogging or reading magazines and books for political information. Thus, the most significant media use differences pertained to use of the Internet, social networking, and YouTube, with younger voters using these media sources much more than did older voters.

In addition to using the Internet and social networking sites more often than did older voters, younger voters also found the Internet and social network media to be significantly more useful for acquiring political information. Younger voters also found TV, magazines, books, and blogs to be significantly more useful than did older voters. In fact, younger voters

Table 5.1 Primary Factor Loadings of Motives

	Factor 1	Factor 2	Factor 3	Factor 4	Factor 5	Factor 6
To see what a candidate would do if elected	.83	.22	.06	−.07	.11	.09
To see how candidates stand on issues	.78	.32	−.02	−.08	.08	−.06
To help make up my mind about how to vote in an election	.77	.23	.04	−.05	.04	.07
To help me decide about important issues	.76	.28	.09	.10	.08	−.05
To judge what political leaders are like	.75	.13	.00	−.03	.18	.20
To keep up with the main issues of the day	.74	.28	.10	−.12	.14	.05
To remind me of my candidate's strong points	.74	.13	.20	.13	.09	.01
To find out about how issues affect people like myself	.71	.21	.11	.12	.12	−.05
To judge who is likely to win an election	.66	.08	.18	.08	.25	.10
For unbiased viewpoints	.61	.20	.16	.31	.06	−.23
To enjoy the excitement of an election race	.57	.15	.39	.14	.26	−.03
Because it is easier to get information	.35	.72	.09	−.05	.08	.12
Because I can use it anytime	.27	.71	.24	−.01	.07	.20
Because it's convenient	.22	.70	.08	.07	−.06	.10
Because I can search for information for as long or as short as I want	.26	.70	.14	.08	.14	.26
To see what is out there	.34	.64	.03	.07	.27	.06
To search for information	.44	.61	.01	−.02	.12	.11
Because I just like to use it	.17	.59	.37	.08	.11	.25

Because it provides a new and interesting way to do research	.21	.59	.32	.21	.25	-.06
Because it is exciting	.19	.20	.83	.20	.19	.15
Because it is thrilling	.14	.17	.81	.26	.17	.19
Because it peps me up	.13	.13	.77	.29	.21	.15
Because it amuses me	.18	.30	.65	.08	.13	.35
So I won't have to be alone	.01	.01	.18	.82	.04	.26
Because it makes me feel less lonely	-.02	.03	.14	.79	.08	.24
Because I want someone to do something for me	.14	.00	.18	.73	.22	.12
To give my input	.26	.15	.13	.14	.81	-.00
To participate in discussions	.21	.14	.10	.10	.77	-.06
Because I can express myself freely	.15	.18	.29	.26	.62	.21
Because I enjoy answering other people's questions	.23	.03	.25	.15	.62	.25
When I have nothing better to do	.01	.21	.18	.24	.02	.78
Because it passes the time away, particularly when I'm bored	-.04	.23	.22	.26	.09	.77
Because it gives me something to occupy my time	.06	.25	.23	.24	.12	.71
Eigenvalue	6.78	4.43	3.39	2.85	2.73	2.50
% variance explained	19.94%	13.03%	9.98%	8.38%	8.02%	7.34%
Mean	3.36	3.52	2.46	1.71	2.40	2.63
SD	.86	.84	1.06	.80	.98	1.13
Cronbach's alpha	.93	.90	.91	.82	.81	.86

Table 5.2 T-Test for Equality of Means of First-Time Eligible and Older Voters on All Variables

	Age groups				
	First-time voters		Older voters		
	M	SD	M	SD	t
Conservatism	2.90	0.68	3.17	0.76	3.99***
Self-efficacy	3.09	0.55	3.20	0.58	2.15*
Knowledge	0.54	0.22	0.61	0.22	3.45***
Cynicism	3.45	0.59	3.60	0.62	2.71**
Elaboration	3.15	0.86	3.15	0.76	0.31
Involvement	4.97	1.10	5.04	1.10	0.61
Likelihood to vote	4.61	0.85	4.64	0.92	0.31
Information seeking motive	3.67	0.78	3.34	0.89	4.16***
Political evaluation motive	3.51	0.82	3.17	0.89	4.24***
Pass time motive	2.93	1.11	2.23	1.03	7.06***
Entertaining arousal motive	2.67	1.05	2.19	1.00	5.09***
Self-expression	2.55	0.96	2.21	0.99	3.52***
Gainful companionship motive	1.82	0.82	1.57	0.76	3.45**
Use television	3.65	1.07	3.72	1.12	0.66
Use radio	2.03	0.95	2.70	1.20	6.83***

Use newspapers	3.07	1.11	3.39	1.11	3.07**
Use magazines	2.38	1.05	2.35	1.11	0.27
Use Internet	4.01	1.08	3.18	1.41	7.18***
Use books	1.59	0.81	1.60	0.90	0.24
Use YouTube	2.95	1.34	2.08	1.34	6.97***
Use social networking sites	2.46	1.28	1.53	0.96	8.68***
Use blogs	1.82	1.08	1.66	1.08	1.59
Television usefulness	3.98	0.99	3.77	1.07	2.00*
Radio usefulness	3.07	1.00	3.16	1.07	0.93
Newspapers usefulness	3.97	0.92	3.80	1.02	1.86
Magazines usefulness	3.06	1.00	2.84	1.04	2.24*
Internet usefulness	4.34	0.89	3.70	1.22	6.37***
Books usefulness	2.63	1.13	2.25	1.11	3.66***
YouTube usefulness	3.31	1.16	2.27	1.36	8.86***
Social networking usefulness	2.73	1.19	1.78	1.11	8.80***
Blogs usefulness	2.90	1.14	2.04	1.20	7.84***
Discuss politics face-to-face	2.79	0.72	2.96	0.84	2.37*
Discuss politics online	1.81	0.87	1.71	0.96	1.19

Note: *p < .05, **p < .01, ***p < .001.

found each of the media (with the exception of radio) more useful than did older voters, even though older voters indicated they used some of these media more often than did younger voters.

Motives for Seeking Political Campaign-Related Fare

Younger voters were significantly more motivated to seek political information about the campaign. We identified six motives for seeking campaign-related political fare: political evaluation, information seeking, entertaining arousal, gainful companionship, self-expression, and to pass the time. Younger voters measured significantly higher on all six motives. The most salient motives for acquiring campaign-related fare among both groups were for political evaluation and information seeking. Interestingly, the third most salient motive for accessing political campaign content for both groups was to pass the time. Therefore, although younger voters were more motivated to seek political information, the most salient reasons for doing so were very similar for both groups of potential voters.

Individual Differences

There were several significant differences between first-time eligible and older voters. Specifically, older voters were significantly more conservative, politically self-efficacious, and knowledgeable about the candidates' positions on major campaign issues. They also were more cynical about politics and politicians. Despite the significant differences noted, a review of the mean values on each of the measures suggests that the differences between the two groups on these variables, in most cases, were not drastic.

Although older voters were more knowledgeable of the candidates' positions on issues, they did not elaborate on (e.g., think about) political information more than first-time eligible voters did. In addition, there were no significant differences between older and first-time eligible voters in their level of involvement with campaign fare or their reported likelihood to vote. The results did suggest that older voters discussed politics more than did first-time voters. However, those discussions tended to occur in face-to-face settings. Neither group indicated that they tended to discuss politics online and there was no significant difference between the groups on the measure of online discussion.

The focus here was to compare first-time eligible and older voters' choice and perceived usefulness of various media for presidential campaign fare. To get a more refined picture of age differences in the use of social and other media, we segmented the sample into different age brackets to see if a less gross age division would shed greater light on the media choice differences among voters of different age groups. The results of this post-hoc analysis are summarized in Table 5.3.

Table 5.3 Ranked Order of Sources of Political Information by Age Group

18–21	*22–35*	*36–55*	*56+*
1. Internet	1. Internet	1. TV	1. TV
2. TV	2. TV	2. Newspapers	2. Newspapers
3. Newspapers	3. Newspapers	3. Internet	3. Radio
4. YouTube	4. YouTube	4. Radio	4. Magazines
5. Soc. Networks	5. Radio	5. Magazines	5. Internet
6. Magazines	6. Magazines	6. YouTube	6. Books
7. Radio	7. Soc. Networks	7. Books	7. YouTube
8. Blogs	8. Blogs	8. Blogs	8. Blogs
9. Books	9. Books	9. Soc. Networks	9. Soc. Networks

Note: Each column reflects the rank order of media used (ranked from most often used to least often used).

The results suggest that, as voters age, their media use was concentrated among fewer media. Older voters reported that they relied on fewer media for political information. Younger voters, on the other hand, tended to use more media more often. Participants over the age of 55, in particular, relied predominantly on what could be termed more traditional media: TV, newspapers, radio and magazines. Participants under the age of 36 also tended to rely on TV, but most often used the Internet for political information.

Social media did play a larger role for younger voters. Although social media were not a predominant source of political information, younger participants, particularly those under 21, did use social media for political information more often than did older participants. Participants over 36 rarely used social media for political information. The potential implications of these results are discussed below.

Discussion

Although the Internet and specific social network sites were used by first-time eligible voters significantly more often than these sources were used by older voters, the 2008 presidential campaign certainly was not a campaign that suggests we should count older media out just yet. Television was still a major source of political information among all participants in the study. In fact, it was used by first-time eligible voters as often as it was used by older voters. This is consistent with prior research that has indicated that newer media such as the Internet have supplemented rather than supplanted traditional media such as television as a major news source (e.g., Althaus & Tewksbury, 2000). In 2000, fewer people relied on newspapers and TV networks for political election news (Farnsworth & Owen, 2004). But, the Internet was not yet a major source of election news. Among first-time eligible voters in our study, however, the Internet had displaced TV as the most often used source of political campaign information.

Media choices tended to change as respondents reached their mid-30s. Respondents under the age of 36 reported that they used the Internet, TV, newspapers, and YouTube most often. For those over 36, TV and newspapers were the most used media sources. Among participants 36 and over, social networking sites were the media least used for acquiring campaign fare. After YouTube, social networking sites were the next most often used media source of political information for first-time eligible voters. However, these social media were not a significant source of information for older voters.

Audience-centered perspectives such as uses and gratifications posit that people turn to media that they perceive as best satisfying their needs and desires (Rubin, 2009). First-time eligible voters in this study were more motivated to use media for political information and found most of the media sources used to be more useful in that regard than did older participants. This has potentially important implications for future campaigns.

In the context of politics, it is logical to assume that people will turn to media they perceive as most useful for satisfying their needs or desires for which they seek political information. Participants in this study 55 and younger reported that they found the Internet and newspapers to be the most useful sources of political campaign information (see Table 5.4). Participants over the age of 55 found TV and newspapers to be the most useful. The perceived usefulness of newspapers among all age groups suggests we should not yet discount the continued importance of traditional media.

Moreover, the findings emphasize the need to devote more attention to differentiating the Internet's functions. Younger voters turned to the

Table 5.4 Ranked Order of Perceived Usefulness for Media Sources by Age Group

18–21	22–35	36–55	56+
1. Internet	1. Internet	1. Newspapers	1. TV
2. Newspapers	2. Newspapers	2. Internet	2. Newspapers
3. TV	3. TV	3. TV	3. Radio
4. YouTube	4. YouTube	4. Radio	4. Magazines
5. Radio	5. Radio	5. Magazines	5. Internet
6. Magazines	6. Magazines	6. Books	6. Books
7. Blogs	7. Blogs	7. YouTube	7. Blogs
8. Soc. Networks	8. Soc. Networks	8. Blogs	8. YouTube
9. Books	9. Books	9. Soc. Networks	9. Soc. Networks

Note: Each column reflects the rank order of perceived usefulness of various media for information about the presidential campaign (ranked from most useful to least useful).

Internet as a whole more than they did to the individual functions of social media and video sharing. Of course, the broader category of the Internet encompasses all Internet use, which includes material delivered via the Web from traditional media sources. Researchers have been suggesting for some time that we cannot consider the Internet to be a single overarching medium, and that researchers should consider Internet functions separately (Bimber, 2000). Even the subcategories of the Internet contain distinctive differences. In the case of social networks, obtaining information from friends on a MySpace page may be far different than obtaining information from a political blog or a network news organization's Web site. Similarly, accessing user-generated content on YouTube may be far different than obtaining a video from one of the official presidential campaign sites.

The new media environment calls into question the underlying definitions and assumptions of media content and delivery. It is worth remembering that audiences can migrate at will to media they perceive as better at satisfying their needs and desires. News may be important to readers, but its most popular delivery system may be the Internet, not newspapers. TV news and advertising may be important to viewers, but YouTube may be the new delivery system of choice for them. At some point, YouTube will be replaced with a more attractive or perceived useful mechanism. Clearly, media choice is not stagnant, and younger voters, at least in the framework in this study, appear to be leading the way in terms of new media adoption. The results here suggest that younger voters are more motivated than older ones to seek out political information, to use a different mix of media to find it, and to find a variety of media to be more useful. But usefulness is in the eye of the beholder, and the measure of usefulness itself doesn't presume any judgment of the quality of the information received. We did not ask participants to describe the political content they obtained, and future scholars should pay more attention to the actual content of political messages in this expanded media environment.

Cultivation researchers have suggested that newer media do not necessarily provide new information but simply repackage traditional media fare (Morgan, Shanahan, & Signorielli, 2009). In this study, first-time eligible voters were watching about the same amount of traditional TV as were their older counterparts, but also were using YouTube. If what they were watching on YouTube was traditional TV fare produced by the usual sources, then they may have been more immersed in TV political content than were older participants. Similarly, participants of all ages acquired political information from printed newspapers, but younger participants used the Internet more. If younger participants were reading online newspapers for political information, they too may have been more immersed in traditional newspaper content than older voters.

Thus, existing research on the impact of traditional media content—or content produced by traditional media sources—will still be relevant in newer media environments.

We did not examine the relationships among variables on which the age groups were compared. However, even the descriptive differences between these groups led us to speculate on the following.

The results regarding media choice may suggest that voters tend to use media with which they are most familiar. Younger voters grew up in the Internet age. Thus, it isn't surprising that the Internet was their most widely used medium for political information. On the other hand, older voters who came of age in a different media environment relied on TV, newspapers, radio, and magazines, and have not yet embraced the social media phenomenon to stay informed about politics. Even among younger voters, it may be a small group of early social media adopters who are the ones using social media sites specifically as a political information source—at least as of the 2008 presidential campaign. But, this could change as even younger people who are growing up with social media become of voting age and adopt sites like MySpace, Facebook, and YouTube as their media of choice.

As for individual characteristics, first-time eligible voters were less cynical than their older counterparts. They saw themselves as involved, interested in political fare, and likely to vote, but less self-efficacious than did older participants. Future researchers need to devote more attention to links between these individual characteristics and the use of a growing number of available media. At least one study found social media use to be a negative predictor of political cynicism (Hanson, Haridakis, Wagstaff, Sharma, & Ponder, 2009).

More importantly, the availability of political information in the social networking spaces may be a way for providers of political media content (e.g., newspapers, television stations, and the campaigns themselves) to grab the attention of first-time eligible voters. This is a demographic that news organizations and political campaigns have long tried to attract and that is vital to the future of politics and democracy.

This study suggests that the Internet, TV, and newspapers are still the "big 3" among all age groups in terms of media sources for politics. But, younger voters are including the newer social media as part of their media mix. If that trend continues, the political wars of the future may play out more and more in these mediated spaces as the voters now using them continue to age, and the number of social media users and Web sites grow.

References

Althaus, S. L., & Tewksbury, D. (2000). Patterns of internet and traditional news media use in a networked community. *Political Communication, 17,* 21–45.

Austin, E. W., & Pinkleton, B. E. (2001). The role of parental mediation in the political socialization process. *Journal of Broadcasting & Electronic Media, 45,* 221–240.

Banwart, M. C. (2007). Gender and young voters in 2004: The influence of perceived knowledge and interest. *American Behavioral Scientist, 50,* 1152–1168.

Barr, K. (2008, October). Young voters will make history on election day. *Politics,* 23–25.

Benjamin, L. M. (1987). Broadcast campaign precedents from the 1924 presidential election. *Journal of Broadcasting & Electronic Media, 31,* 449–460.

Berelson, B. R., Lazarsfeld, P. F., & McPhee, W. N. (1954). *Voting: A study of opinion formation during a presidential campaign.* Chicago: University of Chicago Press.

Bimber, B. (2000). The study of information technology and civic engagement. *Political Communication, 17,* 329–333.

Bynner, J., & Ashford, S. (1994). Politics and participation: Some antecedents of young people's attitudes to the political system and political activity. *European Journal of Social Psychology, 24,* 223–236.

Campus, D., Pasquino, G., & Vaccari, C. (2008). Social networks, political discussion, and voting in Italy: A study of the 2006 election. *Political Communication, 25,* 423–444.

Carr, D., & Stelter, B. (2008, November 2). Campaigns in a web 2.0 world. *New York Times,* 1.

Chaffee, S. H., & Kanihan, S. F. (1997). Learning about politics from mass media. *Political Communication, 14,* 421–430.

Chaffee, S. H., & Yang, S. (1990). Communication and political socialization. In O. Ichilov (Ed.), *Political socialization, citizenship education, and democracy.* New York: Teachers College, Columbia University, pp. 137–157.

Cohen, N. (2008, January 21). Campaign reporting in under 140 taps. *New York Times,* 3.

Cornelis, I., Van Hiel, A., Roets, A., & Kossowska, M. (2009). Age differences in conservatism: Evidence on the mediating effects of personality and cognitive style. *Journal of Personality, 77*(1), 51–88.

Delli Carpini, M. X. (2000). Gen.com: Youth, civic engagement, and the new information environment. *Political Communication, 17,* 341–349.

Doppelt, J. C., & Shearer, E. (1999). *Nonvoters.* Thousand Oaks, CA: Sage.

Edmonds, T. (2008, October). Time to rock the youth vote myth. *Politics,* 25–27.

Eveland, W. P., Jr. (2004). The effect of political discussion in producing informed citizens: The roles of information, motivation, and elaboration. *Political Communication, 21,* 177–193.

Farnsworth, S. J., & Owen, D. (2004). Internet use and the 2000 presidential election. *Electoral Studies, 23,* 415–429.

Fisher, P. (2008). Is there an emerging age gap in US politics? *Society, 45,* 504–11.

Garramone, G. M., Harris, A. C., Pizante, G. (1986). Predictors of motivation to use computer-mediated political communication systems. *Journal of Broadcasting & Electronic Media, 30,* 445–457.

Hall, M. (2009, April 16). Internet engaged people in '08 election, survey shows. *USA Today,* Section: News, 8a.

Hanson, G., & Haridakis, P. (2008). YouTube users watching and hearing the news: A uses and gratifications approach. *Journal of Electronic Publishing, 11*. Retrieved August 3, 2009 from http://quod.lib.umich.edu/cgi/t/text/text-idx?c=jep;cc=jep;view=text;rgn=main;idno=3336451.0011.305.

Hanson, G., Haridakis, P., Wagstaff, A., Sharma, R., & Ponder, J. D. (2009, August). *The 2008 presidential campaign: Political cynicism in the age of Facebook, MySpace and YouTube*. Paper presented at the annual convention of the Association for Education in Mass Communication, Boston, MA.

Haridakis, P. M. (2006). Self-disclosure, immediacy, involvement and parasocial interaction. *Ohio Communication Journal, 41*, 69–97.

Haridakis, P. & Hanson, G. (2009). Social interaction and co-viewing with YouTube: Blending mass communication reception and social connection. *Journal of Broadcasting & Electronic Media, 53*, 317–335.

Johnson, T. J., & Kaye, B. K. (2003). Around the world wide web in 80 ways. *Social Science Computer Review, 21*, 304–325.

Jowett, G. S., & O'Donnell, V. (2006). *Propaganda and persuasion* (4th Ed.). Thousand Oaks, CA: Sage.

Kaid, L. L. (2002). Political advertising and information seeking: Comparing the exposure via traditional and Internet media channels. *Journal of Advertising, 31*, 27–35.

Kaid, L. L. (2004). Political advertising. In L. L. Kaid (Ed.), *Handbook of political communication research*. Mahwah, NJ: Erlbaum, pp. 155–202.

Kaid, L. L., McKinney, M. S., & Tedesco, J. C. (2007). Political information efficacy and young voters. *American Behavioral Scientist, 50*, 1093–111.

Kaid, L. L., & Postelnicu, M. (2006). Credibility of political messages on the Internet: A comparison of blog sources. In M. Tremayne (Ed.), *Blogging, citizenship and the future of media*. New York: Routledge, pp. 149–164.

Kaye, B. K., & Johnson, T. J. (2002). Online and in the know: Uses and gratifications of the web for political information. *Journal of Broadcasting & Electronic Media, 46*, 54–71.

Kaye, B. K., & Johnson, T. J. (2004). A web for all reasons: Uses and gratifications of Internet components for political information. *Telematics & Informatics, 21*, 197–223.

Lasswell, H. D. (1948). The structure and function of communication in society. In L. Bryson (Ed.), *The communication of ideas*. New York: Harper, pp. 37–51.

Lazarsfeld, P. F., Berelson, B., Gaudet, H. (1944). *The people's choice: How the voter makes up his mind in a presidential campaign*. New York: Duell, Sloan, & Pearce.

Learmonth, M. (2008, November 10). One-way media lost the election as cable, interactive dominated. *Atlantic Monthly, 1*.

Lee, K. M. (2006). Effects of Internet use on college students' political efficacy. *CyberPsychology & Behavior, 9*, 415–422.

Leshner, G., & Thorson, E. (2000). Over reporting voting: Campaign media, public mood, and the vote. *Political Communication, 17*, 263–278.

McLeod, J. M., & Becker, L. B. (1974). Testing the validity of gratification measures through political effects analysis. In J. G. Blumler, & E. Katz (Eds.), *The uses of mass communication: Current perspectives on gratifications research*. Beverly Hills, CA: Sage, pp. 137–164.

Mehrabian, A. (1996). Relations among political attitudes, personality, and psychopathology assessed with new measures of libertarianism and conservatism. *Basic and Applied Social Psychology, 18,* 469–491.

Mogan, M., Shanahan, J., & Signorielli, N. (2009). Growing up with television. In J. Bryant & M. B. Oliver (Eds.), *Media effects: Advances in theory and research* (3rd Ed.). New York: Routledge, pp. 34–49.

Morrell, M. E. (2003). Survey and experimental evidence for a reliable and valid measure of internal political efficacy. *Public Opinion Quarterly, 67,* 589–602.

Niemi, R. G., Craig, S. C., & Mattei, F. (1991). Measuring internal political efficacy in the 1988 national election study. *American Political Science Review, 85,* 1407–1413.

Papacharissi, Z., & Rubin, A. M. (2000). Predictors of Internet use. *Journal of Broadcasting & Electronic Media, 44,* 175–196.

Pempek, T. A., Yermolayeva, Y. A., & Calvert, S. L. (2009). College students' social networking experiences on Facebook. *Journal of Applied Developmental Psychology, 30,* 227–238.

Perse, E. M. (1990). Involvement with local television news: Cognitive and emotional dimensions. *Human Communication Research, 16,* 556–581.

Pinkleton, B. E., & Austin, E. W. (2001). Individual motivations, perceived media importance, and political disaffection. *Political Communication, 18,* 321–334.

Pinkleton, B. E., & Austin, E. W. (2004). Media perceptions and public affairs apathy in the politically inexperienced. *Mass Communication & Society, 7,* 319–337.

Pinkleton, B. E., Austin, E. W., & Fortman, K. K. J. (1998). Relationships of media use and political disaffection to political efficacy and voting behavior. *Journal of Broadcasting & Electronic Media, 42,* 34–49.

Pinkleton, B. E. Um, N.-H., & Austin, E. E. (2002). An exploration of the effects of negative political advertising on political decision making. *Journal of Advertising, 31*(1), 13–25.

Rubin, A. M. (1983). Television uses and gratifications: The interactions of viewing patterns and motivations. *Journal of Broadcasting, 27,* 37–51.

Rubin, A. M. (2009). Uses-and-gratifications perspective of media effects. In J. Bryant & M. B. Oliver (Eds.), *Media effects: Advances in theory and research* (3rd Ed.). New York: Routledge, pp. 165–184.

Scheufele, D. A. (2002). Examining differential gains from mass media and their implications for participatory behavior. *Communication Research, 29,* 46–65.

Seelye, K. Q. (2007, June 14). YouTube passes debates to a new generation. *New York Times,* A27.

Speilman, F. (2008, January 8). Young voters here register to vote in record numbers. *Chicago Sun-Times.* Retrieved August 18, 2009 from www.suntimes.com/news/politics/obama/731066,obama10808.article.

Spinda, J. S. W., & Haridakis, P. M. (2008). Exploring the motives of fantasy sports: A uses-and-gratifications approach. In L. W. Hugenberg, P. M. Haridakis, & A. C. Earnheardt (Eds.), *Sports Mania: Essays on fandom and the media in the 21st century.* Jefferson, NC: McFarland & Company, pp. 187–199.

Strama, M. (1998). Overcoming cynicism: Youth participation and electoral politics. *National Civics Review, 87*(1), 71–77.

Sweetser, K. D., & Kaid, L. L. (2008). Stealth soapboxes: Political information efficacy, cynicism and uses of celebrity weblogs among readers. *New Media & Society, 10*(1), 67–91

Tedesco, J. C. (2006). Web interactivity and young adult political efficacy. In W. P. Williams & J. C. Tedesco (Eds.), *The Internet election: Perspectives on the web in campaign 2004*. Lanham, MD: Rowan & Littlefield, pp. 187–202.

Thelwall, M. (2008). Social networks, gender, and friending: An analysis of MySpace member profiles. *Journal of the American Society for Information Science and Technology, 59*, 1321–1330.

Vincent, R. C., & Basil, M. D. (1997). College students' news gratifications, media use, and current events knowledge. *Journal of Broadcasting & Electronic Media, 41*, 380–392.

Wells, J. D. (2008). A voice in the nation: Women journalists in the early nineteenth century south. *American Nineteenth Century History, 9*, 165–182.

Wyatt, R. O., Kim, J., & Katz, E. (2000). How feeling free to talk affects ordinary political conversation, purposeful argumentation, and civic participation. *Journalism & Mass Communication Quarterly, 77*, 99–114.

Yang, J., & Stone, G. (2003). The powerful role of interpersonal communication in agenda setting. *Mass Communication & Society, 6*, 57–74.

Zaichkowsky, J. L. (1985). Measuring the involvement construct. *Journal of Consumer Research, 12*, 341–52.

Chapter 6

When Bloggers Attack

Examining the Effect of Negative Citizen-Initiated Campaigning in the 2008 Presidential Election

Timothy K. F. Fung, Emily Vraga, and Kjerstin Thorson

In the 2008 elections, citizen commentary on political campaigns became more widespread than ever before. Political bloggers expounded on candidate strategy and policy, average citizens were able to post their own comments on newspaper stories even at some of the country's biggest media outlets, and social networking sites offered quick and easy routes to share political thoughts with the world (or at least the world as defined by your own limited readership). Not only was it relatively easy to create and maintain a political blog oneself, but the opportunities blogs offered for individuals to simply add their voice to the cacophony of others made this type of expressive participation easier than ever. And people took advantage of these opportunities: more and more people reported turning to political blogs and social networking sites for campaign information, especially younger adults (Pew, 2008).

But not all of these political postings were wild celebrations of a particular candidate or policy. Many bloggers wrote posts attacking candidates of the opposing party or even candidates from their own party during the presidential primaries. In fact, blogs have become formats in which the opposing party's candidates and policies can be attacked in a highly negative and combative fashion (Koop & Jansen, 2009). In the pre-Internet era, most of the political attacks visible to mainstream audiences were those conducted by or sponsored by the candidates, their parties, or interested groups in the form of political advertising. Today, the growth of blogs has expanded negative campaigning, becoming an option for any partisan with a computer and an Internet connection.

While negativity in campaigning has attracted a great deal of scholarly attention (Ansolabehere & Iyengar, 1995; Brooks & Geer, 2007), less is known about how attacks carried out and disseminated by citizens not affiliated with a campaign will be interpreted by other citizens. This study draws on social emotion theories (Smith 1993, 1999) as a framework to examine how weaker and stronger candidate supporters respond to attacks carried out by an unknown blogger. Previous research has shown that attacks on one's own in-group (such as an attack on Barack Obama witnessed by an Obama supporter) can arouse negative emotions in response and that these emotions will be felt more strongly by those who identify most strongly with the in-group of "Obama supporters." Going beyond this simple amplification of effects among strong identifiers, we use the results of an experimental study to argue that weak and strong identifiers may also evaluate an attack differently, leading them to experience a different set of emotions.

This study extends previous work on the social emotion model by considering the perspective of the individual with regards to a political attack. While an attack might provoke negative emotions for those whose in-group is being attacked, a reader coming from the other perspective—seeing a blogger attack a candidate they both oppose—might appraise the situation positively and thus experience positive emotions. Furthermore, whether positive or negative emotions are invoked in an individual is likely to lead to different actions taken in response. While most research has examined the role of negative emotions like anger and disgust (Nabi, 2002; Thorson, Fung, & Vraga, 2008), this study extends existing research to determine whether positive emotions such as pride can also lead people to take action.

The Effects of Negative Political Attacks

During any election campaign, potential voters are exposed to an extraordinary array of political messages. While many of these messages focus on issues and policy or promote the qualities of a particular candidate, a great number of campaign-related media messages adopt a more negative tone. News coverage of campaigns often focuses on the strategic motivations underlying candidates' and campaigns' actions, leading to increased cynicism and distaste for the political process (Cappella & Jamieson, 1997; Mutz, 2007). Candidates and their proxies continue to create and disseminate messages attacking their opponents, devoting large sums of campaign funds to various forms of negative advertising.

Recent election cycles have seen the rise of blogs as a new forum for political discussion and, in many cases, political attacks. Whereas traditionally the ability to engage in public political attacks was strictly the domain of well-funded candidates and their powerful allies, online political forums have made it possible for the average citizen to disseminate political critiques, a few of which may gain a wide readership. Political blogs are analogous to the partisan press of the nineteenth and early-twentieth centuries (Kerbel & Bloom, 2005). Like those early newspapers, many blogs are blatantly partisan, and are designed to advocate and motivate more than to inform the citizenry with careful, reasoned political dialogue.

The effects of these online, citizen-generated political attacks are not yet well understood, but the literature investigating the effects of negative advertising provides a useful starting point. Recent research suggests that emotional response to candidate advertisements plays a large role in persuasion (Chang, 2001; Brader, 2005; Huber & Arceneaux, 2007). Emotional appeals work differently depending on whether positive or negative emotions (such as enthusiasm or fear) are elicited: enthusiasm reinforces existing partisan loyalties while fear makes people susceptible to persuasion from the opposition (Brader, 2005). Advertising cues and strategies influence this emotional response: supportive advertisements encourage the arousal of positive emotions, while attack ads often produce negative feelings (Chang, 2001; Thorson, Christ, & Caywood, 1991).

Persuasive appeals can provoke a diversity of emotional reactions in their targets, which can further influence their response. Negative advertisements created by candidates—specifically attack advertisements —have been shown to arouse negative emotional responses (Chang, 2001) and influence evaluations of both the sponsoring candidate and the victim of the attack (Roese & Sande, 1993; Kaid & Boydston, 1987; Pinkleton, 1997; Garramone, 1985; Haddock & Zanna, 1997). Similarly, blog posts that attack the reader's own political position have been shown to arouse negative emotions and highlight partisan identity (Thorson, et al., 2008).

In addition to enabling average citizens to initiate political attack and to disseminate political critiques, the relative anonymity and lack of constraints on expression in the blogosphere can in some cases lead to political attacks that adopt an acrimonious tone (Koop & Jansen, 2009). These inflammatory and hostile political attacks tend to include name-calling, contemptuous references, and derision of the opposition (Brooks and Geer, 2007). Political scholars (Kingwell, 1995) regard this particular type of political attack as discursive incivility because this form of expression promotes disrespect of oppositional views rather than making an attempt to understand others' views and to respect the rights of others.

This incivility online raises concerns about how bloggers' tone in their expression of disagreement may affect readers' emotional responses and democratic development. A recent experiment (Hwang, Borah, Namkoong, & Veenstra, 2008) examined blog readers' emotional reactions and attitude toward political disagreement by manipulating the tone of a blogger's commentaries on a balanced mainstream news story and the blogger's partisanship. The results showed that uncivil political blogs posts aroused a set of negative emotions: anger, contempt, disgust, and frustration. These negative emotional responses, in turn, decreased in open-mindedness and increased in attitude certainty when participants read the blog postings that did not "match" with their political ideology.

Another recent experimental study (Thorson, et al., 2008) examined the effects of an uncivil, attacking message on group identification and polarization. The findings indicated that uncivil messages provoke negative emotional responses among partisans, which in turn mediated changes in partisan identification dependent on whether the respondents identified with the attacking or the attacked group. Research therefore suggests that political messages not only arouse emotional response, but that the nature of that reaction depends on characteristics of the message, including tone and position.

Social Emotion Model

But how do political messages cause emotional response? Appraisal theories (Frijda, Kuipers, & Ter Schure, 1989; Roseman, 1984; Scherer, 1988; Smith & Ellsworth, 1985) propose that emotions are results of cognitive interpretations and evaluations of an event based on a number of dimensions, such as whether an event or a situation appears to be consistent or inconsistent with an individual's goals and desires, the causal agent of the event, and the relative power of the individual compared to other individuals or groups. These cognitive appraisals of the dimensions of a particular event combine to produce a specific and targeted emotion in response. For example, positive emotions such as pride generally are aroused when situations are congruent with individuals' goals and are caused by others, while negative emotions such as anger are elicited when situations are incongruent with individuals' goals, caused by others, and perceived as controllable by oneself.

In addition, emotions direct individuals' behaviors (Frijda, Kuipers, & Ter Schure, 1989; Roseman, Wiet, & Swartz, 1994). Each specific emotion is associated with a particular action tendency distinct to that emotion. For instance, the arousal of anger drives individuals to move against the obstacles (including other individuals) interfering with their own goals.

Drawing on self-categorization theory and social identity theory, Smith (1993, 1999) applies appraisal theory to explain emotional and behavioral reactions in an intergroup context. As posited by self-categorization theory and social identity theory, both social and personal aspects constitute an individual's self-identity (Turner, 1985). When an individual's social identity is activated, that individual will no longer perceive him or herself unique, but instead as a member of a group and emphasize the common attributes among other group members (Smith, 1993, 1999). Group identity and membership, hence, become part of the self-concept, and events that harm or favor the in-group are in some sense equivalent to events that harm or favor one's self. Therefore, group members may experience emotions on behalf of an in-group, just as they would feel fear, anger or disgust on their own behalf (Mackie, Devos, & Smith, 2000).

This linkage between emotions and action tendency in appraisal theories also applies to the intergroup context, with arousal of specific intergroup emotions leading to associated intergroup behaviors.

Social Emotion Model and Negatively Valenced Political Messages

From the perspective of the blog reader, the social emotion model predicts that when a candidate supporter is exposed to blog commentary attacking a candidate (either a preferred or an opposing candidate), the blog reader's social identity as a candidate supporter will be activated. As a result, an individual blog reader will perceive himself/herself as part of the Obama (or McCain) supporters group. Because group identity is part of the self, any behaviors that harm (or are in favor of) the group will be cognitively processed as equal to a harm (or favor) to oneself. Individuals will experience specific emotions toward the blogger according to their appraisal of the blog commentaries.

In the case of exposure to a blog commentary attacking a preferred candidate, blog readers are more likely to appraise the blog commentaries as harmful to their goals and desires (i.e., that their preferred candidate win the election), caused by out-group members, and as causing harm to their group and self. With the combinations of these appraisals, supporters exposed to an attack are more likely to experience anger (Roseman, Spindel & Jose, 1990):

> H1: When candidate supporters are exposed to blog commentary attacking their own preferred candidate, they will feel angrier at the blogger.

Furthermore, when blog readers are exposed to uncivil blog commentaries, they should respond negatively. Incivility, such as contemptuous references, derision of the opponent, and disrespect of oppositional views (Brooks & Geer, 2007), violates social norms for polite behavior (Mutz, 2007). These uncivil blog commentaries are likely to be perceived as more aggressive, intimidating, and hostile, heightening individuals' anger at the blogger:

> H2: When individuals are exposed to uncivil blog commentary, they will feel angrier at the blogger.

As delineated in appraisal theory, the same events or situations may lead to different specific emotions dependent upon an individual's subjective evaluations and interpretations. Blog readers may appraise attacking blog commentary differently when the target is the candidate they oppose.

Instead, these readers may find these commentaries consistent with their goals (i.e., increasing the chance of their preferred candidate to win the election) by exposing the demerits of the opponent. Meanwhile, the in-group blog readers may perceive the blogger to be acting as a surrogate of the group (and of one's self) to fight for their preferred candidate and thus experience positive emotions for the blogger pursuing group goals:

H3:   When candidate supporters are exposed to blog commentary attacking the opposing candidate, they will feel more proud of the blogger.

While individuals may feel proud of a blogger who is attacking an oppositional candidate because it is consistent with their motivations and goals, incivility still violates injunctive norms regarding proper political and deliberative behavior (Mutz & Reeves, 2005). Therefore, exposure to an uncivil blogger should decrease feelings of pride in the blogger:

H4:   When individuals are exposed to uncivil blog commentary, they will feel less proud of the blogger.

But not all candidate supporters are created equal. Supporters differ in their level of commitment to a particular candidate, which has important consequences for intergroup emotions and behaviors. One study suggests that strong in-group identifiers were more likely to experience anger toward the out-group and to take action against it (Mackie, et al., 2000). A more recent study has shown that emotional reactions of anger and their associated offensive action tendencies were more pronounced when participants perceived the victims of harmful behaviors and themselves to be part of the same group (Yzerbyt, Dumont, Wigboldus, & Gordijn, 2003). Therefore, we ask:

RQ1:   Does candidate preference strength interact with target of attack, such that higher identifiers experience stronger anger when they were exposed to the blog commentary attacking their own preferred candidate?

RQ2:   Does candidate preference strength interact with target of attack, such that higher identifiers experience stronger pride when they were exposed to the blog commentary attacking the opposing candidate?

RQ3:   Does candidate preference strength interact with incivility, such that higher identifiers experience stronger anger when they were exposed to uncivil blog commentary?

RQ4: Does candidate preference strength interact with incivility, such that higher identifiers experience less pride when they were exposed to uncivil blog commentary?

However, it also seems likely that variations in identity strength may lead to substantively different appraisal of events and situations in addition to weaker or stronger versions of the same appraisal. In other words, lower identifiers and higher identifiers may evaluate the same event or situation differently, leading them to experience different specific emotions with different action tendencies (Roseman, et al., 1990). The underlying reason is that the evaluations and interpretations of events govern whether the emotion will be felt (Vraga, Thorson, Fung, & Meyer, 2009) and which specific emotion will be felt. Along the cognitive appraisal dimensions, lower identifiers and higher identifiers may interpret the blogger's commentary differently in terms of consistency with their goals and desires, and differently in whether the commentary favors or disfavors the group. Therefore, lower identifiers and higher identifiers may experience different specific emotions and action tendencies based on their different interpretation of events.

We expect that the emotional experience will mediate the impact of social identity on specific action tendencies. According to appraisal theory, specific emotions promote certain behaviors (Roseman, et al., 1990). Therefore, we predict that action tendencies of blog readers are conditioned according to their emotional experience related to their social identity (i.e., to which candidate support groups they belong) and the target of the blogger's attack:

H5: Emotional experience of blog readers will mediate the effect of social identity on specific action tendencies.

RQ5: Do lower identifiers and higher identifiers experience different specific emotions and associated action tendencies when they are exposed to different blog commentary?

Method

Our hypotheses were tested in an experiment embedded in a Web survey in which participants viewed a fictitious news story about the 2008 presidential campaign accompanied by commentary from a fictitious political blogger. The sample consisted of students from undergraduate courses at two large universities in the Midwestern United States and was fielded during the last two weeks in October and the first week in November, ending fielding the day before the presidential election. All potential participants were contacted by e-mail and given the Web site of the online survey. A total of 398 students participated in the experiment. The mean age was 20.16 (SD = 1.80), with 25.4 percent male subjects. In terms of candidate support, 22.1 percent were John McCain supporters whereas 69.1 percent were Barack Obama supporters and 8.8 percent supported neither candidate.

Design and Procedure

The study used a 2 (Civility of tone: civil vs. uncivil) × 2 (Target of attack: preferred candidate vs. opposing candidate) between-subjects design. Respondents read a news story about the 2008 presidential election campaign, which was written to emulate journalistic practice by providing a balanced summary of the campaign strategies of the two presidential candidates (Barack Obama and John McCain). The article, attributed to *USA Today*, described the use of an electoral map targeting strategy and negative advertising by both presidential candidates. The content of the news story remained consistent across both experimental conditions.

The campaign news story was embedded in a post on a fictitious Web blog. The blog commentary was written to critique the campaign strategies used by the presidential candidates. To ensure an equal number of subjects in the conditions of either their own or the opposing candidate being attacked, we randomized based on pre-test candidate preferences. Before exposure to our experimental stimulus, we asked participants' whether their preferred presidential candidate was Barack Obama, John McCain, or neither. Subjects were randomized on the basis of this candidate preference to be exposed to blog commentary either attacking their own preferred candidate or attacking the opposing candidate. Meanwhile, respondents were randomized into conditions where the tone of criticism was either civil or uncivil. Participants who reported neither support for Obama or McCain (N = 35) were excluded from this analysis, as we would have no expectation that participants who did not have a candidate preference would have any relevant identity attachment.

To create the civility manipulation, we shifted whether the blogger's commentary made civil or uncivil references to the campaign strategies used by a presidential candidate (Brooks & Geer, 2007). In the civil condition, the critique of the news story maintained a respectful tone (i.e., "Right off the bat, let's be clear: This is a perfect example of McCain/Obama's political strategy. He says he cares about the country as a whole but really he's focused on voters in the few states that matter for winning."). In the uncivil condition, while the terms of the argument remained the same, the blogger used derogatory terms and insulting language when referring to opponents of the blogger's position (i.e., "Right off the bat, let's be clear: This is a perfect example of McCain/Obama's manipulative tactics. He pretends to care about the country as a whole but really he only gives a crap about voters in the few states that matter for winning.").

Measures

Candidate preference strength. Candidate preference strength was measured in two parts. We first asked respondents to indicate which presidential candidate they support, then measured identity strength by asking respondents to indicate how strongly they support the candidate on a 11-point scale ranging from 0 being very little to 10 being very strong (M = 7.72, SD = 1.85). A median split was then used to create two candidate preference groups: low identifiers (n = 155) vs. high identifiers (n = 208). On an 11-point scale, data was split at 8 on strength of candidate preference for lower identifiers (M = 5.97, SD = 1.96) and higher identifiers (M = 9.02, SD = .84). The median of the candidate preference strength in our study rested on a relatively high level on an 11-point scale. The major reason is likely that we fielded the study in the two weeks before the presidential election. Therefore, our respondents had mostly determined their vote choice and were committed to their candidate. One of the purposes of this chapter is to examine the effect of identity strength on intergroup emotions and behaviors, and the election period provides an appropriate time frame to test the effect.

Emotions towards the blogger. The emotional responses towards the blogger (i.e., anger and pride) was measured by the family of concepts that index varying degrees of anger (e.g., angry, irritated) and pride (e.g., pleased, proud and enthusiastic) (Dillard, Kinney, & Cruz, 1996; Dillard & Peck, 2000; Yzerbyt, et al., 2003). Respondents were asked to rate to what extent the blogger's commentary had made them feel these emotions. Seven emotion items, measured on an 11-point scale ranging from 0 being not at all to 10 being a great deal, were submitted to a principal components analysis with direct oblmin rotation. The factor analysis confirmed the presence of two clearly distinguishable sets of items. The two different emotions accounted for 81.09 percent of variance. The first factor, which accounted for 60.19 percent of variance, included angry, disgusted, irritated, and revolted. These items were averaged to create an index for anger at the blogger (M = 4.73, SD = 2.63, Cronbach's alpha = .92). Another factor, which accounted for 20.90 percent of variance, included pleased, proud and enthusiastic on the 11-point scale. These items were averaged to create an index for proud of the blogger (M = 2.73, SD = 2.34, Cronbach's alpha = .86).

Action tendencies toward the blogger. To measure action tendencies, respondents answered two sets of items adopted and modified from Yzerbyt, et al. (2003). To measure offensive action, two items were used asking respondents to rate their level of agreement on an 11-point scale with two statements: "I would like a chance to respond to the blogger's comments" and "I would like a chance to get back the blogger," which were averaged to create an index (M = 3.79, SD = 2.30, inter-item correlation = .56). To measure mockery, respondents rated their level of agreement with two separate items: "I thought the blogger's comments were ridiculous" and "While I was reading, I was making fun of the blogger's comments," which were also averaged to create an index (M = 4.98, SD = 2.24, inter-item correlation = .70).

Results

The data analysis was conducted in two parts. The hypotheses and research questions (H1–H4 and RQ1–RQ4) examining the effects of candidate preference strength and the manipulations on emotional responses were tested by analysis of variance (ANOVA). These analyses lay the groundwork for the second part of the analysis, an examination of the indirect effects of the manipulations of tone and target of attack on action tendencies (H5 and RQ5).

Effects on Emotional Responses

Hypotheses 1 and 2 examined the effects of target of attack and civility of commentary. The results of the analysis indicated that the main effect of target of attack was significant, $F(1, 345)$ = 145.34, p < .001, partial (η^2 = .30. Blog readers who were exposed to commentaries attacking their preferred candidate (M = 6.05) experienced higher levels of anger toward the blogger than those who were exposed to commentaries attacking the opposing candidate (M = 3.29). A significant main effect of civility of tone also was observed, $F(1, 345)$ = 4.44, p < .05, partial (η^2 = .01. This finding suggests that individuals who were exposed to uncivil blog commentaries felt angrier at the blogger (M = 4.92) than those who were exposed to civil commentaries (M = 4.44). These findings, thus, provided support for both H1 and H2. However, the effect of the target of attack was qualified by candidate preference strength. An interaction of target of attack by candidate preference strength (RQ1) was observed, $F(1, 345)$ = 22.83, p < .001, partial (η^2 = .06. High identifiers who saw their own candidate attacked were significantly angrier (M = 6.84) than low identifiers who saw their candidate attacked (M = 5.29). There is also a main effect of candidate preference strength $F(1, 345)$ = 3.93, p < .05, partial (η^2 = .01, such that people with stronger candidate preferences reported more anger at the blogger (M = 4.91) than those with weaker candidate preferences (M = 4.45), but no interactive effect between civility of tone and candidate preference strength emerged (RQ2), $F(1, 345)$ = .81, $n.s.$ Thus, the ANOVA analyses on anger suggests that high and low identifiers react differently to exposure to partisan attack in terms of their level of anger at the blogger, but are not differentially affected by level of incivility.

Another ANOVA was conducted to examine the effects of these same variables on the feelings of pride for the blogger. Significant main effects of target of attack, $F(1, 343) = 73.23$, $p < .001$, partial ($\eta^2 = .18$, and civility tone, $F(1, 343) = 4.48$, $p < .05$, ($\eta^2 = .01$, were found. Individuals who were exposed to commentaries attacking their opposing candidate felt more proud ($M = 3.67$) of the blogger than those who were exposed to commentaries attacking their preferred candidate ($M = 1.77$). Also, individuals who were exposed to uncivil commentaries felt less proud of the blogger ($M = 2.48$) than those who were exposed to civil commentaries ($M = 2.95$). These findings provided support for H3 and H4. However, the effect of attack again varied by candidate preference strength, $F(1, 343) = 17.59$, $p < . 001$, partial ($\eta^2 = .05$. This suggested that the effect of the target of the attack was more substantial among higher identifiers compared to lower identifiers (RQ3). Higher identifiers felt more proud of the blogger ($M = 4.26$) when they were exposed to commentaries attacking their opposing candidate than lower identifiers ($M = 3.07$). There is, however, no interactive effect between candidate preference strength and civility (RQ4), $F(1, 343) = .52$, *n.s.*

In short, the results indicated that civility of tone and the target of attack trigger specific emotional responses, suggesting our message manipulation successfully aroused emotions. Our results confirmed all four of our hypotheses. More importantly, the impact of the target of the attack varied according to candidate preference strength, suggesting that higher and lower identifiers responded differently in their emotional arousal depending on the message characteristics—in particular, exposure to either an attack on the preferred or opposing candidate (answering RQ1 and RQ3). These findings provide a foundation for the second part of our analysis, which more closely investigates how different levels of identi-fication with one's preferred candidate and the characteristics of blog commentaries provoke specific emotions, leading to associated action tendencies.

Lower Identifiers' vs. Higher Identifiers' Differences in Action Tendencies

To test the multi-group model of lower candidate identifiers and higher identifiers on the relationship between exposure to uncivil blog com-mentary, attack on candidates, emotional response, and action tendencies, a series of path analysis models were run in Mplus. A maximum likelihood robust estimator was used in this analysis to protect against non-normality in the data. To answer our research question, the multi-group method of testing different models based on strength of candidate preference was employed. Participants were divided into two groups based on their candidate preference strength: higher identifiers vs. lower identifiers.

To test whether emotional reactions and action tendencies differed depending on whether individuals were lower identifiers or higher identifiers with their candidate, a series of multi-group path models were estimated. First, for each group a constrained model was estimated that required path coefficients for both groups to be equal. The constrained models were then compared to the unconstrained counterpart, where the path coefficients for each group were freely estimated. In order to argue that the two groups differ, the constrained model needed to produce a significant decline in model fitness over the unconstrained model. Chi-square difference tests revealed that a significant difference between the two was observed, with the unconstrained model providing better model fit (χ^2 = 38.883, df = 11, p < .001). Goodness of fit statistics for the constrained model and unconstrained model are reported in Table 6.1.

The path coefficients for lower identifiers and higher identifiers are reported in Figure 6.1. The findings show a similar pattern between lower identifiers and higher identifiers in terms of provoking anger towards the blogger. When lower identifiers and higher identifiers were exposed to blog commentaries attacking their own preferred presidential candidates, members in both groups experienced anger toward the blogger, leading to a higher tendency to engage in offensive and mockery actions against the blogger, providing support for H5.

However, for feelings of pride, the findings show distinctive patterns of effects from the blog message manipulations, emotional responses, and action tendencies between lower identifiers and high identifiers. Higher identifiers were more proud of the blogger when they read a blogger who attacked the opposing candidate, and this effect was strengthened when the attack on the opposing candidate was also uncivil in tone. Further,

Table 6.1 Multi-Group Path Analysis with Path Coefficients Constrained to Equality and Unconstrained Model Between Low Candidate Identifiers and High Identifiers

	Constrained model	Unconstrained model
Chi-square (df)	60.573***, (23)	21.69*, (12) (p = .041)
Chi-square difference test		
CFI	.940	.985
TLI	.907	.954
AIC	7173.652	7156.772
RMSEA	0.095	.067

Note: *p < .05, **p < .01, ***p < .001.

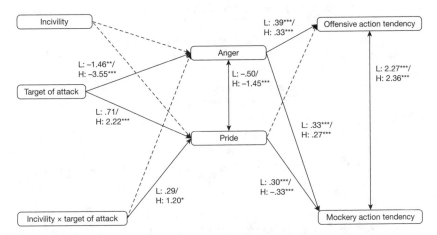

Figure 6.1 Multi-groups model of lower identifiers/higher identifiers with path coefficients

the arousal of pride for both lower and higher identifiers made these individuals significantly less likely to engage in mockery of the blogger and his commentary, but did not impact their decision to take offensive action.

Discussion

Drawing upon the social emotion model, the purpose of our study was two-fold: (1) to examine the effect of citizen-based negative campaigns on blog readers in different candidate support groups during the presidential election campaign and (2) to explore the patterns of specific emotions and associated behaviors between weak and strong group identifiers when exposed to partisan, attacking blog commentaries. Our results indicate that a partisan attack, even from someone not affiliated with the campaign, can produce specific emotional responses and associated action tendencies, but these effects differ based on strength of candidate preference.

Specifically, the findings from our ANOVA analyses show that our message manipulations produced specific emotions. Respondents who were exposed to an uncivil tone were more likely to experience anger and less likely to feel pride toward the blogger. We suspect that the uncivil remarks of the blogger were considered a violation of social norms for interpersonal behavior and that these cognitive appraisals of the message further induced emotional arousal (Vraga, et al., 2009).

Our ANOVA analyses also pointed to the consequential effect of the target of attack on specific emotions. When the respondents in the candidate support group were exposed to blog commentaries attacking their preferred presidential candidate, they likely appraised such commentaries as harmful to their group (lowering the chance for their preferred candidate to win the election). Hence, group members were more likely to experience feelings of anger toward the blogger. While both higher and lower identifiers reported feeling angry at the blogger when they were exposed to an attack on their preferred candidate, the strength of this effect was dependent on their level of affiliation. An interaction between attack and candidate preference strength indicates that higher identifiers felt angrier when exposed to an attack than lower identifiers.

In contrast, when individuals were exposed to blog commentaries attacking the opposing candidate, they may find such behaviors contribute to fulfilling their own goals and desires (i.e., helping their preferred candidate win the election). Thus, people exposed to a blogger attacking an opposed candidate reported more feelings of pride. However, this effect was qualified by the strength of candidate preference. In the ANOVA analyses, the results showed that the effect of target of attack increased as their strength of candidate preference increased. This finding provided the basis for us to further investigate specific emotions patterns and associated behaviors between lower identifiers and higher identifiers.

The structural equation analyses reinforce these results. Both lower identifiers and higher identifiers felt anger at the bloggers when they were exposed to blog commentaries attacking their own preferred candidate, leading to both groups to engage in offensive actions against the blogger and mockery of the blogger and his comments. These findings suggest that both weaker identifiers and stronger identifiers have similar interpretations of the blogger's behaviors and the commentaries as harmful to their own group and their preferred candidate. However, only higher identifiers were more likely to feel proud of the blogger, especially when the blogger's attack of the opponent was uncivil.

The arousal of pride among only higher identifiers has several possible explanations. It may be that a positive emotion like pride has a higher threshold than negative emotions like anger, requiring higher levels of group commitment to activate. Future research should examine whether positive and negative emotions do in fact have different thresholds for activation. An alternative explanation suggests that more investment in the group and its goals are needed before individuals are able to condone violations to social norms. In other words, higher identifiers not only countenanced, but reported feeling proud when an in-group member—in this case, a blogger—attacked the opposing candidate in an uncivil manner. Given that both incivility and overt attack of others violate social taboos, these characteristics tend to lower ratings of the person authorizing the attack (Mutz & Reeves, 2005; Roese & Sande, 1993; Chang, 2001). But highly motivated individuals, such as those deeply attached to their group membership, may be willing to discount these norms and not only support, but also credit, an uncivil attack on the opponent.

Although our manipulations of the blog characteristics, such as the target of an attack and the civility of tone, did not provoke as strong an emotional response among lower identifiers, when these emotions are in fact aroused, they lead to the same action tendencies as among high identifiers. When angered, both higher and lower identifiers are increasingly willing to engage in offensive action, including the desire to respond to the blogger and to mock the blogger. Similarly, when both groups do feel proud of the blogger, they are less willing to mock him and do not show any tendencies towards offensive action. Specific emotions are in fact linked to particular actions in response, regardless of group identity strength (Frijda, et al., 1989). Anger appears to provoke both types of response—offensive reactions and mockery. However, pride not only decreases mockery, but also does not encourage further offensive action. It may be that individuals who see a blogger attacking the opposing candidate no longer feel the need to respond themselves. If participation and discussion is in fact partly motivated by a desire to take corrective action by addressing assumed misperceptions of others (Rojas, 2007), the attack of the blogger performs this function, relieving others of the necessity for offensive action.

Perhaps the most important contribution made by this study is to demonstrate that the same situation can be appraised differently depending on one's particular group identity and his/her identity strength (i.e., weaker or stronger identifier). Group identity and identity strength lead to different cognitive appraisals of the same event, resulting in different emotional responses. In our study, an attack on Barack Obama by a blogger aroused anger among Obama supporters and pride on the part of strong McCain supporters (and vice versa). The different discrete emotions aroused by our manipulations led to different reported action tendencies. Even for members of the same in-group, an uncivil attack by a blogger on a candidate one opposes may look different depending on how strongly you identify with the group of candidate supporters. A moderate Barack Obama supporter might have squirmed at reading an uncivil attack against John McCain while a strong Obama supporter appeared to have cheered the blogger.

It was somewhat surprising to find that incivility alone was not a strong predictor in our path analyses. In our path analyses, the only effects of incivility are to amplify the effects of an in-group member's attack on feelings of pride for higher identifiers. Incivility had no effect among lower identifiers, nor did it predict anger, either on its own or in combination with attack. There are several possible explanations for the lack of impact from incivility. It may be that our manipulations of civility were not strong enough to produce effects. To create the civility manipulation, we changed words and phrases to adopt more insulting and derogatory language, but these changes may not have altered overall perceptions of tone. A second possibility arises from the context of the study, fielded in the two weeks prior to the 2008 election. During the end of a campaign, political attack is likely to be a strong cue, overwhelming the tone of that attack. Although the civility manipulation attempted to maintain a more respectful tone, it still clearly critiqued the candidate's strategy as ineffective and manipulative. In a highly involved context, attack may be the most salient cue to spur appraisals, regardless of level of civility.

Another limitation of the study is our median split for higher versus lower identifiers. Our ANOVA analyses suggested that strength of partisan support has an important interactive effect with exposure to attack on arousal of emotions in response. Using a median split allowed us to maintain a relatively equal number of respondents in each of the groups, but the high level of identification in the sample as a whole means that even "lower identifiers" had relatively high levels of candidate support. When thinking about the campaign context, these inflated support levels make sense. In the final weeks leading up to the election, supporters on both sides of the campaign were likely to feel strong preferences for their candidate and be highly involved in the campaign. That said, differences in emotional response did emerge between higher and lower group identifiers, indicating that there is value to treating these groups separately. Strong identifiers responded with more emotional arousal as a result of the manipulations, both with stronger feelings of anger and with the arousal of pride (which is not apparent) among lower identifiers. Future research should re-examine the impact of strength of group identification on an issue that promotes lower levels of involvement among the population as a whole, allowing for larger differences between high and low identifiers to emerge.

In sum, fielding the study during the final stages of the 2008 election is both a contribution to and a limitation of our research. The authors of this chapter deliberately chose a topic and a context in which involvement and interest would be high to ensure the sample of college students would be engaged in the topic. That said, election campaigns (and especially the final weeks of those campaigns) are not representative of general levels of enthusiasm. Future research should re-examine these key questions using other issues and contexts to determine their effects, as well as replicating the study with adults, whose preferences may be more settled and less malleable.

Conclusion

Ultimately, this study provides a unique, social psychological perspective on citizen-based negative campaigning in elections. With an increasing number of voters relying on political blogs as the sources of information of election campaigns (Pew, 2008), it is important to examine the potential effects of negative campaign tactics initiated by ordinary citizens in the blogosphere. If citizen-initiated attacks that are not endorsed by the major political parties and candidates are ineffective in provoking emotional response or altering intended behaviors from those reading the attacks, the greater ease of expression that online settings provide may not actually be affecting the nature of public discourse.

However, this study indicates that is not the case. This study's findings suggest that exposure to attacks on candidates, even by an unaffiliated political blogger, generates feelings of anger among readers who support the candidate and, in turn, motivates supporters to take offensive and mocking actions against the blogger. Unfortunately these offensive responses may spur a vicious cycle of attack between candidate support groups, rather than facilitating open-minded discussion in the blogosphere. Furthermore, incivility in an attack on the opposition engendered pride among strong supporters and decreased mockery, thus tacitly encouraging such discursive incivility. Therefore, while exposure to an attack on a preferred candidate versus one on an oppositional candidate may produce different emotional responses, both of these responses may discourage healthy democratic debate. If the citizens who are most likely to take advantage of the new expressive opportunities offered online are also the ones most likely to invoke uncivil and attacking language, greater citizen participation in the debate may ultimately prove detrimental to a more deliberative public sphere online.

Acknowledgement

We would like to thank Hans Meyers for his assistance in data collection.

References

Ansolabehere, S., & Iyengar, S. (1995). *Going negative: How attack ads shrink and polarize the electorate.* New York: Free Press.

Brader, T. (2005). Striking a responsive chord: How political ads motivate and persuade voters by appealing to emotions. *American Journal of Political Science, 49*(2): 388–405.

Brooks, D. J., & Geer J. G. (2007). Beyond negativity: The effects of incivility on the electorate. *American Journal of Political Science, 51*(1), 1–16.

Cappella, J., & Jamieson, K. (1997). *Spiral of Cynicism: The press and the public good.* New York: Oxford University Press.

Chang, C. (2001). The impact of emotion elicited by print political advertising on candidate evaluations. *Media Psychology, 3:* 91–118.

Dillard, J. P., & Peck, E. (2000). Affect and persuasion: Emotional responses to public service announcements. *Communication Research, 27,* 461–495.

Dillard, J. P., Kinney, T. A., & Cruz, M. G. (1996). Influence, appraisals, and emotions in close relationships. *Communication Monographs, 63*, 105–130.

Frijda, N. H., Kuipers, P., & Ter Schure, E. (1989). Relations among emotion, appraisal, and emotional action readiness. *Journal of Personality and Social Psychology, 57*(2), 212–228.

Garramone, G. M. (1985). Effects of negative political advertising: The roles of sponsor and rebuttal. *Journal of Broadcasting and Electronic Media, 29*(2), 147–159.

Haddock, G., & Zanna, M. P. (1997). Impact of negative advertising on evaluations of political candidates: The 1993 Canadian Federal Election. *Basic and Applied Social Psychology, 19*(2), 205–223.

Huber, G. A., & Arceneaux, K. (2007). Identifying the persuasive effects of presidential advertising. *American Journal of Political Science, 51*(4), 957–977.

Hwang, H., Borah, P., Namkoong, K., & Veenstra, A. (2008). *Does civility matter in the blogosphere? Examining the interaction effects of incivility and disagreement on citizen attitudes*. Paper presented at the International Communication Association, Montreal, Canada.

Kaid, L. L., & Boydston, J. (1987). An experimental study of the effectiveness of negative political advertisements. *Communication Quarterly, 35*(2), 193–201.

Kerbel, M. R. & Bloom, J. D. (2005). Blog for America and civic involvement. *The Harvard International Journal of Press/Politics, 10*(3), 3–27.

Kingwell, M. (1995). *A civil tongue: justice, dialogue, and the politics of pluralism*. University Park, PA: Pennsylvania State University Press.

Koop, R., & Jansen, H. J. (2009). Political blogs and blogrolls in Canada: Forums for democratic deliberation? *Social Science Computer Review, 27*, 155–173.

Mackie, D., Devos, T., & Smith, E. (2000). Intergroup emotions: Explaining offensive action tendencies in an intergroup context. *Journal of Personality and Social Psychology, 79*(4), 602–616.

Mutz, D. C. (2007). How the mass media divide us. In P. S. Nivola & D. W. Brady (Eds.), *Red and Blue Nation? Volume one*. Washington, DC: Brookings Institute Press, pp. 223–248.

Mutz, D.C., & Reeves, B. (2005). The effects of televised incivility on political trust. *American Political Science Review, 99*, 1–15.

Nabi, R. L. (2002). Anger, fear, uncertainty, and attitudes: A test of the cognitive-functional model. *Communication Monographs, 69*(3), 204–216.

Pew Research Center For the People & the Press. (2008). *More than a quarter of voters read political blogs*. Report from the Pew Research Center for the People & the Press, Washington, DC.

Pinkleton, B. (1997). The effects of negative campaign comparative political advertising on candidate evaluations and advertising evaluations: An exploration. *Journal of Advertising, 26*(1), 19–29.

Roese, N. J., & Sande, G. N. (1993). Backlash effects in attack politics. *Journal of Applied Social Psychology, 23*(8), 632–653.

Rojas, H. (2007). *"Corrective" actions in the public sphere: How perceptions of media effects shape online behaviors*. Association for Education in Journalism and Mass Communication conference, Washington, DC, August 9–12.

Roseman, I. J. (1984). Cognitive determinants of emotions: A structural theory. In P. Shaver (Ed.), *Review of personality and social psychology* (Vol. 5). Beverly Hills, CA: Sage, pp. 11–36.

Roseman, I. J. Spindel, M. S. & Jose, P. E. (1990). Appraisal of emotion-eliciting events: Testing a theory of discrete emotions. *Journal of Personality and Social Psychology, 59*, 899–915.

Roseman, I. J., Wiet, C., & Swartz, T. S. (1994). Phenomenology, behaviors, and goals differentiate discrete emotions. *Journal of Personality and Social Psychology, 67*, 206–221.

Scherer, K. R. (1988). Criteria for emotion-antecedent appraisal: A review. In V. Hamilton, G. H. Bower, & N. H. Frijda (Eds.), *Cognitive perspectives on emotion and motivation*. Boston: Kluwer, pp. 89–126.

Smith, E. R. (1993). Social identity and social emotion: Toward new conceptualizations of prejudice. In D. M. Mackie (Ed.), *Affect, cognition, and stereotyping: Interactive processes in group perception*. San Diego, CA: Academic Press, pp. 297–315.

Smith, E. R. (1999). Affective and cognitive implications of a group becoming part of the self: New models of prejudice and of self-concept. In D. Abrams & M. A. Hogg (Eds.), *Social identity and social cognition*. Oxford, England: Basil Blackwell, pp. 183–196.

Smith, C. A., & Ellsworth, P. C. (1985). Patterns of cognitive appraisal in emotion. *Journal of Personality and Social Psychology, 48*, 813–838.

Thorson, E., Christ, W. G., & Caywood, C. (1991). Effects of issue-image strategies, attack and support appeals, music, and visual content in political commercials. *Journal of Broadcasting and Electronic Media, 35*(4), 465–486.

Thorson, K., Fung, T. K., & Vraga, E. (2008). *How you feel makes you what you are: Partisan reactions to political incivility online*. Paper presented at the annual conference of Association for Education of Journalism and Mass Communication, Chicago, IL, August 2008.

Turner, J. C. (1985). Social categorization and the self-concept: A social cognitive theory of group behavior. In E. J. Lawler (Ed.), *Advances in group process; Theory and research*. Greenwich, CT: JAI Press.

Vraga, E. K., Thorson, K., Fung, T. K., & Meyer, H. K. (2009). *Emotions vs. cognitions? Testing competing models of response to a media message in predicting participation*. Paper presented at the annual conference of Association for Education of Journalism and Mass Communication, Boston, MA, August 2009.

Yzerbyt, V., Dumont, M., Wigboldus, D., & Gordijn, E. (2003). I feel for us: The impact of categorization and identification on emotions and action tendencies. *British Journal of Social Psychology, 42*, 533–549.

Chapter 7

New Voices and New Voters

Ethno-Technology in Reactions to Candidate Messages in the 2008 Campaign

Hyun Jung Yun, Amy E. Jasperson, and Sindy Chapa

Across the two disciplines of political science and mass communication, research examines how growing ethnic minorities in American society have the potential to change the political landscape and to shape future trends in U.S. elections. This study investigates ethnic minorities, whose populations are increasing rapidly and whose proportion of eligible voters exceeds marginal differences for most electoral victories at the state and national levels. Ethnic minority groups' increasing social and political importance in the U.S. has received more attention in the last couple of presidential elections. Further, the presence of an African-American Democratic Party nominee raised levels of racial and ethnic consciousness and changed the picture of the American political process in the 2008 presidential election.

Similarly, young voters received increased attention as an important voting bloc in the 2008 presidential election. According to a report on youth voting by the Center for Information and Research on Civic Learning and Engagement (2008), also known as CIRCLE, youth turnout rose to 52–53 percent in the 2008 presidential election with 23 million young voters under the age of 30 coming out to the polls on Election Day. This represented an increase of 3.4 million young voters over 2004. The Pew Research Center found that 66 percent of young voters supported Barack Obama, "making the disparity between young voters and other age groups larger than in any presidential election since exit polling began in 1972" (Keeter, Horowitz, & Tyson, 2008, para. 1). Keeter, et al. (2008) see this pattern as evidence of a generational shift; while young voters were not decisive for Barack Obama in all states, the authors noted that younger voters also had an influence on their older parents.

In addition, the Pew study found that young voters are more racially and ethnically diverse than in the past. In 2008, young voters were 62 percent non-Hispanic White, 18 percent Black and 14 percent Hispanic; in 2000, 74 percent of young voters were identified as non-Hispanic White. The CIRCLE study cited exit polls as revealing that young voters are more diverse than older voters, with Latinos making up 11 percent of young voters (compared to 6 percent of the entire electorate), and African-Americans making up 19 percent of young voters (relative to 13 percent of the entire electorate) in the 2008 election. In addition, many ethnic and racially diverse youth were first-time voters; 45 percent of 18–29 year old Black youth were first-time voters, and 61 percent of young Latinos were first-time voters, compared with 37 percent of young White first-time voters (CIRCLE, 2008).

These statistics call for greater analysis of this young, ethnically-diverse group of new voters who have the potential to change the American political landscape, in order to determine how they react to candidate campaign messages. Our research aims to broaden our understanding of political communication during campaigns by examining the responses of young voters to candidate advertising messages with attention to race/ethnicity during the 2008 presidential election. We ask whether young racial and ethnic minority voters respond differently to political advertising messages from candidates Barack Obama and John McCain than young majority voters. Past research discovered some differences in the effect of advertising messages on young ethnic minority and majority voters in 2004 (Jasperson & Yun, 2007). Do we see similar or amplified results for 2008, a racially charged campaign with a relatively young, African-American Democratic Party candidate?

Along with the diversity of young voters, the Internet has reshaped the pattern of political communication of this new generation (Vromen, 2008). Such research argues for focusing on race and ethnicity in the new media era, in order to develop a more comprehensive picture of the impact of political campaign communication on a new generation of voters.

Theoretical Approach

Ethnicity in Political Communication

Ethnicity is one of the key variables that scholars investigate when examining political attitudes and behavior in American campaigns. Non-Hispanic Whites, African-Americans, and other ethnic minorities, including Asians, Hispanics, and other multi-racial groups reflect race-based political opinion and behavior cleavages (Steele, 2007). Previous research in the field of minority political communication finds that ethnic minorities' political activities tend to be initiated by ethnicity-based mobilization activities. Therefore, ethnic and racial identities matter, and leaders serve as gatekeepers for their own ethnic groups (Shaw, de la Garza, & Lee, 2000).

Studies argue that a shared sense of community within their own ethnic groups and internal ethnic coalitions are much more important for minorities than social interaction or cooperation in broader non-ethnic organizations. In addition, political mobilization initiated by in-group leaders is more successful than by out-group leaders. In other words, ethnic minority voters are more likely to rely on personal cues rather than on political issues in their political decision-making (Abrajano, 2005; Rodriguez, 2002, pp. 65–89; Shaw, et al. 2000).

Stereotypes also have a strong effect on evaluations of political candidates. When voters' demographic characteristics, such as race or religion, are congruent with political candidates, preference toward the candidates increases; however, if political candidates' traits are not shared, then antagonism toward the target candidate tends to increase (Berinsky & Mendelberg, 2005). These studies highlight the importance of racial and ethnic cues in political decision-making and the significance of learning more about how younger voters respond to these cues.

Ethnic group dynamics in political communication are important for American campaign politics because ethnic groups are a key component of candidates' winning coalitions. For instance, Hispanics, the largest ethnic minority in the U.S., constitute 15 percent of the U.S. population and about 9 percent of eligible voters (U.S. Census Bureau, 2007). According to the Pew Hispanic Center, a little more than half of the Latino population identify themselves as Democrats and about 23 percent support Republicans. However, 34 percent do not identify themselves with any political party (Taylor & Fry, 2007). This latter group of uncommitted Latino voters has great potential to change the results in U.S. elections that are often determined by only marginal voting differences.

Ideologically, compared to non-Hispanic White Americans in the U.S., ethnic minorities are more likely to lean to the liberal side of the ideological spectrum. Among minority groups, Hispanic and Asian political preferences are more evenly dispersed across the ideological continuum from left to right relative to African-Americans, who lean strongly to the left. More interestingly, there is a deviation in some ethnic minorities' ideological and practical political stances. For instance, ideologically conservative Latinos still prefer more government spending and higher taxes. In addition, while Latinos overall are slightly more likely to lean conservative ideologically and are more socially conservative, they are more likely to vote for Democratic candidates (Erikson & Tedin, 2007; Rodriguez, 2002, pp. 45–64). We may legitimately expect to see more movement after exposure to advertising messages among Hispanics relative to other minority or majority youth voters. Different ethnic backgrounds and nationalities have a great deal of societal variations and the differences are reflected in their political preferences (de la Garza, Falcon, & Garcia, 1992; Rodriguez, 2002; Shaw, et al., 2000). Overall, there is no decisive or monolithic picture capturing ethnic minorities' political attitudes and behavior in political campaigns. Therefore, it is important to analyze various minority groups to investigate differences that exist in candidate appraisals.

Recent research has found that new political information has a differential impact on majority and minority voters. After exposure to ads and television debates, ethnic minorities in non-battleground states tend to be much more influenced by incoming political messages than non-Hispanic White Americans in non-battleground states. This tendency is stronger for Hispanic Americans compared to other ethnic minorities, such as African-Americans, Native Americans, and other multi-racial groups. Generally, political information has the ability to influence minorities' political attitudes and behaviors more than those of non-Hispanic White Americans (Jasperson & Yun, 2007; Shaw, et al., 2000; Yun, 2009).

The Internet in Political Communication

The Internet has been defined as an accessible resource with strong research capabilities, rich interaction, and powerful support for effective learning (Bourret, 2000; Lykourentzou, Giannoukos, Mpardis, Nikolopoulos, & Loumos, 2009; Nichols, 2008). In the political communication context, the medium is seen as a force for democracy aimed at increasing voters' interest and participation (Vromen, 2008). In recent years, the Internet has become a powerful tool for seeking out information, especially for the new generation of voters (Anstead & Chadwick, 2008; Bennett, 2007; Lupia & Philpot, 2005). Exposure to candidate Web sites, e-news, chat rooms, blogs, podcasts, Facebook, and Twitter has increased motivation and learning about political campaigns (Kraushaar, 2009; Lupia & Philpot, 2005; Williams, Trammell, Postelnicu, & Landreville, 2005). For instance, political blogs facilitate further learning by providing directives to external links with additional information (Williams et al., 2005).

Bill Clinton's 1992 presidential campaign was the first to use the Internet as it was considered a non-traditional medium (Bimber & Davis, 2003). At the time, political consultants claimed the Internet might be an essential instrument for strategic communication in political campaigns. However, it has proven to be an even more powerful and multi-dimensional tool. It has gradually begun to replace traditional television news as the major source of political communication and has also provided other forms of media, that were once obsolete or facing extinction, the ability to return in a new form, such as the case of the political editorial cartoons which have now taken the form of animated Flash cartoons on the Internet (Baumgartner, 2008; Lordan 2005).

The Internet has many advantages in terms of disseminating information (Bimber & Davis, 2003). Later, scholars claimed the Internet was a superior venue not only in terms of cost and time efficiency, but also as a strategic communication tool. Internet users tend to search proactively for political information, are better informed and are politically less cynical (Kaid, 2002; Tedesco, 2007). However, Bimber and Davis (2003) maintain that the Internet merely reinforces a candidate's audience of supporters and has a minimal effect on undecided voters. Likewise, Park and Perry (2007) argue that campaign Web sites were generally effective for supporting reinforcement rather than mobilization. Yet, Lupia and Philpot (2005) suggest the Internet is the most useful mass medium in engaging and informing undecided young adults more effectively. They found that exposure to political sites and the perceptions that a Web site was effective (convenience, speed, currency, and resources) increased interest and participation of those young adults.

Not surprisingly, in an attempt to reach younger voters, candidates have increased their campaign presence and activities online (Bennet, 2007). In 2008 President Obama targeted younger voters by using Facebook, a social network site, as a new strategic communications tool. On the other hand, the Internet can be used as a tool to distort political communications as well. The lack of regulation on information exchange online makes the situation worse in terms of transparent communication (Kaid & Jones, 2004). In addition, accuracy is a problem. Internet users are easily exposed to pictures or posters that are exaggerated and distorted and users can be exposed to cynical and extreme opinions. This type of information can create misperceptions and misinformation, especially for people who use the Internet as their primary source of information. Selective source accessibility can reinforce biases toward political candidates and issues (Bimber & Davis, 2003; Iyengar & McGrady, 2007, pp. 107–109).

Ethno-Technology in Political Communication and Candidate Evaluations

Cultural differences are also reflected in patterns of media consumption. According to Yun and Park (2008), reliance on "new media" is more prevalent among ethnic groups with collective, interactive, masculine, value-oriented, or emotionally more proactive cultures than ethnic groups living in individualistic or unequal social-structural cultures. For example, Asians are more likely to be open to new media such as the Internet and African-Americans prefer traditional media such as TV and radio (Yun & Park, 2008). In addition, ethnic minorities in the U.S. are more likely to use new media technology to search out political information beyond mainstream news coverage. Non-Hispanic White Americans utilize both new and traditional media sources (Yun & Park, 2008). Cultural differences in relation to ethnic groups' orientations toward the social structure (Hofstede, 2001) influence these differences in the use of media.

Political affiliation (Merritt, 1984) and social groups (Hogg & Turner, 1987; Ray & Lovejoy, 1986) influence individuals' candidate preferences. Social identity theory explains an individual's tendency to like those who are similar and dislike those who are different (Shinnar, 2008). This theory suggests that groups' identifications are established by comparing the individuals' in-group against their out-group. Race is an important part of social identity, particularly for understanding communication behaviors of minorities. Ethnocentrism refers to the tendency to view one's own ethnic group as superior relative to other ethnic groups (Senior & Bhopal, 1994; Shimp & Sharma, 1987). Highly ethnocentric people accept those who are culturally similar and reject or even dislike those who are different (Hogg & Turner, 1987; Ray & Lovejoy, 1986). Therefore, individuals make more negative evaluations of out-group members than for in-group members.

In addition, a recent study makes a new assertion about the relative effect of race on individuals' out-group evaluations. The findings of Kaiser and Pratt-Hyatt (2009) were consistent with previous research in reasserting that non-Hispanic Whites have a more negative attitude toward Blacks than toward other ethnic groups, yet the authors claim this is due to individuals' perceptions that Blacks are a strongly identified minority group. By comparing non-Hispanic Whites' attitudes toward different racial groups, the authors find that non-Hispanic Whites express more negative attitudes toward strongly identified racial minorities than toward weakly identified minorities. Therefore, we expect that race and ethnicity will influence candidate likeability. Specifically, we propose that the greater the difference between the candidate's and individual's ethnic identity, the more likely individuals will be to dislike the candidate.

Political Ad Effects on Candidate Evaluations

Campaign communications influence political learning, candidate evaluations, attitudes of efficacy and cynicism, and turnout. Exposure to ads shapes audiences' perceptions of targeted candidates' images, informs them about candidates' issues, and influences general political attitudes about political systems and voting choice (Kaid, 1995). Exposure to advertising messages can change candidate evaluations as voters formulate and update their impressions over time (Kahn & Geer, 1994; Kaid, 1998). Benoit, McKinney, and Holbert (2001) argue that exposure to direct political information, such as televised debates, changes viewers' evaluations of the candidates, strengthens confidence in preferred candidates, and determines vote choice. These studies agree that there is a positive correlation between political information and candidate evaluations. In other words, exposure to political advertising, TV debates, and candidate visits increase positive evaluations of political candidates (Kaid, 2004; Shaw, 1999).

Further, individuals who have more information available for making their political decisions are inclined to be supportive of their political leaders (Berman, 1997, p. 110). Individuals who are less informed about politics more frequently shift their political position or preference than individuals who have more political information (Converse, 1962). Further, political ads have a greater influence on those with low information and interest (Cundy, 1986). In addition, political ads change attitudes and stimulate action among people who are more eager to look for political information (Freedman, Franz, & Goldstein, 2004). Although some empirical inconsistencies exist (Chaffee, 1978; Katz & Feldman, 1962), exposure to political information is an important factor in determining voters' candidate evaluations (Kaid, 2002; Payne, Golden, Marlier, & Ratzan, 1989).

Young voters are generally seen as less engaged relative to other age groups so one could legitimately expect to see that exposure to political ads could have a dramatic impact on the candidate evaluations of young voters. In addition, young voters are relatively late in making up their minds about which candidate to support; during the 2008 presidential campaign, only 50 percent of young voters had made up their minds before September 2008 (CIRCLE, 2008). This suggests that there may have been an impact of political ads on the candidate evaluations of young voters during the fall 2008 presidential campaign.

Relative Assessment of Candidates

Kruse and Kendall (1995) introduced the concept of a "relative spectrum" as a theoretical and methodological approach to describe voters' simultaneous evaluations of multiple candidates. The idea of a voter's relative preference for a candidate is assessed by the "leverage," or distance that exists between a preferred candidate and the opposing candidate in a voter's mind. A political candidate is always evaluated in comparison to his or her opponents, and a voter's evaluations of a candidate reflect a relative liking or disliking of competing candidates (Kruse & Kendall, 1995, pp. 149–51). Voters' relative perceptions of candidates eventually become a relative preference, and then antagonism builds toward one candidate over the other (Wrede, 2001). In the evaluation process, voters utilize their preexisting "stereotypes" and "projection biases" to interpret new information about political candidates, thus the path of information accessibility and interpretation is more likely to occur based on impression-driven judgment rather than memory-based information recall (Lodge, McGraw, & Stroh, 1989).

Studies show that voters' positive and negative schematic discrepancies, discriminations, and labels toward different candidates are influenced by voters' given personal factors, such as partisanship, class, and race (Hamill,

Lodge, & Blake, 1985) and the schemata for political candidates are less likely to change over the course of the evaluation process (Fiske & Kinder, 1981). In other words, initial cognitive impressions about candidates tend to integrate new information about the candidates (Wyer & Srull, 1986). Therefore, individuals' initial perception towards different candidates serves as the basis of cognitive preferences, and new information simply enhances a voter's relative political preference of different candidates (Lodge, et al., 1989).

Individuals use difference criteria to judge candidates, putting varying weights on candidates whom they like and dislike. Voters' *relative* standards toward different candidates are core elements in candidate evaluations. Therefore, the process of candidate evaluations is more likely a comparative and multidimensional spatial decision (Moskewitz & Stroh, 1996).

Based on the studies outlined above, several hypotheses and corollaries are suggested:

First, related to ethno-technology and candidate evaluation:

H1: Voters' race/ethnicity influences their feelings toward the candidates as measured by feeling thermometers.

H1a: Given racial similarity, African-American voters will be most favorable toward Barack Obama.

H1b: Given racial difference, non-Hispanic White voters will be least favorable toward Barack Obama.

H2: Voters' Internet use influences their feelings toward the candidates.

H3: The patterns of ethno-technology, variations in Internet use by different ethnic groups, influence voters' feelings toward the candidates.

Next, related to ethno-technology and attitude change after exposure to ads:

H4: Voters' race/ethnicity moderates the impact of political ad exposure on changes in feelings toward the candidates.

H4a: After ad exposure, African-American voters will become more favorable toward Barack Obama.

H4b: After ad exposure, non-Hispanic White voters will become less favorable toward Barack Obama.

H5: Voters' Internet use moderates the influence of political ads on changes in feelings toward the candidates.

H6: Internet use by different ethnic groups moderates the influence of political ads on changes in feelings toward the candidates.

Finally, related to ethno-technology and relativism:

H7:   Voters' race/ethnicity influences their relative appraisals of different candidates.

H8:   Voters' Internet use influences their relative appraisals of different candidates.

H9:   Internet use by different ethnic groups influences their relative appraisals of different candidates.

H10:   Voters' race/ethnicity moderates the influence of political ad on their relative appraisals of different candidates

H11:   Voters' Internet use moderates the influence of political ad on their relative appraisals of different candidates.

H12:   Internet use by different ethnic groups moderates the influence of political ads on their relative appraisals of different candidates.

It is important to examine these hypotheses in the context of young voters. Given that they are more racially and ethnically diverse than older generations or even past groups of young voters, and that they vary in their use of new sources of political information, will this study find racial and ethnic variations in the reactions of voters to new information about the candidates? The literature suggests that this study could find some interesting distinctions, with important insights for understanding candidate appraisal.

Method

Data

Members of the Uvote inter-university research team collaborated to gather national data simultaneously during the 2008 presidential campaign season. The research team conducted political ad experiments from September 22 to 24, the beginning of the peak general election campaign season in the 2008 presidential election in 19 different locations across different states in the U.S.[1] Experiment participants were asked to fill out a pre-test questionnaire and were exposed to a series of political ads sponsored by Barack Obama and John McCain: one positive issue ad, one negative issue ad, one positive image ad, and one negative image ad for each general election candidate.[2] After exposure to the ads, participants were asked to fill out a post-test questionnaire. The questionnaire included questions about demographic factors, political attitudes, previous political information exposure, and media use. The data was collected through a paper and pencil format in physical locations as well as through online responses. Pilot studies in both offline and online formats found that there was no statistically significant difference between the two formats.

Sample

From among a sample size of 929, 38.6 percent of respondents (n = 358) were male, and 61.4 percent (n = 570) were female. The average age of the sample was 20.97 years old (SD = 4.82), with 40.9 percent (n = 373) identifying as Democrats, 31.8 percent (n = 290) identifying as Republicans, and 27.4 percent (n = 250) identifying as Independents. Among the sample, 6.5 percent (n = 60) were Asian-Americans, 64.3 percent (n = 597) were Anglo-Americans, 7.5 percent (n = 70) were African-Americans, 14.9 percent (n = 138) were Hispanic Americans, and 6.9 percent (n = 64) were multi or other racial groups.

Measures

Ethnicity can be categorized in a number of ways. Adopting the wisdom of previous research such as National Election Studies and modification of other scholars, this study used ethnic categories of Asian-American, non-Hispanic White American, African-American, Hispanic American, and other or multi-racial groups.

The Use of Technology in individuals' political communication is a methodologically cumbersome concept to define since there are multiple types of communication utilizing technology, such as political blogging, podcasting, and information exchanges in online social network sites (e.g., Twitter) or through personal devices such as cellular phones. In addition, the frequency and intensity of technology use is even more problematic because different types of technology are not comparable. Internet use, however, is the basis of most types of individuals' technology use in general political information searching (Chadwick, 2006). This study includes Internet use as a dichotomous variable—whether or not an individual uses the Internet to search for political information—in order to avoid unnecessary over-representation of or double counts for the same technology-initiated political communication.

Candidate favorability was measured using feeling thermometers toward Barack Obama and John McCain before and after political ad exposure on the scale of 0 (cold/unfavorable) to 100 (warm/favorable). This thermometer is similar to the one traditionally used by the National Election Studies to measure attitudes toward the candidates (Rosenstone, Kinder, Miller, & the National Election Studies, 1997). In order to measure the *change in favorability* after political ad exposure, the difference between pre-test feeling thermometers and post-test feeling thermometers toward each of the candidates was calculated.

The concept of the *relative spectrum,* as discussed in the literature review, is measured by the discrepancy between feeling thermometers of one candidate relative to the other. Participants' feeling thermometers toward Barack Obama were subtracted by the feeling thermometers toward John McCain in both pre- and post-political ads exposures. The "leverage," or gap between the two candidates, was used as the relative spectrum score. Therefore, a positive number indicates a relative warmth toward Barack Obama over John McCain. The *change in the relative spectrum,* the difference between pre-test discrepancy between Barack Obama and John McCain and post-test discrepancy between Barack Obama and John McCain, was also measured to see if exposure to political ads influenced the relative preference for the candidates. Demographic factors, such as age, party identification, and gender, and previous political information exposure (on the scale of 1 = never, to 5 = a lot) are also included in the analyses to control any mediating and moderating effects.

Results

Ethno-Technology in Candidate Preferences

After controlling for all demographic factors, ethnicity showed a statistically moderate impact in explaining voters' initial attitude toward Barack Obama ($F[4, 889] = 2.262, p \leq .061$) and stronger impact for post-test attitudes toward John McCain ($F[4, 887] = 9.567, p \leq .001$) after ad exposure. A Least Significant Difference (LSD) contrasts test found that Barack Obama had more positive evaluations from African-Americans, multi-racial groups, and Asian-Americans than from non-Hispanic White Americans. Non-Hispanic White Americans' attitudes toward Barack Obama were significantly more negative compared to attitudes of ethnic minorities ($F[4, 831] = 3.451, p \leq .008$) (see Tables 7.1 and 7.2 and Figure 7.1a). After participants were exposed to political ads, the same test for John McCain found that he received the least favorable evaluations from African-Americans and had the most positive evaluations from Non-Hispanic Whites and Hispanic Americans ($F[4, 829] = 9.567, p \leq .001$) (see Tables 7.1 and 7.2 and Figure 7.1d). These results suggest that H1 and its corollaries are confirmed for the most part with African-American voters rating Barack Obama much warmer than non-Hispanic Whites and Hispanic voters under an un-manipulated condition. Results suggest that ad exposure seemed to make the relative African-American voters' antagonism and non-Hispanic Whites and Hispanic Americans' likeability toward John McCain more distinctive (see Tables 7.1 and 7. 2 and Figures 7.1a–7.1d).

Internet use was an important influence on candidate evaluations, and it interacted with voters' ethnicity to influence attitudes toward the ethnic minority candidate, Barack Obama, confirming H2 and H3. Findings

Table 7.1 Political Ads Exposure and Candidate Evaluations by Ethnicity and Technology Communication

	Pre-test				Post-test			
	Obama		McCain		Obama		McCain	
	Mean	SD	Mean	SD	Mean	SD	Mean	SD
Asian Americans	54.75	33.72	47.27	25.06	61.22	28.49	40.79	22.45
No-Internet use	65.16	25.35	38.08	20.77	67.20	25.04	38.60	20.64
Internet use	47.09	37.27	54.03	26.06	56.82	30.39	42.45	23.92
Non-Hispanic White Americans	48.36	35.49	48.31	29.20	61.82	28.82	52.28	29.47
No-Internet use	58.90	29.73	49.15	30.61	59.80	29.82	49.58	29.64
Internet use	46.23	36.19	48.14	28.93	62.23	28.63	53.20	29.43
African Americans	59.41	45.63	45.43	39.89	65.41	40.24	17.23	21.30
No-Internet use	92.53	18.34	25.53	24.81	93.12	18.07	22.59	25.25
Internet use	46.61	46.69	53.11	42.12	54.70	41.44	15.12	19.44
Hispanic Americans	53.69	37.84	49.36	29.77	65.40	29.14	45.17	29.79
No-Internet use	71.91	18.36	40.78	25.04	70.43	18.94	44.77	25.14
Internet use	49.74	39.83	51.17	30.47	64.34	30.82	45.25	30.74
Other or multi-racial groups	56.84	39.83	43.96	34.79	63.24	34.92	37.04	34.18
No-Internet use	84.10	19.50	25.50	26.71	84.20	19.03	25.40	25.46
Internet use	50.78	40.78	48.07	35.29	58.58	36.07	39.62	35.55
Ethnic total	50.84	36.87	47.93	30.20	62.64	30.12	47.36	30.40
No-Internet use total	66.29	28.36	42.75	28.93	66.93	28.30	43.33	28.59
Internet use total	47.10	37.73	49.18	30.39	61.61	30.47	48.34	30.76

Table 7.2 Ancova Tests on Candidate Evaluations and Repeated Measures GLM of Ethno-Technology on Changes in Candidate Evaluation

Factors	Pre-Obama		Pre-McCain		Post-Obama		Post-McCain		Changes in Obama evaluation		Changes in McCain evaluation	
	F	Sig	F	Sig	F	Sig	F	Sig	F	Sig	F	Sig
Intercept	39.233	0.000	73.962	0.000	164.963	0.000	99.672	0.000	61.718	0.000	0.557	0.456
Age	0.315	0.575	2.044	0.153	0.384	0.536	3.054	0.081	0.001	0.970	0.031	0.861
Previous political information exposure	130.009	0.000	1.916	0.167	0.254	0.615	2.154	0.143	192.095	0.000	0.111	0.739
Ethnicity	2.262	0.061	1.877	0.112	0.939	0.440	9.567	0.000	2.242	0.063	1.698	0.148
Internet use	32.278	0.000	8.372	0.004	5.451	0.020	0.275	0.600	19.987	0.000	6.747	0.010
Party ID	16.371	0.000	3.542	0.029	13.854	0.000	18.807	0.000	1.488	0.226	3.795	0.023
Gender	1.454	0.228	0.499	0.480	2.702	0.101	4.020	0.045	0.142	0.707	0.926	0.336
Ethnicity *Internet use	2.755	0.027	1.956	0.099	2.141	0.074	0.136	0.969	0.287	0.887	1.856	0.116
Ethnicity *party ID	1.348	0.216	2.397	0.015	1.119	0.348	3.413	0.001	0.554	0.816	1.225	0.281

Ethnicity *gender	1.604	0.171	0.252	0.908	1.635	0.163	0.739	0.566	1.698	0.148	0.216	0.930
Internet use *party ID	1.267	0.282	1.668	0.189	2.587	0.076	0.082	0.921	2.291	0.102	2.389	0.092
Internet use *gender	0.064	0.800	0.000	0.982	0.329	0.566	0.115	0.734	0.252	0.616	0.039	0.844
Party ID *gender	0.442	0.643	0.262	0.770	0.682	0.506	0.565	0.568	0.341	0.711	0.646	0.525
Ethnicity *Internet use *party ID	0.981	0.444	1.730	0.099	1.312	0.241	0.949	0.467	0.443	0.875	0.825	0.566
Ethnicity *Internet use *gender	1.784	0.130	0.078	0.989	1.290	0.272	0.373	0.828	0.104	0.981	0.308	0.873
Ethnicity *party ID *gender	1.745	0.095	0.482	0.848	2.270	0.027	0.397	0.904	0.897	0.508	0.670	0.697
Internet use *party ID *gender	0.710	0.492	1.379	0.252	0.391	0.677	1.959	0.142	0.979	0.376	0.363	0.696
Ethnicity *Internet use *party ID *gender	0.727	0.628	0.347	0.912	1.215	0.296	1.004	0.421	0.857	0.526	0.161	0.987

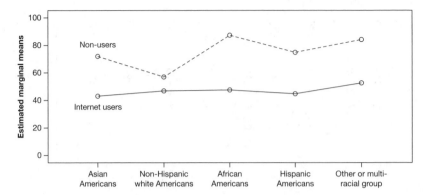

Figure 7.1a Ethno-technology in Obama pre-test evaluation

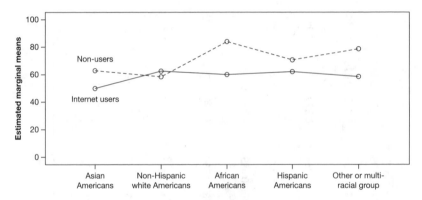

Figure 7.1b Ethno-technology in Obama post-test evaluation

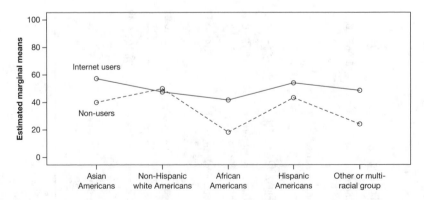

Figure 7.1c Ethno-technology in McCain pre-test evaluation

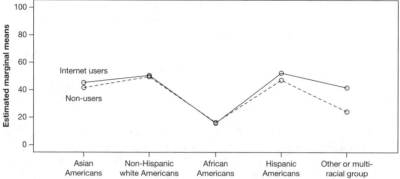

Figure 7.1d Ethno-technology in McCain post-test evaluation

show that individuals' Internet use was consistently associated with reduced likeability for Barack Obama (in the pre-test $F[1, 889] = 32.278$, $p \le .001$; in the post-test $F[1, 893] = 5.451$, $p \le .020$). According to LSD contrast tests, both before ($F[1, 831] = 45.919$, $p \le .001$) and after ($F[1, 835] = 9.031$, $p \le .003$) ad exposure, individuals who used the Internet for searching out political information tended to evaluate Barack Obama more negatively compared to people who had never used the Internet for such a search. Among different ethnic groups, only non-Hispanic White American Internet users and non-users showed no significant difference in their evaluations of Barack Obama ($F[4, 889] = 2.755$, $p \le .027$). After viewing political ads, only non-Hispanic White American Internet users were more likely to evaluate Barack Obama positively versus the non-users, although the difference is moderate ($F[4, 893] = 2.141$, $p \le .074$) (see Tables 7.1 and 7.2 and Figures 7.1a and 7.1b). In contrast, Internet users initially tended to be more positive toward John McCain than non-users ($F[1, 892] = 8.372$, $p \le .004$), but the tendency faded away after ad exposure and did not vary across different ethnic groups (see Tables 7.1 and 7.2 and Figures 7.1c and 7.1d).

Political Ads Exposure and Ethno-Technology in Candidate Preference Vulnerability

After participants were exposed to political ads and demographic factors were controlled, different ethnicity groups tended to be consistent in their candidate preferences. A repeated-measures General Linear Model (GLM) confirmed that voters of different ethnicities were not likely to change their feelings toward candidates after exposure to political ads. African-Americans still had the most positive feelings for Barack Obama while non-Hispanic White and Hispanic Americans were persistently more supportive of John McCain than other ethnic groups. Rather than moderating the influence of political ads on voters as H4 posited, ethnicity was a strong barrier to the external influence of political messages, and thus not likely to change attitudes of people within an ethnic boundary (see Tables 7.1 and 7.2 and Figures 7.1a–7.1d).

Internet use had strong and consistent effects on changes in voters' candidate evaluation as hypothesized. According to a repeated-measures GLM, although Internet users were still more negative about Barack Obama than non-users, Internet users increased their warmth toward Barack Obama after exposure to ads ($F[1, 887] = 19.987, p \leq .001$). In contrast, Internet users were more positive initially about John McCain than non-users, but political ad exposure significantly reduced Internet users' warmth toward John McCain ($F[1, 884] = 6.747, p \leq .010$). Therefore, H5 was confirmed. After controlling for other demographic factors and previous political information, Internet use was a significant indicator associated with voters being influenced by new information and it moderated the effects of ad messages. However, the interactive relationship between ethnicity and Internet use did not show any effect on voters' attitude changes toward either candidate (see Tables 7.1 and 7.2 and Figures 7.1a–7.1d).

Ethno-Technology in Relative Candidate Preferences and Attitude Vulnerability

As both H7 and H8 predicted, ethnicity and Internet use were key factors that maintained voters' varying assessments of different candidates. The preferences of different ethnic groups were consistent throughout the campaign. In the un-manipulated condition after controlling for other demographic factors, a repeated-measures GLM found that different ethnic groups were very distinctive in their relative liking of Barack Obama over John McCain. As expected, the relative preference for Barack Obama over John McCain was the greatest for African-Americans and was the least for non-Hispanic White Americans ($F[4, 884] = 2.485, p \leq .042$). After different ethnic groups were exposed to political ads, African-Americans still expressed the strongest relative preferences for Barack Obama versus John McCain, and non-Hispanic White Americans showed the least difference, or smallest preference gap between the two candidates ($F[4, 882] = 5.492, p \leq .001$). A repeated-measures GLM confirmed that these participants' relative evaluations of Barack Obama versus John McCain before and after ad exposure were consistent. Ethnicity blocked the ability of advertising messages to change different ethnic groups' degree of relative preference for one candidate over the other. In other words, the gap between ethnic groups' candidate preference and antagonism remained stable throughout the campaign regardless of campaign messages (see Tables 7.1 and 7.3 and Figures 7.2a and 7.2b).

Table 7.3 Repeated Measures GLM of Ethno-Technology on Relative Candidate Evaluation and Attitude Vulnerability

Factors	Pre-exposure relativism		Post-exposure relativism		Changes in relativism	
	F	Sig	F	Sig	F	Sig
Intercept	2.193	0.139	10.621	0.001	45.532	0.000
Age	0.277	0.599	0.503	0.478	0.091	0.763
Previous political information exposure	34.215	0.000	0.417	0.518	102.679	0.000
Ethnicity	2.485	0.042	5.492	0.000	1.270	0.280
Internet use	26.204	0.000	4.184	0.041	34.430	0.000
Party ID	12.607	0.000	30.437	0.000	4.250	0.015
Gender	0.068	0.795	0.002	0.967	0.325	0.569
Ethnicity *Internet use	3.276	0.011	1.407	0.230	2.304	0.057
Ethnicity *party ID	2.373	0.016	2.854	0.004	1.424	0.182
Ethnicity *gender	0.295	0.881	0.825	0.509	1.212	0.304
Internet use *party ID	1.822	0.162	1.088	0.337	1.173	0.310
Internet use *gender	0.040	0.841	0.463	0.496	0.276	0.600
Party ID *gender	0.020	0.980	0.045	0.956	0.105	0.900
Ethnicity *Internet use *party ID	1.600	0.132	1.264	0.265	0.851	0.545
Ethnicity *Internet use *gender	0.752	0.557	0.494	0.740	0.465	0.762
Ethnicity *party ID *gender	1.045	0.398	1.623	0.125	0.271	0.965
Internet use *party ID *gender	1.434	0.239	1.757	0.173	1.739	0.176
Ethnicity *Internet use *party ID *gender	0.566	0.757	1.635	0.134	1.040	0.398

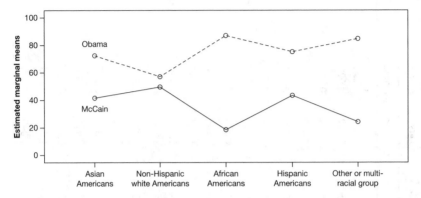

Figure 7.2a Pre-test relative candidate evaluation—Internet non-users

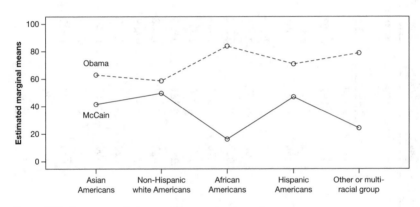

Figure 7.2b Post-test relative candidate evaluation—Internet non-users

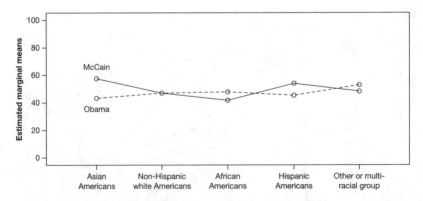

Figure 7.2c Pre-test relative candidate evaluation—Internet users

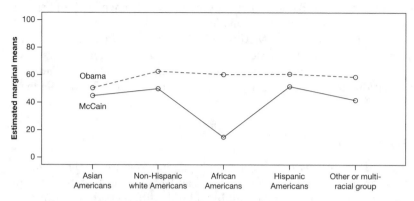

Figure 7.2d Post-test relative candidate evaluation—Internet users

Internet use moderated political message effects and affected changes in relative evaluations of candidates as hypothesized in H11. Internet users showed no noticeable preference for one candidate over the other, but non-users expressed stronger preference for Barack Obama against John McCain ($F[1, 884] = 26.204, p \leq .001$). After political advertising exposure, however, Internet users became more positive about Barack Obama but remained the same toward John McCain, while non-users increased their preference for Barack Obama ($F[1, 882] = 4.184, p \leq .041$). According to a repeated-measures GLM, new campaign messages turned Internet users' relative perceptions about Barack Obama over John McCain to significantly more positive. However, the warmer evaluations toward Barack Obama were constant before and after political ads among voters who did not use the Internet for their political information search ($F[1, 878] = 34.430$, $p \leq .001$) (see Tables 7.1 and 7.3 and Figures 7.2a–7.2d).

The combined effects of ethnicity and Internet use, namely ethno-technology, created discrepancies in voters' attitudes toward different candidates ($F[4, 886] = 3.276, p \leq .011$). African-American Internet users showed the greatest gap between the relative appraisals of Barack Obama and John McCain, and non-Hispanic White American Internet users showed the smallest difference in their relative evaluations of the two candidates compared to any other combination of different ethnic groups and Internet use. Although it was weak, ethno-technology moderated the effects of political advertising on relative perceptions toward Barack Obama and John McCain ($F[4, 878] = 2.304, p \leq .057$). All ethnic groups that did not use the Internet for political information searches were very stable in their relative evaluations of the two candidates, even after political ad exposure. However, Internet users from all ethnic groups amplified their preference for Obama over McCain after viewing advertising messages to varying degrees. African-American Internet users significantly amplified their preference for Barack Obama over John McCain while non-Hispanic White Americans showed the smallest increase in relative preference for Barack Obama over John McCain. Other ethnic minority Internet users, such as Asian and Hispanic Americans, fell in between the first two groups, showing increasing discrepancies in their relative candidate evaluations to a moderate degree (see Tables 7.1 and 7.3 and Figures 7.2a–7.2d).

Discussion

The findings of this research highlight several key points. First, young voters are not a monolithic group. Race and ethnicity did matter for their appraisals of political candidates. In addition, different ethnic groups use new media to different degrees and in different ways, with important consequences for their political attitudes and beliefs, depending upon the range and type of information to which they are exposed. These points suggest further attention to these variables in future studies focusing on young voters.

As predicted, this study shows that race and ethnicity are strong predictors of candidate preference. Race and ethnicity did matter for young voters and they tended to support the candidate who belonged to their in-group. African-Americans were more favorable than other young voters toward Barack Obama, their in-group candidate, and non-Hispanic Whites were less positive (although still favorable). Hispanic voters showed more ambiguous trends. They did not appear to identify with Barack Obama as a racial minority candidate and reflected preferences closer to non-Hispanic Whites. However, further research should investigate this group in more detail, as the literature is unclear in its predictions. The results seem to echo the ambiguity of the literature.

As additional evidence for the strength of race/ethnicity, individuals' appraisals of candidates were not likely to be changed by incoming political information from political ads. In a race-sensitive election (Steele, 2007), ethnicity seemed to be the most consistent and reliable indicator for candidate evaluations. A relative preference for Barack Obama was very distinctive among ethnic minorities, especially for African-Americans, and the degree of difference was consistent regardless of new information contained in political ads. This finding confirmed previous researchers' studies on homogeneous and ethnic minority political communication as well as variations in political attitudes and patterns among different ethnic groups (Erikson & Tedin, 2007; Shaw, et al., 2000). Minorities who are often isolated from mainstream campaign information rely on preexisting political perceptions and stereotypes rather than responding to new, incoming information (Erikson & Tedin, 2007, pp. 204–205). However, it is important to note in this case that the lack of change could be explained by the fact that exposure to new information simply reinforced minorities' preexisting preferences for Barack Obama.

The most interesting changes were seen in relation to those young voters who use the Internet for political information searches. Internet users were more negative toward Barack Obama than non-users, but exposure to political advertising increased Internet users' evaluations of him. Internet users were more positive toward John McCain than non-users, yet ad message decreased Internet users positive assessments toward John McCain. This finding suggests that those who use the Internet for political information search potentially self-selected sites that provided only a one-sided perspective on Barack Obama and/or John McCain. Potentially, young voters who seek out political information on the Internet are looking for a particular ideological alternative to the mainstream television and print media's perspective on politics. Further, as noted in the literature, it is possible that the Internet as an unregulated medium provided more negative images of Barack Obama than the mainstream media. A cursory check of Internet ads from this campaign shows that campaigns and parties created ads for the Internet attacking the opposing candidate that were not aired on television. For those voters who typically use the Internet to gather their political information, they could have been exposed to new information about Barack Obama through the political ads designed for the mainstream audience. This new information led to a change in their favorable evaluation of Barack Obama.

In addition, television is an emotional medium that allows personalities to connect with viewers in a different way than the Internet may allow. As mentioned in the literature review, past studies show that likeability generally increases upon exposure to the candidate. All groups increased their favorability toward Barack Obama after exposure to political ads, while favorability toward John McCain decreased after viewing ads. It is possible that this finding highlights a difference in candidate personality. It could concomitantly suggest an important communication difference in medium, with the ability to convey warmth through large screen, up-close images of candidates. As a new medium, the Internet may not be as effective in communicating or transferring emotion from candidate to voter.

The fact that different ethnic groups are more or less likely to use the Internet in a political information search suggests that different groups of voters expose themselves to different types of information. Variation in tone toward the candidates is just one variable that could differ depending upon the type of media selected as a source of political information. Further investigations of differences in young voters' political attitudes need to take the variables of race/ethnicity and Internet use into account when studying contributing factors.

This research helps to fill the theoretical and methodological gap in political communication that has been often explored only from the perspective of mainstream political structures or from the perspective of individual communication. Theory-oriented political approaches to minority political dynamics and application-oriented minority communication research contributes to both theoretical and methodological interdisciplinary study.

The research focus on minority political communication in the new media era is normatively essential for socially responsible research. Ethnic political communication with attention to the Internet as a communication channel is an area in need of further study. Previous research looks primarily at political communication with a focus on ethnic majorities and mainstream or "traditional" media. Further research on ethnic minorities and new communication channels should improve our understanding of the impact and the effectiveness of political messages aimed at a diverse range of target voters. More broadly, this research aligns with scholarly efforts to include and to expand the study of ethnic minorities in studies of American campaign politics.

Notes

1   Locations of experiment research: Abilene Christian University; Akron University; Chapman University; College of New Jersey; Columbia College; Consumnes River College; Dominican University; Emerson College; Iowa State University; Texas State University; University of Colorado; University of Florida; University of Kansas; University of Missouri; University of New Haven; University of Ohio; University of Texas at San Antonio; Virginia Tech; Virginia Polytechnic Institute

2   Lists of political advertising stimuli: 1. Positive issue on Obama—Community Organizer, Health Care; 2. Positive image on McCain—maverick, good leadership; 3. Negative image on McCain—same as Bush; 4. Negative image on Obama—international celebrity; 5. Negative issue on McCain—no plan for economy, no understanding of technology; 6. Negative issue on Obama—unskilled leadership to handle international crises and enemies; 7. Positive image on Obama—optimistic changes for middle classes; 8. Positive image and issue on McCain—Positive leadership and experience in economic crises.

References

Abrajano, M. A. (2005). Who evaluates a presidential candidate by using non-policy campaign messages? *Political Research Quarterly*, 58(1), 55–67.

Anstead, N., & Chadwick, A. (2008). Parties, election campaigning, and the Internet toward a comparative institutional approach. In A. Chadwick & P. N. Howard (Eds.), *Handbook of internet politics*. London: Routledge Press.

Baumgartner, J. C. (2008). Polls and elections: editorial Cartoons 2.0: The effects of digital political satire on presidential candidate evaluations. *Presidential Studies Quarterly*, 38(4), 735–758.

Bennett, W. L. (2007). Changing citizenship in the digital age. *Civic life online: Learning how digital media can engage youth*. The John D. and Catherine T.

MacArthur Foundation Series on Digital Media and Learning. Cambridge, MA: The MIT Press, pp. 1–24.

Benoit, W. L., McKinney, M. S., & Holbert, R. L. (2001). Beyond learning and persona: Extending the scope of presidential debate effects. *Communication Monographs*, 68(3), 259–273.

Berinsky, A. J., & Mendelberg, T. (2005). The indirect effects of discredited stereotypes in judgments of Jewish leaders. *American Journal of Political Science*, 49(4), 845–864.

Berman, E. M. (1997). Dealing with cynical citizens. *Public Administration Review*, 57(2), 105–112.

Bimber, B., & Davis R. (2003). *Campaigning online: The internet in the U.S. elections*. New York: Oxford University Press.

Bourret, A. (2000). A learning experience. *CMA Management*, 74(5), 24–28.

Chadwick, A. (2006). *Internet politics: States, citizens, and new communication technologies*. New York: Oxford University Press.

Chaffee, S. (1978). Presidential debates—Are they useful to voters? *Communication Monographs*, 45, 330–346

CIRCLE, (2008). Young voters in the 2008 presidential election. *Center for information and research on civic learning & engagement*. Retrieved September 27, 2010, from www.civicyouth.org.

Converse, P. E. (1962). Information flow and the stability of partisan attitudes. *Public Opinion Quarterly*, 26(4), 578–599.

Cundy, D. T. (1986). Political commercials and candidate image. In L. L. Kaid, D. Nimmo, & K. R. Sanders (Eds.), *New Perspectives on Political Advertising*. Carbondale, IL: Southern Illinois University Press, pp. 210–234.

de la Garza, R. O., Falcon, A., & Garcia, F. C., (1992). *Latino voices: Mexican, Puerto Rican, and Cuban perspectives on American politics*. Boulder, CO: Westview Press.

Erikson, R., & Tedin, K. (2007). *American public opinion: Its origin, content and impact* (7th Ed.). New York: Longman Press.

Fiske, S. T., & Kinder, D. R. (1981). Involvement, expertise, and schema use: Evidence from political cognition. In N. Cantor & J. F. Kihlstrom (Eds.), *Personality, cognition, and social interaction*. Hillsdale, NJ: Lawrence Erlbaum Associates, pp. 171–192.

Freedman, P., Franz, M., & Goldstein, K. (2004). Campaign advertising and democratic citizenship. *American Journal of Political Science*, 48(4), 723–741.

Hamill, R., Lodge, M., & Blake, F. (1985). The breadth, depth, and utility of class, partisan, and ideological schemata. *American Journal of Political Science*, 29(4), 850–870.

Hofstede, G. (2001). *Culture's consequences, comparing values, behaviors, institutions, and organizations across nations*. Thousand Oaks, CA: Sage Publications.

Hogg, M. A., & Turner, J. C. (1987). Social identity and conformity: A theory of referent informational influence. *European Social Psychology*, 2, 139–182.

Iyengar. S., & McGrady, J. A. (2007). *Media politics: A citizen's guide*. New York: W. W. Norton & Company.

Jasperson, A., & Yun, H. J. (2007). Political advertising effects and America's racially diverse newest voting generation. *American Behavioral Scientist, 50*(9), 1112–1123.

Kahn, K., & Geer, F. (1994). Creating impressions: An experimental investigation of political advertising on television. *Political Behavior, 16*(1), 93–116.

Kaid, L. L. (1995). Measuring candidate images with semantic differentials. In K. Hacker (Ed.), *Candidate images in presidential election campaigns.* Westport, CT: Praeger, pp. 131–134.

Kaid, L. L. (1998). Videostyle and the effects of the 1996 presidential campaign advertising. In R. E. Denton, Jr. (Ed.), *The 1996 presidential campaign: A communication perspective.* Westport, CT: Praeger, pp. 143–159.

Kaid, L. L. (2002). Political advertising and information seeking: Comparing exposure via traditional and Internet channels. *Journal of Advertising, 31*(1), 27–35.

Kaid, L. L. (Ed.) (2004). *The handbook of political communication research.* Mahwah, NJ: Lawrence Erlbaum Associates.

Kaid, L. L., & Jones, C. A. (2004). The new U.S. campaign regulations and political advertising. *Journal of Political Marketing* 4 (3), 105–110.

Kaiser, C. R., & Pratt-Hyatt, J. S. (2009). Distributing prejudice unequally: Do whites direct their prejudice toward strongly identified minorities? *Journal of Personality and Social Psychology, 96*(2), 432–445.

Katz, E., & Feldman, J. J. (1962). The debates in light of research: A survey of surveys. In S. Kraus (Ed.), *The great debates: Kennedy vs. Nixon, 1960.* Bloomington: Indiana University Press, pp. 173–223.

Keeter, S., Horowitz, J. & Tyson, A. (2008, November 12). Young voters in the 2008 election. *Pew Research Center for People & the Press.* Retrieved September 27, 2010, from http://pewresearch.org/pubs/1031/young-voters-in-the-2008-election.

Kraushaar, J. (2009). Online news leads presidential campaign news cycle. *Journalism Studies, 10*(3), 435–438.

Kruse, D., & Kendall, K. E. (1995). A rashomonian approach to the study of image construction. In K. L. Hacker (Ed.), *Candidate images in presidential election.* Westport, CT: Praeger, pp. 145–152.

Lodge, M., McGraw, K., & Stroh, P. (1989). An impression-driven model of candidate evaluation. *The American Political Science Review, 83*(2), 399–419.

Lordan, E. J. (2005). *Politics, ink: How cartoonists skewer America's politicians, from King George III to George Dubya.* Lanham, MD: Rowman & Littlefield.

Lupia, A., & Philpot, S. T. (2005). Views from inside the net: How websites affect young adults' political interest. *The Journal of Politics, 67 (4)*, 1122–1142.

Lykourentzou, I., Giannoukos, I., Mpardis, G., Nikolopoulos, V., & Loumos, V. (2009). Early and dynamic student achievement prediction in e-learning courses using neural networks. *Journal of the American Society for Information Science and Technology, 60*(2), 372–380.

Merritt, S. (1984). Negative political advertising: Some empirical findings. *Journal of Advertising, 13*(3), 27–38.

Moskewitz, D., & Stroh, P. (1996). Expectation-driven assessments of political candidates. *International Society of Political Psychology, 17*(4), 695–712.

Nichols, M. (2008). E-learning in the context, in the E-primer series. *E-learning In the Context (Creative Common Org.)*. Retrieved September 27, 2010, from http://akoaotearoa.ac.nz/sites/default/files/ng/group-661/n877-1--e-learning-in-context.pdf.

Park, H., & Perry, J. L. (2007). Do campaign web sites really matter in electoral civic engagement? Empirical evidence from the 2004 post-election internet tracking survey. *Social Science Computer Review, 22*(2), 190–212.

Payne, J. G., Golden, J. L., Marlier, J., & Ratzan, S. C. (1989). Perceptions of the 1988 presidential and vice presidential debates. *The American Behavioral Scientist, 32*(4), 425–435.

Ray, J. J., & Lovejoy, F. H. (1986). The generality of racial prejudice. *Journal of Social Psychology, 126*(4), 563–564.

Rodriguez, D. (2002). *Latino national political coalitions: Struggles and challenges.* New York: Routledge.

Rosenstone, S. J., Kinder, D. R., Miller, W. E., & the National Election Studies (1997). *American national election study 1996: Pre- and post-election survey* [Computer file] Ann Arbor, MI: University of Michigan, Center for Political Studies (Producer) and Inter-university Consortium for Political and Social Research (Distributor).

Senior, P. A., & Bhopal, R. (1994). Ethnicity as a variable in epidemiological research. *British Medical Journal, 309*, 327–330.

Shaw, D. R. (1999). The effect of TV ads and candidate appearances on statewide presidential voters, 1988–96. *The American Political Science Review, 93*(2), 345–361.

Shaw, D. R., de la Garza, R., & Lee, J. (2000). Examining Latino turnout in 1996: A three-state validated survey approach. *American Journal of Political Science, 44*(2), 332–340.

Shimp, T. A., & Sharma, S. (1987). Consumer ethnocentrism: construction and validation of the CETSCALE. *Journal of Marketing Research, 24*, 280–289.

Shinnar, R. S. (2008). Coping with negative social identity: The case of Mexican immigrants. *Journal of Social Psychology, 48*(5), 553–576.

Steele, S. (2007). *A bound man: Why we are excited about Obama and why he can't win.* New York: Free Press.

Taylor, P., & Fry, R. (2007, December 25). Hispanics and the 2008 election: A swing vote? *Pre Hispanic Center.* Retrieved September 27, 2010, from http://pewhispanic.org/reports/report.php?ReportID=83.

Tedesco, J. C. (2007). Examining Internet interactivity effects on young adult political information efficacy. *American Behavioral Scientist, 50 (9)*, 1183–1194.

U.S. Census Bureau (2007). *American Fact Finder* (November 11). Retrieved September 27, 2010, from http://factfinder.census.gov/home/saff/main.html?_lang=en.

Vromen, A. (2008). Building virtual spaces: Young people, participation and the Internet. *Australian Journal of Political Science, 43*(1), 79–97.

Williams, A. P., Trammell, K. D., Postelnicu, M., & Landreville, K. D. (2005). Blogging and hyper-linking: Use of the Web to enhance viability during the 2004 US campaign. *Journalism Studies, 6*, 177–186.

Wrede, M. (2001). Yardstick competition to tame the Leviathan. *European Journal of Political Economy, 17*(4), 705–721.

Wyer, R., & Srull, T. K. (1986). Human cognition in its contest. *Psychological Review, 93*, 322–359.

Yun, H. J. (2009). *Geo-ethnic campaign playgrounds: Co-effects of geopolitical competitiveness and ethnic political culture on attitude vulnerability.* Presented at the 67th Midwest Political Science Association Conference, Chicago, IL.

Yun, H. J., & Park, J. H. (2008). Ethno-media technology in political communication. *Business Research Yearbook, 15*(4), 184–189.

Section III

New Technologies and
New Voices in Debates

Chapter 8

CNN's Dial Testing of the Presidential Debates

Parameters of Discussion in Tech Driven Politics

Rita Kirk and Dan Schill

They have been called "dueling EKGs" (Caro, 2008a), "squigglies" (Davies, 2008), the "crawler," "real time response," "surfing the squiggle," and CNN's "thingamajig" (Shearer, 2008). In Australia, the term used is "The Worm." Call it what you will, most people who watched the 2008 presidential debates now have a passing understanding of dial testing. This chapter examines the use of the dials in the 2008 presidential election and explains how the technology affected the way users and viewers processed the debate and the way journalists covered them, returning the people's voice to a place of prominence in the process of choosing a president.

Dial testing is often referred to as an electronic focus group. Within the framework of the 2008 presidential debates, a purposive sample of undecided voters was chosen to represent party affiliation, gender, income level, and ethnicity of such voters. The group watched the direct feed of the debates on a large-screen television while registering individual responses continuously on a hand-held device. The device, which is about the size of a television remote control, permits the user to register reaction to the debates on a 100-point scale. Each second of the debate, researchers collect these data. Data can be viewed in aggregate or broken into demographic categories according to gender or party affiliation. The results are viewed in real time through line graphs projected as an overlay on the debate video, which the participants themselves do not see. Researchers also collect data to questions posed both before and after the debate, as well as conduct focused discussions with participants afterward to help understand participant reactions.

During the 2008 election cycle, CNN, ABC News, CBS News, Fox News, and MSNBC each used dial test groups of undecided voters to assist in their analysis and coverage of the presidential debates. Each used the dial tests in a different way, but it is clear that this long-used instrument of political strategy made its way to prime time news coverage in a prominent way in the 2008 election cycle. CNN chose to project its dial test results live during the general election debates so that viewers could see the same data normally viewed exclusively by researchers, campaigns, and journalists. Data collected by CNN regarding the use of dial tests showed that the dials were one of the major factors driving increased viewer response, especially among a key demographic group: "CNN thinks dial-testing has boosted its debate ratings, helping it reach 9.2 million viewers, more than any other cable news channel and giving it the highest percentage of 25- to 54-year-old viewers (the age group advertisers are most interested in)" (Boyd, 2008, para. 19).

Dial testing itself is not new. In paper and pencil format, the technique currently enhanced by electronic data collection was used by Lazarsfeld and his colleagues in the early election studies of 1940s. In those studies, respondents were shown materials and were then asked to rate an image or phrase on a numeric scale. In electronic form, dial testing gained greater use and precision when in 1984 opinion research firm Columbia Information Systems developed hand-held dials connected to computers. Importantly, it has been used in every election cycle since that time. Further, the technique has been used in jury trials and by film editors, advertisers, and political consultants (see, for example, James Carville's site at DemocracyCorps, which regularly posts analysis of dial tests). Whether fine tuning messages, assessing the effectiveness of argument, gauging the attention-getting power of images, or finding words and phrases that resonate with voters, dial testing has proven to be a useful strategic tool.

While dial tests are not new, neither have they been as fully utilized as they were in Election 2008. CNN experimented with dial research during the 2004 elections on its CNNfn site. Similarly, CNN's Headline News used them in a primary debate in the 2006 election cycle. Other stations (notably, conservative pollster Frank Luntz who often uses dials for FoxNews) have used dial tests previously as well, but have shown only clips of the groups in packaged stories. Like many technologies, in previous elections viewers were not ready for the invasion of technology on their television screens, and their computer bandwidth was insufficient to permit streaming information. Further, television stations were not yet technologically sophisticated enough to make the viewing experience visually appealing.

That changed during the 2008 election for several compelling reasons. The technological issues that retarded use of the technology have been resolved. We live in an age where computer bandwidth is no longer a problem, and many viewers have wireless capabilities that permit them to use their laptops while watching the debate on television. Second, current viewers are used to multitasking. They do many things at once and have developed the capacity to handle multiple information streams simultaneously. Layers of information, including scrolling news lines or stock reports under an onscreen reporter, are commonplace. Third, the news agencies are technologically sophisticated in ways that permit dial test usage. For example, in the first CNN debate to broadcast dial testing live, participants in a remote battleground state watched on a large screen that streamed the debate via a live satellite feed. Data was collected each second, analyzed, and fed back to the CNN news centers in Atlanta and New York where the resulting graph was synced and displayed over the debate for viewers at home with only a three second delay. During one debate, the same thing was accomplished with focus groups in both Nevada and South Carolina sending data simultaneously. The capability to effectively execute these tasks was not available even four years ago. Finally, working across multiple platforms provided a strategic advantage. The 2008 election was highly competitive both among the candidates and the networks that covered them. Airtime was only one means of communication, although an important one. The Internet became an increasingly viable tool for reaching mass audiences. During election 2008, the most frequently cited sources of online political information were news Web sites, with 26 percent of respondents mentioning MSNBC, followed by CNN at 23 percent, and Yahoo News at 22 percent. These three Web sites dominate the online news landscape as 54 percent of those who get their news online cited at least one of these Web sites (Pew, 2008). While these three news sources stood out as information sources, there was also an incredibly "long tail" as Americans cited hundreds of other Web sites as important news sources, led by Google News (9 percent), Fox News (9 percent), AOL News (7 percent), *New York Times* (6 percent), Drudge Report (3 percent), MySpace (3 percent), YouTube (2 percent), BBC (2 percent), USA Today (1 percent), and *Washington Post* (1 percent).

Every outlet looked for an edge over the competition. The CNN experiment began with the process academic researchers implement routinely: reviewing the literature to consider what is at issue. The authors of this paper were intrigued by the fact that the voter's voice played such a diminutive role in journalistic coverage of the debates. A brief review of that literature is included here. Further, we asked what might improve that situation and proposed dial testing to CNN as a means to involve voters and increase news coverage on voter reactions. And, as with all good research, we assessed what worked and did not work, and what we might like to do differently in the future.

Dial Tests in the 2008 Presidential Primary and General Election Debates

Our relationship with CNN began two years prior to the debate when the authors made the pitch to CNN that previous coverage of debates did not aid in voter decision making. Talking heads, even if they are the heads of major political figures, do not make good visuals for the television medium, and the ensuing back-and-forth spin from these analysts often leaves viewers wanting more information. Typically, debates were static events where the candidates talk to a reporter in a predetermined format followed by media analysis of what happened. In the post-debate analysis, three types of media-friendly debate clips dominate coverage: the "gotcha" line where one candidate throws in the zinger that is the quintessential sound bite played repeatedly during the next news cycle; moments when candidates sparred with each other; and moments when a candidate made a mistake. The authors proposed that, while possibly entertaining, these methods of coverage do not aid voter decision making. Instead, the authors proposed using dial tests to solve the "visual problem" while simultaneously providing information on issues that might assist the voters (and reporters) in determining what was really at issue during the debates—at least what was important from the viewpoint of the undecided voter. In this way, the decision about the significant moments in the debate would not be a matter of recall or the few good visual moments of the debate that would serve the needs of television; instead, they would result from data that could identify the moment in the debate when the viewers most strongly agree with a statement, the one where they agreed least with a statement, and the moments when the audience was most divided.

There are three agendas or issues of importance in political debates—candidate, media, and public—and it is the public's agenda that is typically left out of the presidential debate equation (Jackson-Beck & Meadow, 1979; McKinney, 2005). Candidates get free television time to articulate their message. Journalists regulate the debate's format and choose the questions. Yet the public is left to watch the proceedings from the sidelines. Only opinion polls serve as the voice of voters, and those come out well after partisans in spin rooms and television analysts have told viewers how to interpret the debates. Essentially then, the debates are co-created by the candidates and journalists. Studies indicate that these events frequently fall short of public expectations (Carlin, Vigil, Buehler, & McDonald, 2009). The rapid-fire debate formats attempt to cover complicated subjects in a short, 90-minute format. This results in rather generic questions that allow candidates to rely on scripted talking points. Such responses are so general that they frequently fail to reveal new or particularly relevant information for potential voters. Likewise, the questions asked by journalists are often of little interest to the majority of viewers and do not represent public concerns. These are harsh criticisms, but they are backed by research. One study comparing journalists' questions from 1960 through 2000 to polling data of public agenda items revealed that in only one debate (1960) did questions correlate with the public's interests (Benoit & Hansen, 2001). Even the town hall format, which was hailed as an opportunity to introduce the citizen agenda into presidential debates, included voters only as a backdrop to the event

(McKinney, 2005). Town halls are carefully moderated events largely overtaken by journalists who select the questions and questioners in advance, then heavily moderate the event.

Clearly, voters want to be a part of the process. The desire for citizen voice manifested itself in the 2008 CNN/YouTube debate. CNN received 2,989 video submissions of questions people wanted the candidates to answer. By contrast to the questions typically posed by journalists, these questions were anything but detached and unemotional. They reflected the notion that politics really matters in the people's lives and they demanded that candidates talk with them about the problems they face and propose concrete solutions to those concerns.

In previous elections, the voice of the people was conveyed primarily through opinion polls and the occasional "person on the street" interview. While useful, polls do not reveal the depth of voter feelings on an issue. To say that x number of people oppose the war is quite different than the emotional question of a serviceman's wife asking when the "stop-loss" policy will end, a policy that keeps her husband overseas long after he has fulfilled his commitment to serve this nation. And while random interviews can be poignant, they seldom provide the spectrum of opinion that might be useful in decision making.

Most important, polls are not interactive. Those researchers who frame the questions also frame the ideas. In essence, nothing is explored beyond the predetermined set of issues covered by the questionnaire. The researcher, then, presupposes what is at issue, asks questions, and forces people to respond to a predetermined categorical list. Larson (1999) contends that:

> Polls take control of public opinion out of the hands of the public and put it into the 'machinery of polling', keeping political outsiders outside and restricting public debate. Consequently, public opinion is constrained by having polls replace other kinds of expression, and so defined, it addresses the concerns of political experts, which are not necessarily those of the people. By relying almost exclusively on closed-ended questions, the range of opinions measured in polls is limited and their complexity is diminished. Public opinion becomes privatized when it is expressed only to pollsters rather than to a public audience. (p. 133)

Asking a sample of voters closed ended questions, such as "do you have a favorable or unfavorable attitude of the president," does not enact the public agenda in a meaningful way. Further, polls do not demand candidate response. Nor do they challenge a candidate's specific policies or position statements. This is not to say that polls are not a useful tool.

They are. But it does suggest that in the Internet age, the days of static measures and one-way channels of communication are quickly outdated and unsatisfying.

The researchers are convinced that media consumers demand more interaction with candidates and are less content with the traditional passive viewer role. Using dial testing as a technique, audience reactions could be captured and analyzed in real time. They, the voters themselves, would decide what is at issue. No one sets limits on their views and no one has to guess how they respond.

A trial run was conducted during the first New Hampshire debate hosted by CNN and the Hearst/Argyle ABC stations. The impact was immediately recognized. The "squiggly lines" or EKG lines permitted reporters and viewers to determine the issues and statements with which a group of undecided voters most agreed or most disagreed with the candidates, as well as which issues most divided the undecided voters. Those divisions could be parsed along party lines, gender, ethnicity, or religion. The analysis of voter opinions was intriguing and participants reported feeling more engaged in the debates, as we will discuss later. Equally compelling is the way those opinions affected post-debate coverage.

News Coverage of Debates and Its Impact

When the iconic first Nixon–Kennedy debate concluded at 10:30 p.m. eastern daylight time on September 26, 1960, the broadcast networks did not follow the event with news analysis. Instead, they returned to their regularly-scheduled programs: *Jackpot Bowling with Milton Berle* on NBC, the *Original Amateur Hour* on ABC, and a pre-recorded interview between Walter Cronkite and Lyndon Johnson on CBS (Schroeder, 2008). In contrast to the 24-7 news commentary environment in the 2008 election, Americans had to wait until the following morning to read the reviews in the newspaper.

During the election cycles that followed, post-debate coverage dramatically changed. Over the last 16 years, network and cable television stations begin breaking down the key moments in the contest immediately, predicting how the debate will impact the campaign, and allowing pundits from both sides to spin the debate for their candidate. Whole gymnasium-sized rooms are set aside as the Spin Room in a location close by the debate hall that includes multiple microphoned platforms for easy reporter access to the candidates' carefully chosen advocates. Not surprisingly, each of these advocates proclaims victory for their side, and attempts to gain positive coverage for their candidate. Reporters from all mediums, including television, radio, print press and Internet, have easy access to celebrities in the Spin Room, offering more than enough information to fill the post-debate coverage—and do it quickly. In more recent elections, the larger news stations have hired their own partisan analysts to provide point/counterpoint commentary. At times, these exchanges become heated spats that make for great entertainment, but again, provide little information to assist undecided voters.

The major component of the media's coverage of presidential debates is the predicting and assessing the winners and losers (Diamond & Friery, 1987; Kraus, 2000). Political scientists Iyengar and Kinder (1987) describe this strategic coverage:

> This emphasis on the strategic side of campaigns is nowhere more evident than in coverage of the occasional presidential debates. Although the debates are typically crammed with facts, policies, and programs, post-debate coverage has typically concentrated on who won, how each side prepared, and what the ramifications appear to be for each side's chances. (pp. 128–29)

This coverage creates a kind of parallel version of the debate—using a mixture of sound bites from the debate, opinions from experts, and reactions from voters—that may overshadow the audience's original understanding of what it saw (Schroeder, 2008). Content analysis of this post-debate coverage shows that press accounts of debates over-emphasize the negative and the personal and do "not provide voters with an accurate depiction of the debates" (Benoit & Currie, 2001, p. 37). "Gotcha" moments and clips of heated exchanges dominate coverage, while proposals for addressing problems go unanalyzed.

Yet voters look to this coverage to interpret political debates (Kraus, 2000). Longtime political analyst Jeff Greenfield (1980) observes:

> Many of the people watching the debates will not really know what they have seen until the next-day notices tell them . . . Given the arcane nature of most debate questions and answers, the audience tends to be in the position of a theatergoer attending a preview, and saying 'I can't wait to read the reviews so I'll know what I thought of this.' (p. 215)

A sizeable body of research has established Greenfield's point that media coverage of debates can dramatically influence public opinion and can even be more powerful than the debate itself. Chaffee and Dennis (1979) made this point after the 1976 debates: "It may well be that the press's interpretation of the debate . . . is more important in determining the impact on the electorate than is the debate itself" (p. 85).

In order to more fairly cover the debates, then, journalistic practices need to change.

Post-debate coverage clearly affects voter responses. Research on the influence of post-debate journalistic coverage began in a series of effects studies during the 1976 debates between Gerald Ford and Jimmy Carter. Like the studies that followed, these experimental designs compared the attitudes of viewers who watched only the debate to those who were also exposed to the post-debate news coverage. A seminal study of the first 1976 presidential debate found that those polled immediately after the debate declared Carter the winner by a 2–1 margin, whereas those who were questioned a few days after the debate preferred Ford by the same margin, likely due to the intervening negative press coverage of Carter's performance (Lang & Lang, 1978). A similar analysis by Lupfer and Wald (1979) revealed that the group of viewers, who saw no differences between the candidates immediately after the debate, rated Ford more positively when questioned a week later.

An analogous effect was seen in the second presidential debate of 1976, when Ford mistakenly said that "there is no Soviet domination of Eastern Europe, and there never will be under a Ford Administration." Eligible voters interviewed immediately after the debate felt that Ford had won and Carter had lost; however, voters interviewed between 12 and 48 hours after the debate when news coverage highlighted the error said Carter performed better (Patterson, 1980). Thomas Patterson, who conducted the study, concluded that "the passing of time required for the news to reach the public brought with it a virtual reversal of opinion" (p. 123). A comparable study by Steeper (1978) found that over half of those surveyed changed their minds about who won the debate following the post-debate media coverage.

More recent research continues to document this "news verdict" effect (Lemert, Elliott, Bernstein, Rosenberg, & Nestvold, 1991). Immediately after the first 1984 debate, 43 percent of respondents in a CBS/*New York Times* poll thought that Mondale had won compared to the 34 percent who said Reagan was victorious. When the same question was asked two days later, 66 percent of the respondents felt Mondale was the winner, while Reagan's share declined to 17 percent (Geer, 1988). Elliott and Sothirajah (1993) reported that post-debate analysis of the first 1988 debate influenced viewers in the direction of the post-debate commentary. In his study of the second 1988 debate, Lanoue (1991) revealed a similar pattern—that media coverage of the debate colored viewers' views about who won the encounter. Lemert, et al. (1991) conclude their extensive study of 1988 debates by noting, "The candidate judged most favorably in the media verdicts benefits in the survey responses" (p. 255). Similarly, the pro-Bush coverage after the final debate in 2004 led potential voters to negatively alter their attitudes of Kerry and depressed much of the positive bounce Kerry received from his performance in the debate (Fridkin, Kenney, Gershon, & Woodall, 2008). When both candidates receive uniformly positive reviews, the impact is mollified. For example, when Bush and Dukakis received largely favorable post-debate coverage, a study conducted by Lowry, Bridges, and Barefield (1990) did not find that exposure to debate analysis influenced viewers. So, as long as everything is positive, there is little or no effect but when coverage is negative, voters respond. Since journalists are not in the business of public relations, the commentaries are rarely uniformly positive. The evidence of the news verdict effect is compelling.

Importantly, news verdicts can be the result of opinion polling as well. Similar to other types of news coverage, viewers who saw an instant poll by ABC indicating that Dukakis had won the debate were influenced by the poll results (Lowry, et al., 1990). Likewise, credible performances from the Spin Room may have similar effects. McKinnon and Tedesco's (1999) book chapter looking at the 1996 debates found that viewing the post-debate spin following the debate increased the favorable evaluations of both candidates. In short, assessments of the debates will likely be influenced by journalists' coverage regardless of the source of the analysis: analysts, opinion polls, or spin doctors.

There are some limitations to this effect as reported in studies of the 1992, 1996, and 2004 debates. McKinnon, Tedesco, and Kaid's (1993) examination of the third 1992 debate between George H. W. Bush, Bill Clinton, and Ross Perot found that post-debate commentary increased viewer ratings of Perot, decreased ratings of Clinton, and had no effect on evaluations of Bush. This suggests that post-debate media coverage may be influential in voters' evaluation of candidates in certain situations, but cannot be applied to all contexts. Of course, because viewers can access the entire debate directly without a media filter, audiences are not dependent on the news media's framing of the event. They can watch the debate unedited and uninterpreted, turn off the television before seeing the post-debate spin, and make up their own minds. However, many will only watch portions of the debate or not watch the debate at all. These groups of potential voters are the most influenced by the "news verdict" effect. Tsfati (2003) documented this interaction, noting "the power of the media to influence the perception of the winner was strongest when respondents watched little of the programmed debate and weakest when respondents watched large parts of the program" (p. 79). These limitations should be noted, but do not discount the fact that effects have been well documented.

Post-debate coverage impacts viewers' perceptions of the candidates, but such coverage can also encourage voters to be more skeptical of the political process. Media coverage that encourages comparison of candidate performances (such as when candidates are viewed side-by-side on a split screen) instead of issues reduced viewers' political trust. Also, it made it easier for viewers to evaluate the candidates' character (Cho, Shah, Nah, & Brossard, 2009) over substantive issues. In turn, those who view the process negatively are less likely to participate in it. Certainly, the goal of those who cover debates and the networks they work for is dedicated to increased participation, even if the motives for achieving that may vary.

In summary, post-debate media coverage is clearly important because it plays a dramatic role in shaping public opinion of the debate participants. In fact, the ensuing media coverage can be more influential to potential voters than the debate itself. Because of this, what is said after the debate—and who says it—is of critical importance. To improve the process, engaging the public and ensuring that their views are represented as directly as possible is a positive value.

What We Saw at the Debates

Few people are as self-reflexive in their work as journalists. Good journalists seek to improve the credibility of the profession, even if they are also driven by the bottom line. To produce excellent reporting that compels voter attention serves both interests. That is precisely what happened during the 2008 primary and general election debates. Knowing that the debates rarely satisfy either journalists' quest for excellence, or provide a substantive viewing audience that would make them financially lucrative, the major news organizations sought to improve the 2008 debates. Obviously, each network tries to do better than the competition. Sometimes ideas succeed, and sometimes they are of dubious value. But it is important to note that at the beginning of the planning process, executives can only use their best judgment. This account discusses what we learned from the process, and illuminates some of the choices and decisions made.

Dial tests increase viewer interaction and ratings. Data collected by CNN demonstrate that the dial tests serve as provocation for increased Internet response among key demographic groups. Nearly a quarter of Americans (24 percent) say they regularly learned something about the presidential campaign from the Internet (Pew, 2008). The Internet is even more important for younger Americans: 42 percent of those under age 30 say they regularly use the Internet as a source for political information and the Internet is the leading source of campaign information for this age group (Pew, 2008). As previously mentioned, CNN received the highest percentage of 25- to 54-year-old viewers of any television channel. In fact, the *New York Times* reported that in the vice-presidential debate, "In the 18- to 34-year-old demographic, CNN averaged 3.1 million viewers, setting a 28-year record among young viewers" (Stelter, 2008, para. 6). Thus, viewer demand among this key demographic encouraged CNN early in the debate season to continue to use the dials.

Dial tests are effective as a tool of dialogue since they encourage viewers to engage the process. When watching a show in a passive environment, viewers are not called upon to make decisions or assessments. However, when observing a group of voters evaluating the process, they are encouraged to do likewise. The ground of the debate shifts from merely receiving messages to evaluating them.

Further, the use of dial tests promotes active listening. For the graph to have any meaning, viewers must first listen and then consider what the candidates are saying. Similarly, viewers tracking the dial group's reaction can compare their personal evaluation to that of the dial group. In this way, real-time response graphics encourage a type of dialogue between viewers and undecided voters represented by the line. The opinions represented by the graph are another source of information viewers can integrate when forming impressions. This higher-level thinking encourages elaboration and deepens consideration of the candidates' issues and statements.

Part of the reason for the success of the dial testing is that the media environment has changed. The technological sophistication of the public, blended with the capabilities of news organizations to permit multiple outlets for news information and response, marks a shift from previous elections. As mentioned earlier, a significant number of viewers preferred watching the debates on CNN because of the audience response graph. As one critic wrote, "Last night CNN held the attention of 10.6 million viewers who could have tuned in elsewhere if they didn't want all the fixings. So maybe [CNN Vice-President and Producer] Bohrman is onto something" (Chalupa, 2008, para. 16). Not only could viewers watch the dial results on television, they could watch the video stream on Web sites, follow the real-time commentaries of experts, or blog their own responses. CNN capitalized on the technological sophistication by making all the dial test data available live on CNN.com.

Moreover, CNN made the data interactive. With a click of the mouse, viewers could segment the dial group by a number of demographic factors. At one moment, an Internet viewer could divide overall average line graph into lines representing subgroups: male and female; Republican, Democratic, or Independent; or those that make more than $50,000 per year versus those who make less than that amount.

At the very least, the 2008 elections used technology in ways that marked a departure from previous static, rule-based debates and, with the assistance of technology, restored the citizen voice to the proceedings. In an article for the *Washington Post*, Vargas (2008) argued that these technological applications:

... signaled an irreversible shift in campaigning to the kind of two-way communication that many voters have grown to expect. The CNN/YouTube debates, in particular, were thrilling to watch and participate in. They allowed a diverse set of everyday Americans from across the country—not limited to voters seated in a town hall—to ask a variety of questions in creative ways. Yes, it made for better television. But, more importantly, it brought the debate format into the 21st century, where it belongs. (para. 12)

The success of dial testing, then, is the way that it interacts with other components of the media environment to encourage participation.

Many people find dial test information useful. Younger viewers found the dial tests engaging. Rather than static information, the layers of data from the candidates themselves, the dial test results, and the addition in some debates of CNNs pundits giving thumbs up or down visuals during the debate, served to increase attention. CNN Vice-President and Producer David Bohrman noted that younger viewers are "used to dealing with deconstructed information coming at them" and expect equally robust information streams when watching presidential debates (Caro, 2008a, para. 5). On that count, CNN delivered. Strategists who routinely use dial tests note that they provide one more layer of information for voters: "We want as much information as we can get. That's what the Internet is all about" (Luntz in Caro, 8 October 2008b, para. 11).

Rather than a distraction, some people even enjoyed the experience more. "When you see a sporting event, you see and hear the reaction of the crowd, and that doesn't affect your enjoyment of the game" (Bohrman in Caro, 2008b, para. 10). Research on laugh tracks used on situational comedies reveals that reactions from others increase the enjoyment of watching the show (see Cialdini, 1993). Perhaps that is why CNN garnered a large share of the young viewers to watch the debates on their channels.

Certainly, those who watched the debates with dial in hand reported that they paid more attention to the debates. One person in our dial test group in New Hampshire noted that the dials aided in cognitive processing: "Not only did I have to listen to what was being said, I had to think about whether I agreed or not" (Schill & Kirk, research notes). Viewers reported similar responses on their blog sites often questioning why the dials moved on a particular discussion in response to their own feelings on the matter.

The dials are also useful to those who study negative campaign tactics. One blogger noted that negative attacks produced negative reactions from those being dial tested: "If nothing else, it's made it really visually clear to us this election how much the swing voter hates negative attacks" (mk blog response to Davies, 17 October 2008, para. 3). The blogger was correct. Consistently, our research indicates that sniping comments and direct attacks on opponents received negative responses from the undecided voters we studied. Perhaps such comments are useful for the cheering supporters of a candidate who want to stick it to the other side, but as a tool of decision making among undecided voters, such tactics backfired. A participant in an Iowa dial test group was clearly miffed by the negative attacks: "Look, I want to know what someone is going to do to solve these problems. They're serious. I don't give a hoot what one candidate thinks of another. They'd better be concerned what we think. And we want specifics!" (Schill & Kirk, research notes). Another clear example of this was reported from an ABC journalist observing the dial test results from the Republican debate in Manchester, New Hampshire, on January 5, 2008:

> Dials turned down among the Republican-minded focus group during the GOP debate when Arizona Sen. John McCain swiped at former Massachusetts Gov. Mitt Romney as a 'candidate of change.' Fiery debate theater at its best, the focus group assigned McCain the lowest votes of the evening. It was a trend among Republicans and Democrats alike: When it came to political in-fighting within their own party, dials turned down. (Venkataraman, 2008, para. 9)

Dial tests are frequently viewed negatively. The dial test idea did not go without comment. Both late night comedians Stephen Colbert and Jon Stewart ran satirical pieces on their use. Stewart ended one session by commenting that the dials were "a patronizing piece of made-up technology." Nora Ephron on the *Huffington Post* wrote: "This graph on CNN affected me, it affected me so much that I could barely focus on the debate, I was so busy watching the graph. I knew it was completely unreliable and irrelevant, and yet my heart sank and rose according to it" (2008, para. 4).

Media critics are concerned that the dial tests call for immediate responses, not necessarily well considered ones: "Reflection is not an option," lamented one commentator (Caro, 2008a, para. 4). However, there is a distinction between audience reactions to a debate and a doorstep opinion. Doorstep opinions are a concern for pollsters who find that when respondents do not know enough to have an opinion on a question, they will simply make it up. Dial testing does not require respondents to evaluate each argument positively or negatively if they are unsure. In fact, participants are instructed to set their dials in the middle position when they have a neutral opinion and to move the dials only when they react strongly to something that is being said. The 100-point continuous scale also allows respondents great freedom to react with various levels of strength. No doubt, critics are correct when they say that immediate responses are required, but no more so than from pundits and journalists who routinely offer such spur of the moment commentary as the debates unfold.

The ideal method of democratic decision making, as taught in schools and espoused by great political thinkers, is for the voter to engage in serious reflection. There is concern that voters do too little of that. Remedies for shallow thinking are unclear. But there are those who believe that dial testing contributes to poor decision making. For example, "Lipman, who writes the Head of State blog, also said that television's competitive push to be fast rather than deep 'drives people to believe that the way to make decisions about political candidates is the instantaneous gut responses'" (Caro, 2008b, para. 8). The argument is that voters will become accustomed to making decisions based on quick reactions. We would argue that voters already are. Further, since debates are scattered throughout the political season, and no one votes immediately, there is little direct connection between the dial results and voting outcomes. The argument about habit of mind could be valid, but as discussed earlier, dial graphs could also encourage voters to consider the opinions of others and engage in deeper thinking.

Another criticism of the dials is the impact of the visual argument being made. This is an area of research that is not definitive at this time. One blogger for the *Denver Post* expressed concern that the visual images of the dial tests would affect viewer reactions: ". . . in the words of Cliff Zukin, director of the public-policy program at Rutgers University and former head of the American Association for Public Opinion Research, people tend to believe their eyes. Protect democracy. Get rid of live dial-testing data!" (McCarter, 2008, para. 12). Whether they influence viewers or not is unclear. What is clear is that many of the participants gave thoughtful responses in their blogs and even occasionally quoted academic research to justify their position. The question of the impact of visuals is unclear. In similar vein, do dial graphics affect voters? Determining what, if any, effect the visual has on voters should be an area for future study. Once determined, the next question is how much visual information is appropriate?

Even those who did not like the idea of dial testing found that they held their interest and attention. This account by *Chicago Tribune* writer Mark Caro (2008b) is typical of what we heard repeatedly:

> So on Tuesday night, I tuned into the presidential debate on PBS, and the moment when one candidate said something rather snarky, I switched to CNN to see what the lines were doing. I never switched back. Somehow I managed to pay attention to the entire debate even as the green Men's line and orange Women's line snaked up and down.

I was interested to observe that Barack Obama's peaks generally seemed higher than John McCain's and that male viewers appeared more often to be disapproving than the female ones. Was any of this information meaningful or necessary? I can't say. But I did choose to watch it even after my complaining. Maybe what's really going on is this: I've already made up my mind about who's getting my vote, so although I'm interested to hear how both candidates address this country's deepening crises, I'm equally motivated to learn how their rhetoric plays with those who ultimately will decide the election. (paras. 13–20)

The dial tests were an attempt to understand how undecided voters reacted to candidate messages. At the presidential level, debates are not held until late in the campaign. Therefore, most debate viewers have already made up their minds about the candidates and issues they are supporting. This majority group of voters is more interested in seeing how the event is received by voters in swing states than learning about the issues. Dial tests are certainly a better indicator of voter opinion than post-debate conjecture from partisan analysts.

Political elites who closely follow the candidates from the time they surface to Election Day rallies sometimes view the debates as a boxing match where their candidate shows his superiority to the other. Those truly interested in learning what motivates or inspires undecided voters find that the dial results provide insight. Certainly, this is why political consultants regularly use the technique. Persuasion is a key component to winning elections, for once the elites and partisans have taken their position, a close election will be determined by this group of people who decide late in the election cycle and who use the debates as a time to focus on the voting decision. David Paull who runs MSInteractive, the company that builds and supports the dial technology, argues that as much as people wish to dismiss the technology, it reflects the way strategists make decisions every day: "... let's face it, feedback from 30 people in a room here and 30 people in a room there (i.e., focus groups) is how each campaign is making critical decisions every day" (Paull blog response in Caro, 2008b, para. 2). Voters have a right to know that. While scholars may decree this strategy-focused coverage, the reason it is the foundation of election coverage is that the majority of viewers prefers this type of coverage.

Dial tests affect journalists' coverage of the debate. As discussed earlier, post-debate commentary has the potential to affect viewer perceptions of the event. Further, we noted that the citizen voice was virtually absent from that commentary. Dial testing provided a means of injecting voter feedback into the commentary. Like its network counterparts, CNN used the services of experienced commentators to assist in deconstructing the debate. In previous elections, the "spin room"—the room where each candidate lines up notable party and opinion leaders to make the case to the news media that their candidate had performed the best in the debate— provided the bulk of post-debate analysis. The dial test results added another layer to that; one that came from voters rather than political operatives. This is an important distinction. Journalists are certainly knowledgeable about the issues and many are quite effective in observing the nuances of candidates' performances. Perhaps for that reason, they are not representative of voters' opinions who are engaging the political process for the first time. The dial tests as constructed for this election were designed to observe voters who were just beginning to make up their minds. In traditional news coverage, journalists prefer to interview those who have an opinion, not the person who is forming one. The dials added another—and important—element to journalistic coverage: the impressions of undecided voters as they were assessing political information. After all, those are the people to whom the messages are being delivered. Rightfully, their reactions *should* comprise a generous portion of post-debate coverage.

CNN's decision to monitor the decision process is illuminating. While there are those that claim that debates make little or no difference, Carlin and McKinney (1994) argue that "of all the campaign information sources available for voter education, only debates provide voters with an opportunity to view the candidates side-by-side for an extended period of time. Debates are the closest thing to a job interview that candidates and the public will ever experience" (p. 3). Debates, then, become the natural moment to report how the interview is going: how candidates are making their case and how the voters respond.

The depth of analysis available is also notable. After each debate, CNN turned to the dial test groups to get first reactions to the event. Importantly, these groups often lead the CNN coverage. Rather than asking simply who won or lost the debate, coverage also examined attitudinal shifts. Since the researchers conducted pre- and post-test analysis, we were able to assess how each candidate was viewed before and after the event. Strongly positive or negative results were noted and often became the subject of some discussion as Wolf Blitzer lead the discussion with reporters and commentators.

The news hole available for traditional commentator comment was certainly reduced by the time devoted to covering the dial test groups. One blogger humorously noted that the dial coverage reduced the role of commentators who typically dominate post-debate coverage: "I was instantly convinced by the crawler . . . It's like one of those miracle bug sprays you see advertised. It destroys whole worlds of noxious commentators" (John Emerson blog response to Davies, 17 October 2008, para. 1).

To the extent that journalists do indeed affect viewer perceptions, perhaps the lessons gleaned from voters will serve an education function for those running for office. One of those lessons concerns the use of negative attacks. CNN reporter Soledad O'Brien summed this sentiment in her post-election analysis:

> So you can certainly see, Anderson, whenever you heard specifics, sort of ticking off the things that they were interested in doing, the dials would go up, where we saw it go down, it's what we've seen before, negativity, sniping, digs, immediately people would dial down. Our panelists told us frankly they were so interested in getting some substance that they just didn't want to waste time with digs. It really had nothing to do even sort of overall negativity, just don't waste my time and stick to some substance.
>
> (Cooper, 2008, show transcript)

We cannot stress enough that the dial groups consistently revealed that undecided voters do not find the typical mud-slinging negative attack useful. One blogger noted: "If nothing else, it's made it really visually clear to us this election how much the swing voter hates negative attacks" (mk blog response to Davies, 17 October 2008, para. 3).

By contrast, voters explained that they looked for specific, detailed solutions or programs. When audiences did not get specific information, they complained about it. Note this interview by Soledad O'Brien of three focus group participants:

O'BRIEN: You said you wanted specifics on health care. They spent a fair amount of time on health care. Did you—what did you hear? Did you like what you heard?

UNIDENTIFIED MALE: Well, it still was a little muddled. I'm still not real sure what exactly affordability is. And it just still gives me doubt on if health care's issues are going to be solved. I'm not real sure.

O'BRIEN: How did you feel, Cheryl? I know you had felt you didn't get a lot of specifics the last presidential debate. What do you think this time around? And did you hear what you wanted to hear?

UNIDENTIFIED FEMALE: No, I did not. I didn't hear anything at all. I just heard a bunch of, you know, the same old thing, I mean from both candidates, which I was really surprised about. Very disappointed.

O'BRIEN: Disappointed. OK, J.R., you said it was about alternative fuel. And both candidates spent a decent amount of time, probably more than they did in the first debate, talking about that. Did that give you—make you give them high marks?

UNIDENTIFIED MALE: They definitely pinpointed on different aspects of what we could do to, you know, change the economy and go towards the alternative fuels. But I don't think they actually pinpointed the specifics on what I was looking for each one of the candidates to pinpoint on. (O'Brien on *Anderson Cooper*; Cooper, 2008)

Also, our panelists reacted negatively to what they perceived as gimmicks. Take this example of a post-debate exchange between Soledad O'Brien and the dial test audience regarding Joe the Plumber:

O'BRIEN: Let's talk about Joe the plumber, who happens to be a real guy. And not only is he a real guy, he's a real guy here in Ohio. Again, Joe the plumber's stories, everybody dialed down, did not like Joe the plumber.
Liz George, we've given you a mike. Why no resonance with Joe the plumber?
UNIDENTIFIED FEMALE: I appreciated the story. I know a lot of people in his situation. I needed less personal story and more specifics. How are McCain and Obama going to really crack the code on supporting small and medium-sized businesses in this country, because that's really what's going to drive the economic growth. And they just kept going back to telling the story again and again and again.
O'BRIEN: Did you think it was a gimmick, or did you think it was a genuine story and it just wasn't resonating?
UNIDENTIFIED FEMALE: I believe his—his story was genuine but about the third or fourth time I heard it, it started to get gimmicky. (O'Brien on Anderson Cooper, 7 October 2008; Cooper, 2008)

In each of these exchanges, we observe the voter struggling with the information offered to make a decisions about who will earn his or her vote. Negative attacks did not work. Gimmicks did not work. But specific, detailed responses to questions produced positive feedback from those we tested.

Conclusion

One of the major advances of the 2008 elections is the adaptation of technology to the political environment. Despite its many previous uses, 2008 marks the first election where the Internet was fully integrated, even if its role is not fully defined.

These researchers believe that the 2008 CNN dial tests serve as a useful model of how voters might be better engaged in the future. Micah Sifry, co-founder of the non-partisan *TechPresident.com*, noted in a *Washington Post* interview that dial testing is just a beginning. But it is an important step in creating a future environment where the public could voice opinions and encourage candidate adaptation to the will of the people:

> We'd involve the public directly, and in real time, in judging how well the candidates are answering the questions being asked, and we'd include that information in aggregate form. Showing a dial-test line from uncommitted voters in Ohio is just one step in that direction [referring to CNN's innovation] . . . There's no reason why we can't invite everyone to express their responses, in real time, using everything from the Web to old fashioned dial-up phones. And that real-time feedback would be fed back into the debate loop, for the candidates to address. If millions of viewers think a candidate isn't really answering the question, maybe this way we'll get them to be more responsive. (cited in Vargas, 2008, para. 15)

This speaks to one of the key issues of political participation. Voters want to feel that candidates hear what they are saying and respond appropriately: Vox populi (the voice of the people).

References

Benoit, W. L., & Currie, H. (2001). Inaccuracies in media coverage of the 1996 and 2000 presidential debates. *Argumentation and Advocacy, 38*, 28–39.

Benoit, W. L., & Hansen, G. J. (2001). Presidential debate questions and the public agenda. *Communication Quarterly, 49*, 130–141.

Boyd, S. (2008, October 15). *Seriously? Tapped blog.* Retrieved September 27, 2010, from www.propsect.org/csnc/blogs/tapped_archive?month=10&year=2008&base_name=seriously.

Carlin, D. B., & McKinney, M. S. (Eds.). (1994). *The 1992 presidential debates in focus.* Westport, CT: Praeger.

Carlin, D. B., Vigil, T., Buehler, S., & McDonald, K. (2009). *The third agenda in U.S. presidential debates: DebateWatch and viewer reactions, 1996–2004.* Westport, CT: Praeger.

Caro, M. (2008a, October 7). Instant feedback: CNN graph shows what viewers think, but can we digest all that? *Chicago Tribune.* Retrieved September 10, 2009, from http://archives.chicagotribune.com/2008/oct/07/news/chi-talk-cnn-debateoct07.

Caro, M. (2008b, October 8). CNN's debate squiggles strike back. *Chicago Tribune.* Retrieved September 10, 2009, from http://featuresblogs.chicago tribune.com/entertainment_popmachine/2008/10/cnns-debate-squ.html.

Chaffee, S. H., & Dennis, J. (1979). Presidential debates: An empirical assessment. In A. Ranney (Ed.), *The past and future of presidential debates.* Washington, DC: American Enterprise Institute, pp. 75–106.

Chalupa, A. (2008, October 3). *CNN, stop with the screen litter.* Retrieved September 10, 2009, from www.portfolio.com/views/blogs/views?subtype Choice=blog&categoryChoice=views&publishYearMonth=200810&page=31.

Cho, J., Shah, D. V., Nah, S., & Brossard, D. (2009). "Split screens" and "spin rooms": Debate modality, post-debate coverage, and the new videomalaise. *Journal of Broadcasting and Electronic Media, 53,* 242–261.

Cialdini, R. B. (1993). *Influence: The psychology of persuasion.* New York: Quill.

Cooper, A. (2008, October 7). *Anderson Cooper 360.* CNN Transcripts. Atlanta, GA.

Davies, D. (2008, October 17). *Don't scrap the squiggles. Out of the crooked timber of humanity, no straight thing was ever made* (blog site). Retrieved September 10, 2009, from http://crookedtimber.org/2008/10/17/dont-scrap-the-squiggle/.

Diamond, E., & Friery, K. (1987). Media coverage of presidential debates. In J. Swerdlow (Ed.), *Presidential debates: 1988 and beyond.* Washington, DC: Congressional Quarterly Press, pp. 43–51.

Elliott, W. R., & Sothirajah, J. (1993). Post-debate analysis and media reliance: Influences on candidate image and voting probabilities, *Journalism Quarterly, 70,* 321–335.

Fridkin, K. L., Kenney, P. J., Gershon, S. A., & Woodall, G. S. (2008). Spinning debates: The impact of the news media's coverage of the final 2004 presidential debate. *Press/Politics, 13,* 29–51.

Geer, J. G. (1988). The effects of presidential debates on the electorate's preference for candidates. *American Politics Quarterly, 16,* 486–501.

Greenfield, J. (1980). *Playing to win: An insider's guide to politics.* New York: Simon & Schuster.

Iyengar, S., & Kinder, D. R. (1987). *News that matters: Television and American opinion.* Chicago, IL: University of Chicago Press.

Jackson-Beeck, M., & Meadow, R. G. (1979). The triple agenda of presidential debates. *Public Opinion Quarterly, 5,* 173–180.

Kraus, S. (2000). *Televised presidential debates and public policy* (2nd Ed.). Hillsdale, NJ: Erlbaum & Associates.

Lang, G. E., & Lang, K. (1978). Immediate and delayed responses to a Carter-Ford debate: Assessing public opinion. *Public Opinion Quarterly, 42,* 322–341.

Lanoue, D. J. (1991). The "turning point": Viewers' reaction to the second 1988 presidential debate. *American Politics Quarterly, 19,* 80–95.

Larson, S. G. (1999). Public opinion in television election news: Beyond polls. *Political Communication, 16,* 133–145.

Lemert, J. B., Elliott, W. R., Bernstein, J. M., Rosenberg, W. L., & Nestvold, K. J. (1991). *News verdicts, the debates and presidential campaigns.* New York: Praeger.

Lowry, D. T., Bridges, J. A., & Barefield, P. A. (1990). Effects of TV "instant analysis and querulous criticism:" Following the first Bush–Dukakis debate. *Journalism Quarterly, 67,* 814–825.

Lupfer, M., & Wald, K. (1979). An experimental study of the first Carter–Ford debate. *Experimental Study of Politics, 7,* 20–40.

McCarter, J. (2008, October 3). Diary of a mad voter. PoliticsWest. *The Denver Post*. Retrieved September 10, 2009, from www.newwest.net/topic/article/the_sideshow/C530/.

McKinney, M. S. (2005). Let the people speak: The public's agenda and presidential town hall debates. *American Behavioral Scientist, 49*, 198–212.

McKinnon, L. M., & Tedesco, J. C. (1999). The influence of medium and media commentary on presidential debate effects. In L. L. Kaid & D. G. Bystrom (Eds.), *The electronic election: Perspectives on the 1996 campaign communication*. Mahwah, NJ: Lawrence Erlbaum, pp. 191–206.

McKinnon, L. M., Tedesco, J. C., & Kaid, L. L. (1993). The third 1992 presidential debate: Channel and commentary effects. *Argumentation and Advocacy, 30*, 106–118.

Patterson, T. (1980). *The mass media election: How Americans choose their president*. New York: Praeger.

Pew Research Center for the People and the Press (2008, January 11). *Social networking take off: Internet's broader role in campaign 2008*. Retrieved September 10, 2009, from http://people-press.org/reports/display.php3?ReportID=384.

Schroeder, A. (2008). *Presidential debates: Fifty years of high-risk TV*. New York: Columbia University Press.

Shearer R. R. (2008, October). *CNN's "Thingamajig": "Live audience reaction" graphic flat-lined at the presidential debates*. Retrieved September 10, 2009, from www.stinkyjournalism.org/latest-journalism-news-updates-132.php.

Steeper, F. T. (1978). Public response to Gerald Ford's statements on Eastern Europe in the second debate. In G. F. Bishop, R. G. Meadow, & M. Jackson-Beeck (Eds.), *The presidential debates: Media, electoral, and policy perspectives*. New York: Praeger, pp. 81–101.

Stelter, B. (2008, October 3). Big ratings for the V.P. debate. *The New York Times* Political Blog. Retrieved September 10, 2009, from http://thecaucus.blogs.nytimes.com/2008/10/03/big-ratings-for-vp-debate/.

Tsfati, Y. (2003). Debating the debate: The impact of exposure to debate news coverage and its interaction with exposure to the actual debate. *Harvard International Journal of Press/Politics, 8*, 70–86.

Vargas, J. A. (2008, October 8). A timeless debate format? Or a dated one? *Washington Post*. Retrieved September 10, 2009, from http://voices.washingtonpost.com/44/2008/10/08/a_timeless_debate_format_or_a.html.

Venkataraman, N. (2008, January 5). Focus groups spin the dial during debates: "Real time response" reveals voter disdain for party in-fighting. *ABC News*. Internal Release.

Chapter 9

New Media's Contribution to Presidential Debates

Pamela Jo Brubaker

Much like traditional communication technologies of their time, the interactive features of Web 2.0 technologies open the doors for average citizens to participate in the democratic process in ways never thought possible. Hopes for a better democracy have shifted to new media with the anticipation of encouraging participation, giving voices to marginalized groups (Dahlberg, 2007) and producing more informed citizens (Racine Group, 2002; Minow & LaMay, 2008). Web 2.0 technologies add a new dimension to political campaigns whereby citizens can view and listen to political messages as well as produce and distribute the messages themselves. Today, user-generated, video-sharing Web sites like YouTube allow citizens to generate and post their own political or social commentary.

New media's potential for altering the face of political campaigns, particularly political debates, became evident during the 2008 presidential campaign when the social networking Web site YouTube offered users the opportunity to create and post 30-second video questions for potential use in an upcoming presidential primary debate. These debates, which took place during the 2008 presidential primary season in July and November of 2007, were co-sponsored with YouTube and aired by the Cable News Network (CNN). In an effort to better understand new media's contribution to political discourse this study examines the YouTube video questions selected by journalists and aired during the Democratic and Republican CNN/YouTube debates.

Televised Presidential Debates

Televised presidential debates have become an integral part of the political campaign process (Jarmin, 2005). Not only do debates give millions of Americans the opportunity to examine presidential candidates up close, but they help voters solidify their opinions and make a final decision on Election Day. Debates contribute to the political campaign process by providing voters with an opportunity to hear a variety of viewpoints and/or policy or issue proposals, see how the candidates handle themselves under pressure, and judge which candidate appeals are most convincing (Minow & LaMay, 2008).

Exposure to the candidates in intraparty presidential primary debates is particularly important as this is often the first time voters have the opportunity to compare and contrast political contenders face-to-face on the same issues and topics (Benoit, Stein, & Hansen, 2004). During this first phase of the presidential campaign process, when candidates compete to become the front-runner on their political party's ticket, voter perceptions of candidate images are particularly capricious (Becker & McCombs, 1978; Gopoian, 1982). In a quasi-experiment Pfau (1987) studied the impact of the 1984 presidential primary debates on public opinion and found them to be particularly influential on the formation of voter perceptions and attitudes of participating candidates and their character. During the primary season debates have also been said to "affect public perception of a candidate's image—general competency, personal attributes, and character traits" (Trent & Friedenberg, 2007, p. 312). Once opinions are formed, debates elicit incremental changes in voter's perception or reinforce opinions, but when undecided voters are conflicted or uninformed about candidates, debates can have a greater influence in swaying opinions (Racine Group, 2002).

The debate format contributes not only to candidate performances, but to audience perceptions of the candidate's performance (Carlin, Morris, & Smith, 2001; Racine Group, 2002). Prior to the 2008 CNN/YouTube presidential primary debates, presidential debates consisted of face-to-face questions posed by a panel of journalists, a single moderator, and/or audience members (Carlin et al., 2001). In the first televised debates a panel of journalists questioned candidates (Minow & LaMay, 2008). Later, single moderator and town hall formats, which allowed audience members to ask questions, were adopted. In the 1992 presidential election all three debate formats were employed, allowing comparisons of candidate's performance among the various formats. In addition, the type of debate format as well as who participates in the debate contributes to a more casual or formal atmosphere and influences overall perceptions of candidates (Carlin et al., 2001; Hart & Jarvis, 1997). Most often, in multiple candidate debates, the depth of analysis given to questions is minimized. As a result, follow-up questions are sacrificed along with candidates' ability to respond to each question (Racine Group, 2002).

The New Debate Agenda

The importance of selecting appropriate debate questions is underscored by the need to give voters the information they need to make informed choices among political candidates. Studies indicate debate questions are overwhelmingly about issues. A content analysis of the 1976 presidential debates between Senator John Kennedy and Vice President Richard Nixon reveals that 92 percent of the questions were about issues and almost 80 percent of the candidate responses were comprised of issue content (Racine Group, 2002). The substantive nature of mediated debates has always been an issue raised by critics. Prior to the first televised presidential debate in 1960, an editorial in the *Wall Street Journal* speculated that a televised debate would be "rigged more for entertainment than for enlightenment" (as cited in Minow & LaMay, 2008, p. 11):

> Mr. Nixon and Mr. Kennedy will each be trying to bring the audience to his point of view . . . but the danger is that they will be attempting to do this not so much by explanation and logic but by personality projection, charges and counter-charges, empty promises, and plain gimmicks of one sort or another. The fear is that they will not discuss the issues as much as put on a show.
>
> (Minow & LeMay, 2008, p. 11)

It is therefore possible that using new media to construct a new debate format may provide more entertainment value than substantive value and ultimately fail to reveal differences between the candidates' personality, character, previous record, and position on issues.

Although the YouTube debate format eliminated journalists' carefully scripted questions, it empowered journalists with control over selecting those questions the news media felt were most important for candidates to respond to and audiences to hear about. This gate-keeping function is similarly performed by journalists on a daily basis and reflected in the news media today. It is therefore plausible that the selection of debate questions may reflect more journalistic values and norms found in coverage of political campaigns opposed to those issues on the minds of citizens.

Agenda Setting

The news media play a key role in providing information on political issues, and particularly political candidates, to an otherwise uninformed electorate (McCombs & Reynolds, 2009). As candidates compete for the public's attention, the media are relied upon to help individuals weed through an assortment of messages that vie for their attention prior to elections. In their research on agenda setting, McCombs and Shaw (1972) examined how the media influenced perceptions of reality. In a survey of undecided voters in Chapel Hill, North Carolina, answers to perceptions of the key issues of the day were ranked according to the percentage of voters naming each issue. These issues were then compared to a rank-ordered list of key issues covered most often in news stories from nine news outlets of local and national prominence. The resulting correlation between the social and political issues on both agendas provided evidence of the news media's ability to tell audiences what issues were most important and worthy of their attention. Issues or topics can be made more salient through a variety of means, including frequent coverage or inclusion of stories on a specific topic or issue, placing stories in prominent locations and giving valuable space to a story such as the front page of a newspaper or magazine. Later, in revisiting agenda-setting theory, McCombs and Reynolds (2002) further suggested that the "mass media set the agenda of issues for a political campaign by influencing the salience of the issues among voters. Those issues emphasized in the news come to be regarded over time as important by members of the public" (p. 2). Examining the topics discussed during the CNN/YouTube debate is therefore a critical step in understanding those issues the news media find most salient and worthy of the public's attention.

Not only does the news media make issues salient, but they make various aspects of these issues salient. First-order agenda setting as discussed previously, refers to the news media's ability to tell us what to think about; second-order agenda setting—also known as attribute agenda setting—refers to the news media's role in telling us *how* to think about issues. By emphasizing different aspects of these issues to varying degrees, the media ultimately influences how people will think and talk about the issues the debate tells us to think about (Becker & McCombs, 1978; McCombs & Reynolds, 2009). With attribute agenda setting, the more individuals use the media, the more various aspects of the issues high-lighted by the media become accessible and salient to audiences. This is not to be conflated with framing theory, which refers to deliberate judgments about the relevance of information to the current situation, or the applicability of the information to the situation (McCombs & Reynolds, 2009; Tewksbury & Scheufele, 2009).

Research Questions

The 2007 CNN/YouTube debates are among some of the first debates to engage candidates with unedited citizen-generated questions. They are also among some of the most viewed presidential primary debates in history. The first debate, held by Democratic candidates in Charleston, South Carolina, was viewed on CNN by 2.6 million people (Gough, 2007). The subsequent Republican YouTube debate, held in St. Petersburg, Florida, was watched by an unparalleled 4.4 million viewers, more than any other primary debate up to that time in cable news history (Guthrie, 2008).

This study examines the debate questions selected by CNN and YouTube and asked of the Democratic and Republican presidential candidates during the CNN/YouTube debates to determine the substantive quality of the questions, as well as how they might have contributed to or handicapped a more informed electorate. More specifically, what substantive value did the questions offer (e.g., entertainment, information, etc.)? To gain a better understanding of the debate's agenda and the messages presented to audiences, the following research questions are addressed:

RQ1:   What types of citizen-generated questions did CNN and YouTube choose to include in the debates?

RQ2:   Are the questions posed to presidential candidates in the Democratic and Republican CNN/YouTube debates reflective of the most important issues on American's minds at the time of each debate?

RQ3:   Is the debate agenda reflective of the public agenda?

Method

This study employed a content analysis that compares the salient issues and topics addressed during the Democratic and Republican CNN/YouTube debates to answers from Gallup Poll's survey on the most important problems facing the nation, and election polls reported at the time of the debates. Initially, all of the citizen-generated video questions that aired during the CNN/YouTube presidential primary debates were examined, for a total of 71 questions. Video questions for the Democratic debate were submitted between June 10, 2007, and July 22, 2007. Thirty-eight of the 2,989 submissions were selected for inclusion in the July 23, 2007, debate. The Republican debate received nearly 2,000 additional submissions for a total of 4,927 videos questions. Only 33 of these questions were utilized in the November 28, 2007, debate. Eight candidates participated in each of the debates. CNN reporter Anderson Cooper moderated the two-hour debates, which ran uninterrupted, without commercial breaks. Authors of the submitted questions were instructed to be personal and include their perspective, keep their video questions to less than 30 seconds in length, to be original, address their questions to one or all of the candidates, practice standard production techniques such as keeping the camera steady and speaking loudly, and indicate their name and hometown ("Submission criteria: Democrat," 2008a; "Submission criteria: Republican," 2008b). Video questions were retrieved from an online debate archive at CNN.com and analyzed by one coder.

Due to the nature of this novel questioning format it is necessary to examine types of questions asked, how they were asked, and who asked them. The question format was examined (e.g., one or more questioners, animated questioner, no person present, etc.) as well as the questioner's age, gender, and race. The questioner's age was sorted into one of four categories (< 17; 17–35; 36–49; 50+). Age, which was reported on more than half of the questioners' personal YouTube sites, was then compared with a more subjective assessment of the spokesperson's age. When self-reported age was not available, the coder based assessments on a variety of facial cues. Age was analyzed twice during two separate coding sessions to ensure reliability. On a few occasions, when discrepancies were found, the spokesperson's age was analyzed a third time. When watching the videos, other elements that appeared—or did not appear—in the question format were noted, including the use of props, additional video footage, and animation.

Much like other agenda-setting studies that rely on public opinion polls for gauging public attitudes and salient issues on the publics' mind (Beniger, 1978), this study utilized public opinion polls as well as election polls to gain a better understanding of the public agenda. To answer the second research question and determine whether or not the questions posed to presidential candidates in the CNN/YouTube debates were reflective of the most important issues on American's minds at the time of each debate, the issues addressed in each question were compared to public opinion data on the most important issues facing the nation. Each month Gallup publishes reports outlining the response to a national telephone survey whereby participants are asked to respond to an open-ended question, "What is the most important problem facing the nation today?" Responses include a variety of economic and non-economic problems facing the nation. For this portion of the analysis, Gallup Poll results from 2007 are utilized (Newport, 2008).

To answer the third research question and further gauge how the debate agenda reflects the public agenda, election polls published by Gallup Poll and American Research Group, which indicated public support behind the candidates in July 2007 and November 2007, are then compared to candidate-specific comments as well as the number of candidates' responses (see American Research Group, 2007, July; American Research Group, 2007, November; Gallup Poll, 2007, July; Gallup Poll, 2007, November).

Results

Question Format

A greater understanding of the question format provides insight into how messages in the debate were communicated. From this analysis, it is clear that the selection of video questions was not based on professionalism or the use of professional video equipment. Rather, the video quality in the debate questions reflected the tools and technology available to citizens who regularly use YouTube. Most videos were shot from a single vantage point without the use of editing. More extensive knowledge of video creation was evident in two (6.1 percent) Republican and one (2.6 percent) Democratic question, which featured talking, animated characters. The majority of video questions featured bust or head shots of one individual asking the question. More than one person was introduced in 14.2 percent of the videos (Democrat: 4 videos; Republican: 1 video), but only one of these questions featured two people asking the question. This video did not warrant a response from candidates as it was a question about former Vice-President Al Gore potentially running for office. Although Gore did not declare his candidacy in 2008, there were a number of grassroots supporters hoping he would join the race. In another Democratic video music and text were used to convey the question; however, the male questioner was not visible.

Men and younger adults were more likely to be featured in the video questions. In both debates the gender of the questioner was most often male, with 71.8 percent of the questioners being male (Democrat: 68.4 percent; Republican: 75.8 percent) and 22.5 percent female (Democrat: 26.3 percent; Republican: 18.2 percent). One Democratic question had both male and female questioners. Gender was not coded in the three animated questions. A good majority of questioners, or 70.4 percent, were between the ages of 17 and 35 years of age (Democrat: 65.5 percent; Republican: 65.7 percent). Only 14.1 percent (Democrat: 10.5 percent; Republican: 18.2 percent) of the questioners were between the ages of 36–49, and another 14.1 percent (Democrat: 18.4 percent; Republican: 9.1 percent) were 50 or older. One questioner, featured with his father, was younger than 17 (Republican: 1.4 percent). These findings are fairly consistent with reports that indicate video-sharing sites are more popular among men and younger adults (Rainie, 2008). Overall, 81.7 percent of the questioners were Caucasian and 11.3 percent were African-American. Race was not clearly identifiable in 1.4 percent of the videos. Both age and ethnicity were either unidentifiable (e.g., no questioner visible) or irrelevant (e.g., animation) in four (5.6 percent) of the videos.

Types of Questions

In most instances candidates were asked questions that allowed them to explain their stance or position on an issue and what he/she would do about it, if given the opportunity (Democrat: 23/38 questions; Republican: 22/33 questions). Republican candidates were also primary targets of questions that required clarification of prior deeds or statements (Democrat: 1 question; Republican: 6 questions). But a number of the questions had no value in helping viewers understand candidates' policy positions on issues of global or individual importance. Such questions were only aired to expose the nature, character, or beliefs of the men and women running for office and were not particularly relevant or on topics of key importance to the presidential office (Democrat: 14 questions; Republican: 5 questions). Among such questions, Democrats were asked who they would "hypothetically" pick as a Republican running mate and Republicans were asked about their personal gun collection(s).

Questions of self importance. A good portion of the questions reflected individual interests of the questioner. Although video submitters were encouraged to "be personal" ("Submission Criteria: Democrat," 2008a; "Submission Criteria: Republican," 2008b), it was not uncommon to have sentiments personalized and even go so far as to reflect the self interests of the questioner, centering on topics or issues that affect them individually. This finding is similar to public discourse identified in post-debate discussion groups by Carlin and colleagues (2005) following the 2004 presidential election. In their analysis of an online political discussion board and a DebateWatch group, public comments revealed a highly individualistic culture. Instead of providing commentary on those issues that would benefit a broader group, individuals thought the debate was only meaningful when the discussion aligned with those topics that affected individuals personally or the country's domestic problems more directly.

Debate questions were personalized through a variety of means, including the addition of the questioner's affiliation and personal examples. The inclusion of personal elements lent credibility to the questioner and helped illustrate the need for politicians to address the issue at hand. Questioner affiliations ranged from an openly gay Brigadier General who asked a question on gay rights in the military to Darfur refugee workers who asked how the candidates were going to get the African children back to a safe Darfur.

The expectation that the politicians were responsible for and would alleviate an individual's personal problems was also reflected in questions. One Republican questioner wanted to know how candidates planned to keep lead-laced toys out of her home, whereas a Democratic questioner wanted to know what the government was going to do to curb the "boom" of Alzheimer's disease, because "not every parent has two loving sons to take care of them."

Over one third of the videos in both debates (Democrat: 31.6 percent; Republican: 36.4 percent) featured questions that were personalized by the questioner or made particularly relevant and meaningful through the inclusion of props, video footage, or some other creative element. Props such as the Holy Bible, the "stars and bars" flag, and a large semi-automatic weapon served as effective communication devices. The addition of video footage (e.g., toy spacemen on the moon, farm workers, etc.) also helped engage the audience in a short amount of time. One of the more creative videographers asked about the federal deficit and videoed himself in the center of a dollar bill where former presidents typically appear. Others chose to demonstrate their talents in animation. In the Democratic debate a snowman worried that global warming was going to make his snow son melt. The Republican debate featured a talking poster of Uncle Sam who wanted to know if candidates would consider eliminating federal income tax. Humor was not a strong component of the questions and was clearly identifiable in only 13 percent of the videos aired. Despite the novelty of using more creative formats, their use may have distracted audiences from the real issues and inflated the perception of the issues' importance. By couching questions in creative formats or highlighting the question's self-importance, perhaps it is the talking snowman audiences will remember most and not the issues addressed by the questioners.

The Most Important Problem

Questions on economic issues. In July 2007, Gallup Poll responses to the importance of economic concerns facing the nation were at an all-time low for the year at 16 percent; however, in November 2007 when the Republican debate took place American's unease about the economy nearly doubled (31 percent). At the time of both debates, unease about the economy in general along with fuel/oil prices were of greatest concern, with these two topics becoming larger issues by November. Unemployment/jobs topped this list at number three followed by the federal deficit. Lack of money, corporate corruption, taxes, and wage issues were also among the economic concerns (see Newport, 2008).

Despite public opinion about their relative importance, economic issues were not regularly raised during the debate (see Table 9.1). Democrats and Republicans alike addressed a total of four questions on the topic (Democrat: 10.5 percent; Republican: 12.1 percent); however, the Republicans fielded these inquiries earlier in the debate (questions 6–9), after a series of questions on immigration and illegal aliens. Democrats on the other hand fielded economic questions near the latter half of the debate (questions 27, 29–31). Democrats took one question on wage issues, one on the federal deficit, and two on taxes. In what could be considered questions designed to trick and embarrass the candidates or expose their character and potential elitism, the first question about the economy centered on candidates' willingness to be paid the national minimum wage. Another question on the economy came from a questioner who complained he paid taxes on everything and he wanted to know what the politicians would do to remedy his situation. Others wanted to know if their taxes would increase if a Democrat were to take office. Republican questions on economic issues were specific to the national debt and taxes. Questioners wanted to know how the national debt was going to be controlled and the measures candidates would take to decrease this debt (e.g., top three programs candidates would decrease in size). Questions were also raised about the future possibility of eliminating the federal income tax and vetoing any effort to raise taxes.

Questions on non-economic issues. The most important non-economic issues on American's minds in 2007 centered on the war in Iraq, with this conflict being of greater concern in July (35 percent) than in November (24 percent; see Newport, 2008). At the time of the Democratic debate health care, along with immigration/illegal aliens, topped the list of concerns at 14 percent and 11 percent respectively. By November, health care was still the second greatest concern at 12 percent, however, at this time dissatisfaction with government (11 percent) was a greater concern than immigration (7 percent). Additional issues that top this list include ethics/moral/religious/family decline as well as terrorism and education (poor education and access to education). Concerns over the environment, social security, gun control, abortion, and homosexuality/gay rights were identified as being of grave concern by a small minority (≤ 1 percent; see Newport, 2008).

Quality of education was a key issue addressed by Democrats in four questions. The Iraq war, dissatisfaction with government, international problems, election reform/presidential choices, and racism received three questions each. Health care, the energy crisis, and issues of homosexuality/ gay rights all received two questions. The importance of health care should not be minimized, however, as candidates were asked to respond to one set of questions couched in four separate video submissions. Keeping this in mind, the number of questions on health care would have totaled five, but only the first video question in this health care segment was coded. Health care issues ranged from affordable health insurance to coverage for undocumented workers. The environment, foreign aid, and gun control were each addressed in one question. Overall, non-economic issues were addressed in 76.3 percent of the Democratic questions, 16 percent more than in the Republican debate (see Table 9.1).

When it came to educational issues, candidates were asked to address how they would deal with the current education policy, No Child Left Behind, and what their administration would do to raise the standards in public schools. Questions probing candidates about whether or not they have talked to their kids about sex education and if they would consider sending their kids to public or private schools were aimed at exposing the candidate's personal lives and character rather than helping voters learn what the candidate would do if elected.

With regard to the Iraq war questioners wanted to know how candidates would conduct themselves once in office. Not only were they curious about the date troops would be out of Iraq, but they wanted to know how America could pull out of the war now when the country had a

Table 9.1 The Most Important Problems Addressed During the CNN/YouTube Debates

Most Important Problem	July 2007		November 2007		
	Gallup poll %	Dem. debate %	Gallup poll %	Rep. debate %	Both debates %
Economic problems (net)	16	10.5	31	12.1	11.3
		(4)		(4)	(8)
Economy in general	6	0	14	0	0
Fuel/oil prices	4	0	7	0	0
Unemployment/jobs	3	0	4	0	0
Federal budget deficit/federal debt	1	1	2	2	3
Taxes	1	2	1	2	4
Wage issues	1	1	*	0	1
Non-economic problems (net)	86	76.3	77	60.6	69
		(29)		(20)	(49)
Situation in Iraq/war	35	3	24	2	5
Poor health care/hospitals; high cost of healthcare	14	2	12	0	2
Immigration/illegal aliens	11	0	7	4	4
Dissatisfaction with government; poor leadership; corruption	8	3	11	1	4

Education/poor education/access to education	3	4	0	4
Environment/pollution	2	1	0	1
Lack of energy sources; energy crisis	2	2	0	2
International issues/problems	2	3	0	3
Foreign aid/focus overseas	2	1	0	1
Crime/violence	2	0	1	1
Social Security	1	1	1	2
Race relations/racism	*	3	1	4
Guns/gun control	1	1	3	4
Election year/presidential choices/election reform	*	3	3	6
Abortion	1	0	2	2
Homosexuality/gay rights issues	0	2	2	4
"Other" non-economic problems (net)	4	13.2	27.3	19.7
		(5)	(9)	(14)
Total questions posed to candidates		38	33	71

Note: *= Less than 0.5%. Debates = Number of video questions aired on a topic during the CNN/YouTube Democratic and Republican debates that took place on July 23, 2007, and November 28, 2007, respectively. Gallup Poll = Gallup Poll survey results on the most important problem (MIP) facing the nation identified in the July 12–15, 2007, and November 11–14, 2007, polls. Not all issues identified in Gallup's MIP survey are represented in the chart. Gallup Poll's MIP is adapted from Newport, F. (2008, January 11). Americans: Economic issues country's top problem today. *Gallup News Service.* Retrieved from www.gallup.com/poll/103699/Americans-Economic-Issues-Countrys-Top-Problem-Today.aspx#2.

responsibility to get Iraq on its feet. On international problems questioners were interested in whether or not candidates would consider meeting leaders of other countries without precondition during the first year of their administration. On this same topic, Senator Clinton was asked whether a woman president would be taken seriously by Arab and Muslim nations and Senator Gravel was asked to defend or dispel a statement he made regarding all deaths in Vietnam being in vain.

Due to the mixed racial and gender dynamics among candidates in the Democratic debate, equality was a pivotal topic on which questions five through seven focused. Here candidates were asked to address whether African-Americans should receive reparations for slavery and if they thought race played a role in the response to Hurricane Katrina. Senator Obama and Senator Clinton, the only African-American and female candidates, were also asked how they plan to address charges of not being black enough or woman enough.

Dissatisfaction with government and political cynicism were apparent in the initial rounds of the July debate when candidates were asked how they were going to be different from the current administration. This theme was picked up again near the end of the debate when a questioner pointed out that the same two families (Bush and Clinton) would be in charge of the executive branch of government for 28 years if Senator Clinton was elected to two presidential terms. The questioner wanted to know what changes the Senator would bring to the White House. In addition to the direct questions reflecting political cynicism, a cynical tone was evident in queries like those mentioning Democrats "playing political games" with the Iraq war and the need for answers beyond "empty promises" given to refugees at Darfur.

On the topic of energy sources candidates were asked how they were going to decrease energy consumption as well as where they stood on nuclear power. Global warming was the only environmental concern addressed. Much like the Republican debate, Democrats were asked to explain their position on protecting guns.

During the Republican debate 60.6 percent of the questions reflected non-economic issues identified by the Gallup Poll. When it comes to issues on American's minds, Table 9.1 shows Republican issues centered more on immigration/illegal aliens, guns/gun control, and election year/presidential choices/election reform, with immigration inspiring four questions and the other two topics receiving three questions each. This was followed by issues about the Iraq war, abortion, and homosexuality/gay rights, which were each addressed in two questions. The topics of racism, crime/violence, dissatisfaction with government, and social security each received one question in the debate

Immigration was the first issue addressed in the Republican debate. At this time candidates were asked if they would veto amnesty for illegal immigrants and provide immigration reform. Mayor Giuliani and Governor Huckabee were also asked to address prior policies and behavior that assisted or gave benefits to illegal immigrants. The first question on guns queried candidates about their opinions on gun control and was followed by an inquiry about Mayor Giuliani's position on written exams for gun owners. On other issues like the Iraq war, candidates asked tough questions about how they planned to repair America's image in the eye of the Muslim world and whether they would make a long-term commitment to the people of Iraq. Questions were often posed in hypothetical terms in an effort to learn more about candidate's positions on issues or how they would embrace or reject ideas. For example, on the topic of abortion candidates were asked if they would sign a federal abortion ban and if they could articulate the punishment mothers and doctors should receive for violating such a ban.

As in the Democratic debate, political cynicism was apparent in various questions aimed at establishing trust, credibility, and motives of the presidential candidates and the government. One questioner accused Congressman Paul of using the Republican ticket to increase his exposure and then asked if he was really going to run as an Independent. Another accused Mayor Giuliani of exploiting September 11 to help him get to the White House. In addition, both log cabin Republicans and conservative African-Americans questioned why they should support Republican candidates.

Questions on other issues. In the Democratic debate 13.2 percent of the questions were on concerns not identified in Gallup's monthly public opinion poll on the most important problem facing the nation. Questions on "other" issues included those requiring Democratic candidates to explain what he or she likes and dislikes about their opponents. This debate also included two questions on religion, which required candidates to answer what "In God We Trust" means to them and address the concerns of an atheist who feared that non-religious Americans would not be treated equally in a Democratic administration. Near the beginning of the debate Senator Clinton was asked to define liberal and how she would use this term to define herself. Gender equality was subsequently highlighted in another video about women registering for the draft at age 18.

In the Republican debate nearly a third of the questions (27.3 percent) were on issues unrelated to those identified by the Gallup Poll. For Republicans, three of these questions dealt with the allocation or reallocation of funds for expanding the U.S. space exploration program, rebuilding America's infrastructure (roads, bridges, etc.), and eliminating farm subsidies. Much like the Democratic debate, religion was a topic of interest as candidates were asked if they believe "every word of the Holy Bible" and "what would Jesus do" about the death penalty. One candidate had the opportunity to dispel rumors of a conspiracy theory to create a North American Union, whereas the need to halt importing lead-laced toys was brought to candidates' immediate attention.

The Most Important Candidate

The amount of attention given to various candidates throughout the CNN/YouTube debates was indicative of the importance the media placed on each candidate. Election polls at the time of the debates were a direct reflection of the attention given to front-runners. The news media's obsession with giving audiences the perception of a close race often dominates political news coverage, which emphasizes who is ahead or behind in the polls and creates the image of a horse race (Broh, 1980). Subsequently, the horse race metaphor is reflected in favoritism leading candidates received during these interparty presidential debates.

Early in the Democratic debate (question 2), the most important candidates were established when a video questioner addressed Congressman Kucinich and asked why he would be a better president than Senator Clinton and Senator Obama. In July 2007 public opinion polls showed Senator Clinton in a substantial lead over all candidates, with Senator Obama trailing substantially, but still the closest Democratic runner up (Gallup Poll, 2007, July; ARG, 2007, July). Eager to learn what the first woman or first African-American president would do in office, questions on race, gender, and equality were posed to these two front-runners throughout the debate. Additionally, video questioners addressed specific Democratic candidates in six of the 38 questions aired during the debate, whereas the moderator determined who would first answer the other 32 questions. In five of these six questions Senator Clinton was either addressed or acknowledged in the video. Three questions were directed to Senator Clinton whereas Senator Obama and Senator Clinton were both addressed in one question. As was just mentioned, Congressman Kucinich was asked about these two senators in another question. The only other question not specifically addressing Senator Clinton was directed to Senator Gravel who was asked to defend a previous statement. During the debate Senator Obama responded to 17 questions, more than any other candidate in either debate. Senator Clinton and Senator Edwards trailed at 13 and 12 responses respectively. The polls showed Senator Biden, Congressman Kucinich, and Senator Gravel in single digits at the time of the debate. Not surprisingly, these candidates responded to the fewest questions.

At the time of the Republican debate Mayor Giuliani was shown leading public opinion polls (Gallup Poll, 2007, November; ARG, 2007, November). Throughout the Republican debate the former mayor received more attention than any other Republican candidate. This was made apparent in four ways: first, of the seven video questions where questioners directed their inquiries to specific Republican candidates, four of these questions indicated their question was for Mayor Giuliani. Of the eight Republican candidates, only Mayor Giuliani (4 questions), Governor Huckabee (1 question), and Congressman Paul (2 questions) received direct questions asking for greater clarification on prior statements, positions, or actions. In all other instances the moderator determined who would answer the question. Second, not only did the debate open with a question directed to Mayor Giuliani, but it closed on a light note from a questioner who asked him if he was a Red Sox or a Yankees fan. Third, the former mayor of New York was the first candidate to respond to nearly a third of the questions (9 questions). Finally, Mayor Giuliani responded to 13 questions, more than any other candidate in the Republican debate. Governor Romney, Senator McCain, and Senator Thompson each trailed with 12, 11, and 10 responses respectively.

Discussion

In an age of mass communication, most experiences with politicians are mediated through communication technologies such as televisions, radios, computers, or cell phones. As indicated in this analysis, interparty presidential debates using new media offer insight into issues that resonate more with journalists and less with the most important issues on the minds of Americans. The questions CNN and YouTube chose to include in the debate, as well as the candidates that received the most attention, highlights journalists' continued emphasis and reliance on the horse race metaphor, typically used by journalists in political campaign coverage (Broh, 1980). Using this metaphor, the main focus of the debates then becomes the candidates' image, personality, and strategy.

Video questioners' use of professional production elements were not a key factor in the questions CNN and YouTube chose to include in the debates. With only one third of the questions providing any variation on how the questions were asked, those questions engaging a more novel format are more likely to be remembered by audiences. But the minimal number of highly creative or professionally-produced questions demonstrates that most videos were not necessarily chosen for their unique format or production style.

The topics and issues addressed in debate questions were found to reflect the self-interests of the questioners. Although video submitters were encouraged to "be personal," the inclusion of questions of self-interest creates the illusion that politicians are responsible for the questioner's individual problems. Focusing on issues of self-importance also has the potential to inflate perceptions of the problem's importance. Unfortunately, the inclusion of questions of this nature undermines the complexity of issues candidates could have addressed. Additionally, questions on topics of little or no importance to the presidency may acquaint us with the politician him or herself, showcasing the candidate's character and demonstrating how he or she can diplomatically handle pressure.

Questions that reflected the broader more imminent issues on the minds of Americans were not evident in the debate. Dedicating a substantial number of questions to issues like abortion, gay rights, and race relations underscores the importance the media, opposed to the public, places on these issues. In addition, as concern over various issues grew, these issues were not adequately addressed. Even on questions that touched on the most important issues identified by Gallup, debate questions were not necessarily of substantive value and they often centered on topics of self-importance. In their book on the evolution of presidential debates, Minow and LaMay (2008) recommend that televised debates become "less formal and more spontaneous—without canned speeches, and with opportunities for the candidates to question one another and for citizens to question candidates directly" (p. 105). The YouTube questions are certainly less formal than traditional debates and require candidates to sway from scripted campaign speeches, but the topics are not highly relevant or informative on issues of public concern. Does the viewing public need to know if candidates have talked to their kids about sex education, what their gun collection looks like, or if the next president's kids will go to public or private school? Ultimately, questions posed to candidates in the CNN/YouTube debates are more likely to help voters become better acquainted with the personal lives of candidates and allow candidates to dispel rumors and respond to political cynicism. They are also more revealing of the questioners self-interests rather than those issues truly on the minds of Americans. Although these questions are not positioned to help voters understand what presidential candidates will do in the White House, what policies they will change, or the plans and experience they have to help in times of war or economic crises, it could be said that their value lies in helping Americans become better acquainted with the politician they will look to for leadership during the next four years. However, further analysis of all video submissions is needed to understand the full gate-keeping and agenda-setting role performed by journalists in the selection of video questions.

Although the debate agenda did not mirror the public agenda, election polls did reflect the most important candidates in the debate. Interestingly enough, the leading candidates in each partisan race received the most attention. Those watching the debates were made aware that Senator Clinton and Senator Obama were the most important candidates to watch whereas the Republicans were told Mayor Giuliani was the preferred candidate. The news media's reliance on the horse race metaphor is therefore evident in their emphasis on the candidates ahead in the polls (Broh, 1980).

New media have contributed to the debate process by empowering individuals who traditionally viewed or listened to debates with the ability to voice views or concerns on topics salient to them. By encouraging active voter participation in political campaigns, new media technologies are eroding barriers that have traditionally made political debates only a spectator sport. Although citizen-generated debate questions were made available to all YouTube users, by selecting those questions actually posed to candidates, it is still the media we rely upon to perform the gate-keeping and agenda-setting functions that tell viewers what and how to think about the issues. But as demonstrated during the 2008 election cycle, new media have indeed provided a viable outlet where voters can air their ideas for a viewing public.

References

American Research Group (ARG) (2007, July). *USA election polls*. Retrieved December 1, 2008, from www.usaelectionpolls.com/2008/polls/American-Research-Group-National-Polls-July-2007.html.

American Research Group (ARG) (2007, November). *USA election polls*. Retrieved December 1, 2008, from www.usaelectionpolls.com/2008/polls/American-Research-Group-National-Polls-November-2007.html.

Becker, L., & McCombs, M. E. (1978). The role of the press in determining voter reaction to presidential primaries. *Human Communication Research, 4*, 301–307.

Beniger, J. R. (1978). Media content as social indicators: The Greenfield index of agenda-setting. *Communication Research, 5*, 437.

Benoit, W. L., Stein, K. A., & Hansen, G. J. (2004). Newspaper coverage of presidential debates. *Argumentation and Advocacy, 41*, 17–27.

Broh, C. A. (1980). Horse-race journalism: Reporting the polls in the 1976 presidential election. *Public Opinion Quarterly, 44*, 514–529.

Carlin, D. B., Morris, E., & Smith, S. (2001). The influence of format and questions on candidates' strategic argument choices in the 2000 presidential debates. *American Behavioral Scientist, 44*, 2196–2218.

Carlin, D. B., Schill, D., Levasseur, D. G., & King, A. S. (2005). The post 9/11 public sphere: Citizen talk about the 2004 presidential debates. *Rhetoric & Public Affairs, 8*(4), 617–638.

Dahlberg, L. (2007). The internet, deliberative democracy, and power: Radicalizing the public sphere. *International Journal of Media and Cultural Politics, 3*(1), 47–64.

Gallup Poll. (2007, July). *USA election polls*. Retrieved December 1, 2008, from www.usaelectionpolls.com/2008/polls/Gallup-National-Polls-July-2007.html.

Gallup Poll (2007, November). *USA election polls*. Retrieved December 1, 2008, from www.usaelectionpolls.com/2008/polls/Gallup-National-Polls-November-2007.html.

Gopoian, J. D. (1982). Issue preferences and candidate choice in presidential primaries. *American Journal of Political Science, 26*, 524–546.

Gough, P. J. (2007, July 25). CNN's YouTube debate draws impressive ratings. *Reuters*. Retrieved December 1, 2008, from www.reuters.com/article/technology News/idUSN2425835220070725.

Guthrie, M. (2008, January 22). CNN's Democratic S.C. Debate Sets Cable News Record. *Broadcasting & Cable*. Retrieved September 27, 2010, from www. broadcastingcable.com/article/112101-CNN_s_Democratic_S_C_Debate_Sets_ Cable_News_Record.php.

Hart, R. P., & Jarvis, S. E. (1997). Format debate: Forms, styles, and media. *American Behavioral Scientist, 40*(8) 1095–1122.

Jarmin, J. W. (2005). Political affiliation and presidential debates. *American Behavioral Scientist, 49*(2), 229–242.

McCombs, M., & Reynolds, A. (2002). News influence on our pictures of the world. In J. Bryant, & D. Zillmann (Eds.), *Media effects: Advances in theory and research* (2nd Ed.). Mahwah, New Jersey: Lawrence Erlbaum Associates, pp. 1–18.

McCombs, M., & Reynolds, A. (2009). How the news shapes our civic agenda. In J. Bryant, & M. B. Oliver (Eds.), *Media effects: Advances in theory and research* (3rd Ed.). New York: Routledge, pp. 1–16.

McCombs, M., & Shaw, D. L. (1972). The agenda-setting function of mass media. *Public Opinion Quarterly, 36*, 176–187.

Minow, N. N., & LaMay, C. L. (2008). *Inside the presidential debates: Their improbable past and promising future*. Chicago: University of Chicago Press.

Newport, F. (2008, January 11). Americans: Economic issues country's top problem today. *Gallup News Service*. Retrieved September 27, 2010, from www.gallup.com/poll/103699/Americans-Economic-Issues-Countrys-Top-Problem-Today.aspx#2.

Pfau, M. (1987). The influence of intraparty political debates on candidate preferences. *Communication Research, 14*(6), 687–697.

Racine Group. (2002). White paper on televised political campaign debates. *Argumentation and Advocacy, 38*, 199–218.

Rainie, L. (2008, January 9). Pew internet project data memo: Video sharing websites. *Pew Internet & American Life Project*. Retrieved December 1, 2008, from http://pewinternet.org/PPF/r/232/report_display.asp.

Submission criteria: Democrat (2008a). *YouTube.com*. Retrieved June 16, 2008, from www.youtube.com/contest/DemocraticDebate.

Submission criteria: Republican (2008b). *YouTube.com*. Retrieved June 16, 2008, from www.youtube.com/contest/RepublicanDebate.

Tewksbury, D., & Scheufele, D. A. (2009). News framing theory and research. In J. Bryant & M. B. Oliver (Eds.), *Media effects: Advances in theory and research* (3rd Ed.). New York: Routledge, pp. 1–16.

Trent, J. S., & Friedenberg, R. V. (2007). *Political campaign communication: Principles and practices* (6th Ed.). Lanham, MD: Rowman & Littlefield.

Chapter 10

The Biden–Palin 2008 Vice Presidential Debate

An Examination of Gender and Candidate Issue Expertise

Mitchell S. McKinney and Mary C. Banwart

While the term "historic" is frequently invoked to characterize the 2008 presidential election—used to describe Hillary Clinton's primary candidacy as well as Barack Obama's nomination and eventual election—another historic element of the '08 presidential race involved the vice-presidential candidacy of Republican nominee Sarah Palin. Following Geraldine Ferraro's vice-presidential candidacy in 1984, Palin is only the second female candidate to be included on a major-party national ticket. Adding to the historic nature of the 2008 campaign was the vice-presidential debate between Palin and her Democratic opponent Joe Biden. Indeed, approximately 70 million viewers tuned in to watch the Biden *v.* Palin debate, which is the only instance in presidential debate history that a vice-presidential debate encounter attracted more viewers than a debate series' presidential exchanges. The Biden–Palin debate now holds the record as the second-highest-viewed debate in all of televised presidential debate history, surpassed only by the nearly 81 million viewers who tuned in just days before the 1980 election to watch Jimmy Carter and Ronald Reagan in their single debate exchange.[1]

So why would the Palin and Biden vice-presidential debate draw more interest—something that has never happened before in presidential campaign history—than those of their "top of the ticket" running-mates John McCain and Barack Obama? In short, it was Sarah Palin—rather than Joe Biden—who attracted many of the millions of viewers to their television sets on the evening of October 2, 2008, to watch the vice-presidential candidates spar, tuning in especially to see how Palin would perform—if she would embarrass herself—in prime time. From the time that John McCain made his surprise announcement of the little-known governor of Alaska as his running mate on August 29, 2008, media attention focused on Sarah Palin was dominant. The Pew Project for Excellence in Journalism reported that the week of September 1–7, the week following the Palin announcement and the week of the Republican National Convention, was the very first time in the three months since both presidential nominees declared victory at the end of their primary campaigns that more news coverage was focused on the John McCain campaign than on Barack Obama (Jurkowitz, 2008). This news attention was focused mainly on Sarah Palin who was the dominant feature of 60 percent of all campaign stories during the week following the announcement, eclipsing both her party's own presidential nominee John McCain and Barack Obama who was the dominant focus of only 22 percent of the news stories. Overall, in the five-week period that spanned the time of Palin's announcement until just after the vice-presidential debate, from among the four campaign principals (Obama–Biden, McCain–Palin) Sarah Palin won the race for most media exposure during two of these weeks and eclipsed her own presidential running mate in yet a third week. Throughout this entire period, poor Joseph Biden received the least media attention of any of the candidates, with Palin garnering more than three times the total news coverage of her vice-presidential competitor.[2]

While the media's reporting of Palin's inclusion on the Republican ticket was at first mostly positive, at least during the few days of the Republican national convention, the tone and substance of Palin's news coverage quickly turned negative. Specifically, the focus on Palin's family, including her unmarried and pregnant daughter, as well as Palin's not-so-stellar interviews first with ABC news anchor Charles Gibson and then with CBS anchor Katie Couric just days before the VP debate, and even the fall campaign's "lipstick on a pig" controversy,[3] all received more attention by the media than did Palin's public record as Alaska Governor (*Winning the media campaign*, 2008). Overall, while the magnitude of Palin's positive versus negative media coverage is debated, sources regarded as both "liberal" and "conservative" leaning all agree Palin received much more negative than positive media attention. Whatever the exact amount of negative to positive Palin coverage, the Pew analysis (*Winning the media campaign*, 2008) shows that Palin's negative coverage continued to increase throughout the month of September, reaching its peak in the week leading up to the October 2 vice-presidential debate.

Thus, expectations were set for Sarah Palin's historic and much anticipated debate appearance. So, how did debate viewers respond to Palin—and Biden's—debate performance? Our study addresses two specific goals. First, we examine how exposure to the vice-presidential debate affected viewers' post-debate evaluations of the two candidates. We also examine how debate viewers evaluated Sarah Palin's and Joe Biden's issue competencies, particularly the two candidates' perceived expertise and expressed concern for stereotypical masculine (military/economic) and feminine (compassion/women's) issues.

To better understand how debate viewers evaluated the two candidates' issue competencies, our study design combines analysis of national survey data with computerized measurement technology. As a point of comparison with and illumination of our survey data, 27 respondents viewed the debate while using a computerized measurement system that charted debate viewers' second-by-second reactions to the candidates' debate dialogue. While our survey data provides an assessment of the effects of debate exposure in a much more holistic fashion, the second-by-second computerized response measurement allows researchers to determine which specific candidate responses and issue appeals were evaluated highest by debate viewers.

Review of Literature

With the exception of 1960 and 1980, a single vice-presidential debate has been included as part of each televised general-election presidential debate series. Although a small number of studies have examined these vice-presidential exchanges (e.g., Beck, 1996; Drew & Weaver, 1991; Holbrook, 1994, 1996; Kay & Borchers, 1994; Lemert, 1993; Tonn, 1994), the "undercard" debates have clearly received much less attention than their presidential counterparts. Carlin and Bicak (1993) provide a concise summary of vice-presidential debate research, finding the VP debates have unique rhetorical exigencies that demand different candidate message strategies than those used in presidential debates.

In the current study, we seek to examine how citizens' assessments of Sarah Palin and Joe Biden may be altered from viewing the candidates' debate performances. Here, we regard citizens' pre-debate assessments as a measure of expectations that have been formed for each of the candidates prior to the debate event. We are aware of at least one other study (Pfau, 1987) that explores reactions to candidates' debate performances by examining how candidates violate viewers' pre-debate expectations— including both positive and negative violations. Applying Burgoon and Miller's (1985) expectancy theory to a 1984 Democratic primary debate, Pfau (1987, p. 694) found "as predicted by expectancy theory, positive changes in attitudes toward [Jesse] Jackson were based on viewer perception of a positive violation of expectations, and negative changes toward [Gary] Hart were the result of viewer perception of a negative violation of expectations." Similarly, Yawn, Ellsworth, Beatty, and Kahn (1998) examined a 1996 Arizona Republican primary debate, and although their study was not couched in formal expectancy theory, Yawn et al. (1998, p. 155) found "that changes in [candidate] viability, changes in electability, as well as differences between expected and actual debate performance influenced the vote preferences of audience members." Our application of expectancy theory to the Palin–Biden VP debate examines if viewers' pre-debate evaluations or expectations of the two candidates are either confirmed or called into question by their actual debate performances, leading viewers to maintain their pre-debate evaluations (if expectations are confirmed, no significant difference will occur in candidate evaluations after debate exposure), or viewers will alter their pre-debate candidate assessments either positively (if pre-debate expectations are exceeded) or negatively (if pre-debate expectations are violated or not confirmed).

Our first question, regarding viewers' overall evaluation of the two candidates, is also explored based on respondents' sex (female or male) and party affiliation (Democrat, Republican, or Independent) as these key variables may well influence evaluations of the two candidates:

RQ_1:   How does exposure to the vice presidential debate affect viewers' evaluations of Sarah Palin and Joe Biden?

RQ_{1a}:   Do males differ significantly in their evaluations of Sarah Palin and Joe Biden before and after viewing the vice presidential debate?

RQ_{1b}:   Do females differ significantly in their evaluations of Sarah Palin and Joe Biden before and after viewing the vice presidential debate?

RQ_{1c}:   How does party affiliation (including Democrat, Republican, Independent) affect viewers' evaluations of Sarah Palin and Joe Biden's debate performance?

Beyond the few studies of the 1984 George H. W. Bush and Geraldine Ferraro vice-presidential debate (e.g., Hardy-Short, 1986; Rosenberg & Elliott, 1987; Shields & MacDowell, 1987; Sullivan, 1989; Trent, 1994), very little campaign debate research exists that incorporates candidate gender as a central variable of analysis. With female candidates only twice appearing on the presidential-level debate stage—first Ferraro in 1984 and then Palin in 2008—the campaign debate scholarship that has examined the performance of female candidates has either focused on presidential primary debates (e.g., McKinney, Davis, & Delbert, 2009), or lower-level debates that include female candidates engaged in U.S. Senate, House, or gubernatorial debates (e.g., Banwart & McKinney, 2005; Edelsky & Adams, 1990; Hill, 2005). In the current study, our analysis of candidate gender is guided by the work of Huddy and Terkildsen (1993) whose previous research found that gender-belief stereotypes affect expectations of female and male candidates' areas of perceived knowledge and public policy concerns. Our examination of debate viewers' assessments of Palin and Biden's issue expertise is also explored based on respondents' sex (female or male) and party affiliation (Democrat, Republican, or Independent) as these key variables may well influence evaluations of the two candidates issue competencies. The following questions guide our analysis of the vice presidential candidates' issue expertise:

RQ_2: How does exposure to the vice presidential debate affect viewers' assessments of Sarah Palin and Joe Biden's issue expertise?

RQ_{2a}: Do males differ significantly in their evaluations of Sarah Palin and Joe Biden's issue expertise before and after viewing the vice presidential debate?

RQ_{2b}: Do females differ significantly in their evaluations of Sarah Palin and Joe Biden's issue expertise before and after viewing the vice presidential debate?

RQ_{2c}: How does party affiliation (including Democrat, Republican, Independent) affect viewers' evaluations of Sarah Palin and Joe Biden's issue expertise?

Finally, analysis of a sub-set of our study participants who used computerized measurement technology while watching the debate allowed us to evaluate second-by-second responses to the candidates' debate dialogue, assessing reactions to the candidates' specific arguments and issue appeals. Here, we were particularly interested in identifying the top-rated issue appeals for both Palin and Biden, and thus posited a final research question:

RQ_3: Which specific issue appeals made by Sarah Palin and Joe Biden were evaluated most positively during the debate?

Method

Sample

Survey Responses: For this study a total of 515 participants from 11 locations throughout the nation viewed the vice-presidential debate on October 2, 2008.[4] The 90-minute debate between Alaska Governor Sarah Palin and Delaware Senator Joe Biden was held at Washington University in St. Louis, Missouri, and was broadcast nationally by various networks. Gwen Ifill, of PBS's *NewsHour with Jim Lehrer* and *Washington Week*, served as the sole debate moderator and questioner. Our study respondents included 286 (55 percent) females and 229 (45 percent) males. Respondent party identification was distributed as follows: 39 percent ($n = 203$) Democrat, 28 percent ($n = 146$) Republican, and 32 percent ($n = 166$) Independent/other. The mean age of the respondents was 21 ($SD = 4.59$), with respondents ranging in age from 18 to 57. Among the respondents, 64 percent ($n = 330$) identified as Caucasian, 16 percent ($n = 80$) as Spanish or Hispanic, 7 percent ($n = 37$) as African-American, 6 percent ($n = 31$) as multi-racial/mixed-race, and 5 percent ($n = 28$) as Asian or Pacific Islander.

Computerized Responses: In addition to the survey respondents, 27 study participants (11 females, 16 males) drawn from the overall sample provided feedback throughout the entirety of the debate with the use of a computerized dial measurement system. Each of these participants was provided with a hand-held device on which they continuously registered their opinions from 1 (very negative) to 100 (very positive) to what each of the candidates were saying. The dials were connected to one central computer that recorded a numerical response per second for each participant. Data points corresponding to each candidate's responses were isolated and mean scores were calculated for each discrete response segment. Because we were interested in respondents' evaluations of the candidates' issue discussions, we eliminated responses to opening and closing statements from our analysis.

Procedures

The survey respondents for this study were recruited from basic communication and political science courses at the participating universities and received credit for taking part in this research. Their participation was voluntary and anonymous. In each session, the respondents completed a pre-test questionnaire, watched the debate in real time without media commentary either before or after, and immediately following the debate completed a post-test questionnaire. The pre-test questionnaire included demographic items, questions designed to measure respondent's general evaluations of the two candidates, as well as respondents' perceptions of the candidates' ability to handle various issues. The post-test questionnaire included repeat measures of candidate evaluation, and questions relating to the candidates' issue expertise.

Measures

Debate viewers' overall evaluation of the two candidates was measured with a "feeling thermometer" scale used by the National Election Studies to measure candidate favorability (Rosenstone, Kinder, Miller, & the National Election Studies, 1997). Participants were asked to indicate their overall feelings toward each candidate using the standard 0 to 100 feeling thermometer before viewing the debate and again after viewing the debate. A score between 0 and 49 indicates unfavorable feelings, 50 degrees is indicative of a neutral evaluation, and scores ranging from 51 to 100 degrees demonstrates a favorable evaluation of the candidates.

To assess viewers' evaluation of the two candidates' issue abilities, we adapted a nine-item scale measuring stereotypic expectations of female and male candidates' issue expertise developed by Huddy and Terkildsen (1993). These researchers found that gender-belief stereotypes affect expectations of female and male candidates' areas of perceived knowledge and public policy concern. The nine-item issue scale examines issue competencies on military/economic issues and compassion/women's issues. The military/economic issue items asked how well the candidate would handle a military crisis, reduce the budget deficit, deal with leaders in business and industry, and handle the current economic crisis. Compassion/women's issues asked how the candidate would deal with reducing the wage gap between men and women, address children's health care, assist the poor, improve the welfare of children, and deal with the abortion controversy. Participants' perceptions of the candidates' ability to handle the various issues were measured both before and after debate exposure by asking respondents, "Based on what you know about the Vice-Presidential nominees, how well would each handle the following issues." Responses ranged from 1 ("not very well") to 5 ("very well"). Cronbach's alpha reliabilities were acceptable for both candidates on each dimension of this scale.[5]

Analysis

This study's research questions were examined using one-way repeated measures ANOVAs to compare the pre-test and post-test mean scores of the feeling thermometer, and evaluation of the candidates' issue expertise. Paired samples t-tests were conducted as follow up tests for any significant ANOVAs; the Holm's sequential Bonferroni procedure was used to control for familywise error rates across significant pairwise comparisons at the .05 level.

Results

Candidate Evaluation

To respond to the first set of research questions regarding candidate evaluation, one-way within subjects repeated measures ANOVAs were used; the means and standard deviations for each question are reported in Table 10.1. Our first research question asked if exposure to the vice-presidential debate would change respondents' overall evaluation of the two candidates. Mauchly's test indicated that the assumption of sphericity had been violated ($\chi^2 = 1012.18$, $p < .05$), therefore degrees of freedom were corrected using Greenhouse-Geisser estimates of sphericity ($\epsilon = .46$). The results indicated a significant viewing effect, $F(1.38, 709.82) = 60.69$, $p < .001$, multivariate $\eta^2 = .12$. Follow-up paired sample t-tests indicated that Biden's evaluation after respondents viewed the debate was significantly higher ($M = 57.82$, $SD = 28.77$) than before respondents viewed the debate ($M = 49.24$, $SD = 28.14$), $t(514) = 10.81$, $p < .001$. Palin's evaluation after respondents viewed the debate was also significantly higher ($M = 41.76$, $SD = 32.95$) than before respondents viewed the debate ($M = 37.43$, $SD = 32.78$), $t(514) = 5.54$, $p < .001$.

We were next interested in whether males differed significantly in their evaluations of the candidates before and after viewing the debate (RQ1a). Based on Mauchly's test ($\chi^2 = 390.26$, $p < .05$) degrees of freedom were corrected using Greenhouse-Geisser estimates of sphericity ($\epsilon = .48$). The results indicated a significant viewing effect, $F(1.45, 330.93) = 30.22$, $p < .001$, multivariate $\eta^2 = .12$. Follow-up paired sample t-tests indicated that Biden's evaluation after males viewed the debate was significantly higher ($M = 54.66$, $SD = 28.62$) than before males viewed the debate ($M = 47.66$, $SD = 27.81$), $t(228) = 6.08$, $p < .001$. Palin's evaluation after males viewed the debate was also significantly higher ($M = 38.48$, $SD = 31.60$) than before males viewed the debate ($M = 35.82$, $SD = 31.35$), $t(228) = 2.29$, $p = .023$.

The next research question (RQ1b) asked whether females differed significantly in their evaluations of the candidates before and after viewing the debate. Degrees of freedom were corrected based on Mauchly's test ($\chi^2 = 614.79$, $p < .05$), using Greenhouse-Geisser estimates of sphericity ($\epsilon = .45$). The results indicated a significant viewing effect, $F(1.34, 381.12) = 31.76$, $p < .001$, multivariate $\eta^2 = .10$. Follow-up paired sample t-tests also indicated that Biden's evaluation after females viewed the debate was significantly higher ($M = 60.35$, $SD = 28.68$) than before females viewed the debate ($M = 50.51$, $SD = 28.39$), $t(285) = 9.05$, $p < .001$. And, similar to male respondents, Palin's evaluation after females viewed the debate was significantly higher ($M = 44.38$, $SD = 33.82$) than before females viewed the debate ($M = 38.71$, $SD = 33.88$), $t(285) = 5.39$, $p < .001$.

RQ1c asked whether Biden and Palin's evaluations were influenced by respondents' party identification (RQ1c). Degrees of freedom were again

Table 10.1 Evaluation of Palin and Biden Before and After Debate

Candidate evaluation	Joe Biden			Sarah Palin		
	Pre-test	Post-test	Net-change	Pre-test	Post-test	Net-change
	M			*M*		
Overall evaluation	49.24	57.82	8.58***	37.43	41.76	4.33***
Females	50.51	60.35	9.84***	38.71	44.38	5.67***
Males	47.66	54.66	7.00***	35.82	38.48	2.66*
Democrats	49.85	59.09	11.90***	20.36	24.75	4.39***
Republicans	47.40	53.62	6.22***	72.43	74.90	2.47
Independents	50.12	59.96	9.84***	27.51	33.40	5.89***

Note: Higher feeling thermometer scores are more positive.
*$p < .05$; **$p < .01$; ***$p < .001$.

corrected based on Mauchly's test (χ^2 = 723.81, p < .05), using Greenhouse-Geisser estimates of sphericity (ϵ = .52). A main effect emerged for party identification, $F(3.12, 798.91)$ = 96.14, p < .001, multivariate η^2 = .27. Paired samples t-tests indicated that Democrats rated Biden more favorably after viewing the debate than before, $t(202)$ = 7.07, p < .001; and Democrats also rated Palin more favorably after debate viewing, $t(202)$ = 7.07, p < .001. While Republicans viewed Biden significantly more favorably after viewing the debate than before, $t(145)$ = 4.34, p < .001, their evaluations of Palin did not differ based on debate viewing. Independent/other respondents evaluated Biden more favorably after viewing the debate, $t(165)$ = 7.15, p < .001, and also viewed Palin more favorably after debate viewing, $t(165)$ = 3.95, p < .001.

Table 10.2 Evaluation of Biden and Palin's Issue Expertise Before and After Debate

Issue	Joe Biden			Sarah Palin		
	Pre-test	Post-test	Net-change	Pre-test	Post-test	Net-change
	M			M		
Military/economic issues	3.56	4.01	.45***	2.75	2.99	.24***
Compassion/women's issues	3.42	3.85	.43***	3.09	3.15	.06*
Male respondents:						
Military/economic issues	3.56	3.99	.43***	2.70	2.88	.18***
Compassion/women's issues	3.41	3.84	.43***	2.97	2.99	.02
Female respondents:						
Military/economic issues	3.56	4.03	.47***	2.79	3.08	.29***
Compassion/women's issues	3.43	3.86	.43***	3.19	3.28	.09**
Democrat respondents:						
Military/economic issues	3.91	4.45	.54***	2.28	2.42	.14**
Compassion/women's issues	3.78	4.22	.44***	2.74	2.75	.01
Republican respondents:						
Military/economic issues	3.08	3.40	.32***	3.64	4.00	.36***
Compassion/women's issues	2.99	3.40	.41***	3.88	4.00	.12*
Independent respondents:						
Military/economic issues	3.56	4.02	.46***	2.53	2.79	.26***
Compassion/women's issues	3.36	3.81	.45***	2.84	2.89	.05

Note: Scores ranged from 5 ("very well") to 1 ("not very well").
*p < .05; **p < .01; ***p < .001.

Candidate Issue Expertise

Our second research question asked how exposure to the vice-presidential debate affected viewers' assessments of Sarah Palin's and Joe Biden's issue expertise. Candidates were evaluated on two issue dimensions, military/economic issues and compassion/women's issues, prior to respondents' debate viewing and again after debate viewing. In order to answer this research question we conducted two separate analyses. We first conducted a one-way within subjects repeated measures ANOVA, with the dependent variable being evaluations of candidate issue expertise before and after debate viewing (see Table 10.2 for means and standard deviations). We first examined evaluations of military/economic issues; because Mauchly's test indicated that the assumption of sphericity had been violated ($\chi^2 = 972.94$, $p < .05$), degrees of freedom were corrected using Greenhouse-Geisser estimates of sphericity ($\epsilon = .47$). The results indicated a significant viewing effect, $F(1.40, 720.84) = 175.33$, $p < .001$, multivariate $\eta^2 = .26$. Follow-up paired sample t-tests indicated that respondents rated Biden's military/economic expertise significantly higher after debate viewing, $t(514) = 15.04$, $p < .001$, and that they also rated Palin's military/economic issue expertise significantly higher after viewing the debate, $t(514) = 7.72$, $p < .001$.

We next examined the respondents' evaluations of the candidates' compassion/women's issue expertise. Based on Mauchly's test ($\chi^2 = 1039.66$, $p < .05$) we corrected degrees of freedom using Greenhouse-Geisser estimates of sphericity ($\epsilon = .46$). The results indicated a significant viewing effect, $F(1.38, 707.36) = 76.87$, $p < .001$, multivariate $\eta^2 = .13$. Follow-up paired sample t-tests indicated that respondents rated Biden's compassion/women's expertise significantly higher after debate viewing, $t(514) = 16.2$, $p < .001$, and also rated Palin's expertise higher on compassion/women's issues after the debate, $t(514) = 2.06$, $p = .04$.

Males' Evaluation of Candidate Issue Expertise: We were next interested in whether males differed significantly in their evaluations of the candidates' issue expertise before and after viewing the debate (RQ2a). Degrees of freedom were corrected using Greenhouse-Geisser estimates of sphericity ($\epsilon = .47$; Mauchly's test: $\chi^2 = 428.47$, $p < .05$). The results indicated a significant viewing effect, $F(1.41, 321.30) = 98.77$, $p < .001$, multivariate $\eta^2 = .30$. Follow-up paired sample t-tests indicated that males evaluated Biden significantly higher, $t(228) = 10.18$, $p < .001$, and Palin significantly higher, $t(228) = 3.93$, $p < .001$, on military/economic expertise after viewing the debate.

We then tested male responses to the candidates' compassion/women's issue expertise, again correcting degrees of freedom using Greenhouse-Geisser estimates of sphericity ($\epsilon = .47$; Mauchly's test: $\chi^2 = 424.35$, $p < .05$). The results indicated a significant viewing effect, $F(1.42, 323.96) =$

52.39, $p < .001$, multivariate $\eta^2 = .19$. Follow-up paired sample t-tests indicated that while males evaluated Biden significantly higher on compassion/women's issue expertise after viewing the debate, $t(228) = 11.01$, $p < .001$, they did not rate Palin significantly higher or lower on compassion/women's issues following their debate viewing.

Females' Evaluation of Candidate Issue Expertise: Research Question 2b asked whether females differed significantly in their evaluations of the candidates' issue expertise before and after viewing the debate (RQ2b). Again we used one-way within subjects repeated measures ANOVAs to test each set of issues. When testing military/economic issue expertise, Greenhouse-Geisser estimates of sphericity were used to correct degrees of freedom ($\epsilon = .46$; Mauchly's test: $\chi^2 = 543.26$, $p < .05$). The results indicated a significant viewing effect, $F(1.40, 397.95) = 81.74$, $p < .001$, multivariate $\eta^2 = .22$. Follow-up paired sample t-tests indicated that females evaluated both Biden, $t(285) = 11.13$, $p < .001$, and Palin, $t(285) = 6.81$, $p < .001$, significantly higher on military/economic expertise after debate viewing.

When testing compassion/women's issue expertise evaluations, we again used Greenhouse-Geisser estimates of sphericity to correct degrees of freedom ($\epsilon = .45$; Mauchly's test: $\chi^2 = 608.05$, $p < .05$). The results indicated a significant viewing effect, $F(1.35, 384.14) = 29.98$, $p < .001$, multivariate $\eta^2 = .10$. Follow-up paired sample t-tests indicated that females evaluated both Biden, $t(285) = 11.88$, $p < .001$, and Palin, $t(285) = 2.58$, $p = .010$, significantly higher on compassion/women's expertise after debate viewing.

Party Affiliation and Evaluation of Candidate Issue Expertise: The next research question asked whether Biden and Palin's issue expertise evaluations were influenced by respondents' party identification (RQ2c). Using Greenhouse-Geisser estimates of sphericity we corrected degrees of freedom ($\epsilon = .56$; Mauchly's test: $\chi^2 = 602.94$, $p < .05$) to first test military/economic issue evaluations. A main effect emerged for party identification, $F(3.34, 856.01) = 133.62$, $p < .001$, multivariate $\eta^2 = .34$.

Six paired samples t-tests were conducted to follow up on the significant main effect for party identification on military/economic expertise evaluations (see Table 10. 2). The results indicated that Democrats rated both Biden, $t(202) = 11.72$, $p < .001$, and Palin, $t(202) = 2.77$, $p = .006$, significantly higher on military/economic issue expertise after viewing the debate. After debate viewing Republican respondents also rated Biden, $t(145) = 5.61$, $p < .001$, and Palin, $t(145) = 6.50$, $p < .001$, significantly higher on military/economic issue expertise. Finally, as with respondents from the two major parties, Independent/other respondents evaluated Biden, $t(165) = 8.58$, $p < .001$, and Palin, $t(165) = 4.66$, $p < .001$, significantly higher on this issue set after debate viewing.

We next tested evaluations of the candidates on their compassion/ women's issue expertise, and again used Greenhouse-Geisser estimates of sphericity to correct degrees of freedom (ϵ = .52; Mauchly's test: χ^2 = 734.75, p < .05). A main effect emerged for party identification, $F(3.13, 801.27)$ = 101.48, p < .001, multivariate η^2 = .28.

Six paired samples t-tests were conducted to follow up on the significant main effect for party identification on compassion/women's issue expertise evaluations (see Table 10.2). The results indicated that while Democrats did not rate Palin differently on compassion/women's issue expertise based on debate viewing, they did rate Biden significantly higher on this issue set following the debate, $t(202)$ = 10.15, p < .001. On the other hand, Republican respondents rated both Biden, $t(145)$ = 7.73, p < .001, and Palin, $t(145)$ = 2.53, p = .012, significantly higher on compassion/women's expertise following debate viewing. Finally, Independent/other respondents evaluated Biden significantly higher on this issue set after watching the debate, $t(165)$ = 10.14, p < .001, although they did not rate Palin significantly differently.

Moment-by-Moment Candidate Evaluations

In order to respond to RQ3, which asked what issue appeals were viewed most favorably during the actual debate, mean scores were calculated for each candidate's debate responses. An examination was conducted to determine on what issues the candidates were rated the highest through the moment-to-moment dial feedback (see Table 10.3). Here, Joe Biden's highest-rated responses included his attack on Dick Cheney's performance as vice-president and Biden's own interpretation of the vice-presidency, followed by the Obama campaign's position on same-sex benefits, a discussion as to whether Iran or Pakistan poses a greater threat to the U.S., causes of climate change, and a defense of Obama on raising taxes combined with a charge that McCain supported banking industry deregulation. Sarah Palin's highest-rated responses included a brief response that pointed out neither she nor Biden supported gay marriage, followed by a discussion of the Israeli/Palestinian conflict, a defense of John McCain as a military leader, the U.S. military's counterinsurgency strategy in Afghanistan, and whether Iran or Pakistan pose a greater threat to the U.S.

Discussion

The first general conclusion to be drawn from this study's results is that campaign debates do not function as a "zero-sum" game for candidates who debate one another. Unlike the eventual voting decision, debate gains for one candidate do not necessarily come at the expense of another. For

Table 10.3 Moment-by-Moment Evaluations During Vice-Presidential Debate

	M	Debate time
Biden—highest-rated responses:		
Vice-President Cheney/interpretation of the vice-presidency	74.62	1:14:11
Same-sex benefits	71.58	33:45
Iran/Pakistan/who is the greatest threat	67.79	42:39
Causes of climate change	67.75	29:40
Defends Obama on taxes, charges McCain supported deregulation	67.00	11:00
Palin—highest-rated responses:		
Stand on same-sex marriage	56.66	36:28
Israeli/Palestinian conflict	52.52	48:50
Defends McCain, general military	51.26	1:03:34
Military surge, Afghanistan	50.92	57:16
Iran/Pakistan/who is the greatest threat	48.55	44:20

our study's two major measures, for the most part, we see that both Sarah Palin and Joe Biden improved their overall evaluation among debate viewers and also enhanced their perceived issue competencies.

Viewers' overall evaluations of the two candidates—study participants' feeling thermometer scores—showed a significant increase for both candidates following their debate performance. Even though Sarah Palin was able to improve her net evaluation following her debate performance, suggesting she exceeded debate viewers' pre-debate expectations, we certainly find evidence that the pre-debate framing of Palin successfully diminished viewers' expectations for her as her pre-debate evaluation score was substantially lower than Joe Biden's (with Palin pre-debate at 37.43 to Biden's 49.24). While it is also clear, as one would expect, that Palin was viewed much more favorably by Republicans than Democrats (with Republicans assessing Palin at 72.43 pre-debate to Democrats' pre-debate Palin evaluation of 20.36), Democrats still evaluated Sarah Palin significantly higher following her debate performance. Independents' pre- and post-debate Palin evaluation also suggests her debate performance was at least somewhat successful among Independents in helping to diminish the mostly negative frame and low expectations that had been created for her before the debate. While Independent viewers' assessment of Palin was rather low before the debate—yet still not as low as the Democrats—Palin enjoyed her largest net-gain and a significant post-debate increase among Independents (from 27.51 to 33.40), suggesting her debate performance exceeded their pre-debate expectations.

Even more so than Sarah Palin, Joe Biden seemed to have benefited from his debate performance. First, Biden's overall net change from pre- to post-evaluation was nearly twice the size of Palin's net gain (an 8.58 gain for Biden compared to Palin's 4.33 increase). Also, Biden's net change—and a significant increase in each case—was larger than Palin's post-debate net increase among every group (including females, males, Democrats, Republicans, and Independents).

However, when comparing the two candidates' evaluations among the various partisan sub-groups (Democrats, Republicans, and Independents), we find that Republicans felt much more positively about their VP nominee than Democrats felt about their nominee (both before and after debate viewing). While Sarah Palin's post-debate increase among Republicans was not significant (with only a 2.47 net gain), this slight increase must be viewed in light of the rather high pre-debate evaluation Palin received from Republicans (72.43). On the other hand, before they viewed their nominee's debate performance, those identifying as Democrats in this study actually placed Joe Biden *below* the neutral evaluation of 50 degrees (at 49.85). In fact, Biden—both pre- and post-debate—was evaluated *more positively* by Independents than by Democrats (see Table 10.1). One interpretation of party members' evaluations of the two candidates suggest that Republican partisans had a much stronger allegiance to their VP candidate than Democrats felt toward their VP nominee. Yet another interpretation may be that Joe Biden possessed a much stronger appeal to Independent voters than did Sarah Palin. Finally, one might also interpret these data to conclude that Sarah Palin is a much more polarizing figure than Joe Biden. When comparing the two candidates' post-debate evaluations between Democrats and Republicans, we see that partisans' evaluation of Joe Biden is not very far apart (with Democrats evaluating Joe Biden at 59.09 compared to Republicans' 53.62 assessment). There is a very wide gulf, on the other hand, between Republicans' and Democrats' evaluations of Sarah Palin (74.90 Republican assessment vs. the Democrat's 24.75).

In terms of debate viewers' perceptions of the two candidates' issue expertise, specifically the candidates' competency to deal with military/economic issues and also compassion/women's issues, we found that, overall, while both candidates improved their perceived expertise in both policy arenas, Joe Biden's issue competency was bolstered more by his debate performance than was Sarah Palin's perceived expertise. As Table 10.2 reveals, while both candidates received a significant increase in their overall competency assessments for both areas following the debate, Biden's net-change is consistently greater than Palin's net-change across all sub-groups (even among Republican respondents who gave Biden a significant increase in both his military/economic and compassion/women's policy expertise following his debate performance).

Also, our results provide support for Huddy and Terkildsen's (1993) notions of gender-belief stereotypes, where previous research has found that male candidates are typically viewed as being more competent to handle military/economic affairs while female candidates are evaluated more positively on compassion/women's issues. On this front, we find two distinct and opposite patterns regarding debate viewers' evaluations of the two candidates' issue competencies. First, both before and after debate viewing, Joe Biden's perceived credibility to deal with military/economic issues was higher among all groups than his perceived expertise to deal with compassion/women's issues (among Republicans Biden's pre-debate military/economic expertise was also higher than his compassion/women's issue competency, but following a greater net-increase in his compassion/women's issue score his post-debate evaluation in both areas was exactly the same). The pattern of perceived issue competency for Sarah Palin is just the opposite of Joe Biden's. For Palin, both before and after her debate performance, her perceived credibility to deal with compassion/women's issues was higher among all groups than her perceived expertise to deal with military/economic policies (among Republicans Palin's pre-debate compassion/women's issue expertise was also higher than her military/economic issue competency, but following a greater net-increase in her military/economic issue score her post-debate evaluation in both areas was exactly the same).

It is interesting to note, however, that Sarah Palin's debate performance seemed to be much more successful in enhancing her perceived military/economic issue credibility than her expertise in dealing with compassion/women's issues. In fact, her post-debate net increase in issue competency across all sub groups (including male, female, Democrat, Republican, and Independent respondents) was significantly greater for her military/economic issue expertise than for her perceived compassion/women's issue competency (see Table 10.2). Here, our computerized dial responses allow us to better understand exactly where Sarah Palin made her issue expertise gains. As Table 10.3 indicates, four of Sarah Palin's five highest-rated issue appeals during the debate specifically addressed military matters (rather than economic issues), while only one of Joe Biden's highest-rated responses addressed a military issue. As we argue in the next few paragraphs, it appears that Sarah Palin's debate strategy was to downplay compassion/women's issues, while attempting to bolster her expertise in military affairs. This strategy may well have been adopted due to the pre-debate expectations that had been set for both candidates.

Joe Biden's pick as Barack Obama's running mate was attributed largely to his foreign affairs and military knowledge, having served as a long-time member and former chair of the U.S. Senate's foreign relations committee. Sarah Palin, on the other hand, was frequently asked how her service as commander of the Alaska national guard qualified her for possibly serving as our nation's commander-in-chief (Barnes, 2008); and Palin's military *bona fides* were further questioned—and ridiculed—before the debate by her claim, as expressed so powerfully by Tina Fey playing Sarah Palin in a pre-debate *SNL* skit, that "I can see Russia from my house!" Our findings—the combined results of our survey and dial responses—suggest that Sarah Palin was somewhat successful in using her debate performance to enhance her perceived credibility in dealing particularly with military issues.

A closer examination of the two candidates' evaluations in the arena of compassion/women's issues is also warranted. While Sarah Palin did achieve a small increase in her overall compassion/women's issue assessment following the debate, her slight increase on this policy issue dimension is rather conspicuous when compared to Joe Biden's rather large net gain in perceptions of his ability to address compassion/women's issues. In fact, while Biden was awarded a significant post-debate increase by all sub-groups (including Republicans) for his ability to address compassion/women's policies, this was not the case for Palin. While female and Republican respondents overall awarded a significant increase to Palin for her ability to deal with compassion/women's issues following her debate performance, Palin did not achieve significant gains in this issue arena from males overall, Democrats, or Independents. To help explain why Joe Biden may have achieved substantial increases among debate viewers for his perceived compassion/women's issue expertise, much more so than Sarah Palin, we find it helpful to examine the two candidates' actual debate behavior and specific responses in the area of compassion/women's issues. Indeed, our analysis is premised on the assumption that the candidates' debate performances, including their interactions with one another as well as their debate dialogue and arguments, affect viewers' perceptions and attitudes toward the candidates.

When considering potential reasons for changes in the candidates' evaluations regarding compassion/women's issues, we are reminded that study participants' evaluation of this issue area was based on the candidates' ability to address such matters as the wage gap between men and women, children's health care, the overall welfare of children, assistance for the poor, and the controversy over abortion. Throughout the 90-minute debate, while there was no specific discussion of the wage gap between men and women, nor was there any discussion of the abortion issue, the candidates did speak of children in the health care context, discussed promoting the well-being or "welfare" of children, and also touched briefly on assisting the poor and middle-class families (through tax policies). In noting the various ways in which the two candidates touched on the specific issues that relate to compassion/women's policies, it is quite clear that Joe Biden devoted much more attention—and rhetorical force—to compassion/women's issues than did Sarah Palin during the debate. For example, on two different occasions Biden expressed his concern for violence against women, asserting at one point that he "wrote the Violence Against Women Act . . . which John McCain voted against."[6] The only explicit claim made by Sarah Palin regarding "women's" issues was during a discussion of international terrorism (again, an appeal made in the context of military affairs) when she observed that the U.S. must ensure other countries "[have] respect for women's rights."

From the moment of her nomination and throughout the fall campaign, voters frequently saw and learned a great deal about the "hockey mom" Governor of Alaska and her five children. Yet, during her debate with Joe Biden, Sarah Palin seemed to carefully avoid any sort of overt familial appeals or arguments grounded in compassion in relationship to children's issues. In only one response, in which she described her portfolio as John McCain's second-in-command, did Palin make a very indirect reference to the fact that she had a son with Down Syndrome:

> John McCain and I have had good conversations about where I would lead with his agenda, and that is energy independence in America and reform of government overall; and then working with families of children with special needs. That's near and dear to my heart also.

Instead, it was Joe Biden who delivered the most overt appeal relating to compassion and nurturing of children; and his argument was actually framed in somewhat confrontational gendered terms, with Biden directly challenging Palin's apparent advantage in this area:

> Look, I understand what it's like to be a single parent. When my wife and daughter died and my two sons were gravely injured, I understand what it's like as a parent to wonder what it's like if your kid's going to make it . . . But the notion that somehow, because I'm a man, I don't know what it's like to raise two kids alone, I don't know what it's like to have a child you're not sure is going to—is going to make it—I understand. I understand, as well as, with all due respect, the governor or anybody else.

Perhaps even more interesting than his verbal appeal was the manner in which Biden told of his nurturing instincts. As he talked about raising his two kids alone following the death of his wife and daughter, Biden faltered in his delivery when he noted he wasn't sure if his gravely injured son "[was] going to make it," and viewers could tell that he was struggling to hold back tears. For decades, political candidates and leaders have learned the dangers of public emotions and tears (a lesson re-learned by Hillary Clinton in the primary campaign when she *almost* shed a tear). Yet, the results of this study suggest that Biden, with his substantial net-gain in perceptions of his compassion/women's issue expertise, may well have gained from his heartwarming re-telling of his family tragedy and life as a single father (a story that he had repeated numerous times on the campaign stump).

This significant debate moment also illustrates well one of Jamieson's (1988) "double binds" for female leaders. Televised political eloquence provides greater latitude for the adoption of the so-called "feminine style" by male rhetors (employing the expression of nurturing, empathy—even tears—in one's message), while such message strategies are extremely dangerous for the female political rhetor for fear of appearing too emotional or unstable. Specifically in the campaign debate context, the more emoting and nurturing Biden versus the perceptions of a less compassionate Palin seems to confirm Banwart and McKinney's (2005) gendered candidate "debatestyles." In their analysis of mixed-gendered gubernatorial and U.S. Senate campaign debates, Banwart and McKinney found that when female and male candidates meet face-to-face on the debate stage, both seem mindful of gendered stereotypes and approach their debate task by generating a dialogue of "gendered adaptiveness" (a style of debate argumentation in which female candidates incorporate typically masculine attributes and appeals in their debate dialogue just as frequently as their male opponents; and male candidates incorporate typically feminine attributes in their debate dialogue just a frequently as their female opponents).

Overall, the debate performances of Sarah Palin and Joe Biden—and viewer reactions to the candidates—may best be understood when interpreted through the conceptual lens of gendered adaptiveness. First, Sarah Palin seemed most concerned with addressing perceptions and viewer expectations that she lacked credibility in the stereotypical male domain of military affairs—and particularly so as she spared with a long serving U.S. Senator perhaps best known for his foreign affairs expertise. Palin's frequent appeals in this area were met with significant post-debate gains in her perceived military/economic issue credibility. On the other hand, Joe Biden's heartwarming familial homily suggests a concerted strategy to develop his compassion *bona fides*, especially when standing next to only the second female in presidential campaign history to take the stage in a presidential debate, the self-styled "hockey mom" in lipstick. On this front, Biden's debate performance successfully enhanced his compassion/women's issue expertise.

Conclusion

As one of the most important—and watched—events of a truly eventful presidential campaign, the 2008 vice-presidential debate provided a remarkable communication occasion most clearly worthy of analysis. With this debate including Republican nominee Sarah Palin, only the second female ever nominated as part of a national party presidential ticket in the U.S., our study incorporates gender as a central variable of analysis. Specifically, we examined debate viewers' overall evaluation of the two candidates' debate performances, and also evaluation of the candidates' issue competencies in dealing with stereotypical masculine (military/economic) and feminine (compassion/women's) policy concerns. Overall, our findings point to the fact that debates, unlike the actual election, do not function as a "zero sum" game for the candidates—both candidates have the ability to exceed expectations and "win" from their debate performance. Also, our results both confirm and extend previous research relating to gender and politics, and specifically the debate styles adopted by female and male candidates when engaged in mixed-gendered debates. While we are not there yet, we welcome the day when the presence of a female presidential and vice-presidential candidate on the debate stage will be truly unremarkable.

Notes

1   Debate viewership data supplied by Nielsen Media Research can be found at the Commission on Presidential Debate's Web site at www.debates.org. See "Debate History" section.
2   The Pew Research Center's Project for Excellence in Journalism provides a weekly index of news coverage that can be found at www.journalismorg/news_index. Search "Campaign 2008" for weekly reports of news coverage during the 2008 presidential election.
3   The "lipstick on a pig" controversy began when Sarah Palin in her vice-presidential acceptance speech at the Republican National Convention described herself as "your average hockey mom" and then quipped, "You know what they say is the difference between a hockey mom and a pit bull: lipstick." A couple of weeks later while on the campaign trail Barack Obama mocked John McCain's frequently touted assertion that he, along with his running mate from Alaska, would bring change to Washington, DC, to which Obama punned, "you know, you can put lipstick on a pig, but it's still a pig." For many, the Obama retort seemed a play on Palin's hockey mom/pit bull line, and some media pundits accused Obama of insulting Palin, with others even suggesting Obama's remark was a sexist insult. For several days, fueled by the late-night comics as well as the many chattering political pundits, "lipstick on a pig" became the campaign's slogan.
4   The 11 locations included: Gainesville, FL; Ames, IA; Lawrence, KS; Columbia, MO; Chapel Hill, NC; Las Cruces, NM; San Antonio, TX; San Marcos, TX; Abilene, TX; College Station, TX; Milwaukee, WI.
5   Pre-test reliabilities were as follows: Biden military/economic = .87; Palin military/economic = .90; Biden compassion/women's issues = .88; Palin compassion/women's issues = .89. Post-test reliabilities were as follows: Biden military/economic = .87; Palin military/economic = .91; Biden compassion/women's issues = .86; Palin compassion/women's issues = .89.
6   All debate quotes are taken from the official transcript of the 2008 Vice-Presidential debate, available at the Commission on Presidential Debate's Web site at www.debates.org. See "Debate History" section.

References

Banwart, M. C., & McKinney, M. S. (2005). A gendered influence in campaign debates? Analysis of mixed-gender United States senate and gubernatorial debates. *Communication Studies, 56*, 353–373.

Barnes, J. E. (2008, September 6). An important job but focused on Alaska policy. Gov. Palin's role as national guard chief is largely unrelated to foreign affairs. *Los Angeles Times*. Retrieved December 18, 2009, from http://articles.latimes.com/2008/sep/06/nation/na-guard6.

Beck, C. S. (1996). "I've got some points I'd like to make here": The achievement of social face through turn management during the 1992 vice presidential debate. *Political Communication, 13*, 165–180.

Burgoon, M., & Miller, G. R. (1985). An expectancy interpretation of language and persuasion. In H. Giles & R. N. St. Clair (Eds.), *Recent advances in language, communication, and social psychology*. Mahwah, NJ: Lawrence Erlbaum, pp. 199–229.

Carlin, D. B., & Bicak, P. J. (1993). Toward a theory of vice presidential debate purposes: An analysis of the 1992 vice presidential debate. *Argumentation and Advocacy, 30*, 119–130.

Drew, D., & Weaver, D. (1991). Voter learning in the 1988 presidential election: Did the debates and the media matter? *Journalism Quarterly, 68*, 27–38.

Edelsky, C., & Adams, K. (1990). Creating inequality: Breaking the rules in debates. *Journal of Language and Social Psychology, 9*, 171–190.

Hardy-Short, D. (1986). An insider's view of the constraints affecting Geraldine Ferraro's preparation for the 1984 presidential debates. *Speaker and Gavel, 24*, 8–22.

Hill, M. L. (2005). The relationship between candidate sex and pronoun usage in a Louisiana governor's race. *Women & Language, 28*, 23–32.

Holbrook, T. M. (1994). The behavioral consequences of vice-presidential debates: Does the undercard have any punch? *American Politics Quarterly, 22*, 469–482.

Holbrook, T. M. (1996). *Do campaigns matter?* Thousand Oaks, CA: Sage.

Huddy, L., & Terkildsen, N. (1993). Gender stereotypes and the perception of male and female candidates. *American Journal of Political Science, 37*, 119–147.

Jamieson, K. H. (1988). *Eloquence in an electronic age: The transformation of political speechmaking*. New York: Oxford University Press.

Jurkowitz, M. (2008, September 9). *Northern exposure: Palin dominates campaign coverage*. Pew Research Center Publications. Retrieved December 18, 2009, from: http://pewresearch.org/pubs/944/sarah-palin-news-coverage.

Kay, J., & Borchers, T. A. (1994). "Children in a sandbox": Reaction to the vice presidential debate. In D. B. Carlin & M. S. McKinney (Eds.), *The 1992 presidential debates in focus*, pp. 99–108. New York: Praeger.

Lemert, J. B. (1993). Do televised presidential debates help inform voters? *Journal of Broadcasting & Electronic Media, 37*, 83–94.

McKinney, M. S., Davis, C. B., & Delbert, J. (2009). The first—and last—woman standing: Hillary Rodham Clinton's presidential primary debate performance. In T. F. Sheckels (Ed.), *Cracked but not shattered: Hillary Rodham Clinton's unsuccessful campaign for the presidency*. New York: Rowman & Littlefield, pp. 125–147.

Pew Research Center Project for Excellence in Journalism (2008). *Winning the media campaign*. Retrieved December 18, 2009, from http://journalism.org/node/13310.

Pfau, M. (1987). The influence of intraparty debates on candidate preference. *Communication Research, 14*, 687–697.

Rosenberg, W. L., & Elliott, W. R. (1987). Effect of debate exposure on evaluation of 1984 vice-presidential candidates. *Journalism Quarterly, 63*, 55–64, 262.

Rosenstone, S. J., Kinder, D. R., Miller, W. E., & the National Election Studies. (1997). *American national election study 1996: Pre- and post-election survey* [Computer file]. Ann Arbor, MI: University of Michigan, Center for Political Studies (Producer) and Inter-university Consortium for Political and Social Research (Distributor).

Shields, S. A., & MacDowell, K. A. (1987). "Appropriate" emotion in politics: Judgments of a televised debate. *Journal of Communication, 37*, 78–89.

Sullivan, P. A. (1989). The 1984 vice-presidential debate: A case study of female and male framing in political campaigns. *Communication Quarterly, 37*, 329–343.

Tonn, M. B. (1994). Flirting with Perot: Voter ambivalence about the third candidate. In D. B. Carlin & M. S. McKinney (Eds.), *The 1992 presidential debates in focus*. Westport, CT: Praeger, pp. 109–123.

Trent, J. S. (1994). The 1984 Bush–Ferraro vice presidential debate. In R. V. Friedenberg (Ed.), *Rhetorical studies of national political debates*. New York: Praeger, pp. 121–44.

Yawn, M., Ellsworth, K., Beatty, B., & Kahn, K. F. (1988). How a presidential primary debate changed attitudes of audience members. *Political Behavior, 20*, 155–181.

Media Representations and Voter Engagement

Chapter 11

Just a Hockey Mom with a Gun

Competing Views of Sarah Palin on CNN and Fox

Maridith Dunton Miles, Lynda Lee Kaid, and Kendall Sharp

Bias in the media—in particular political bias—continues to be a source of great debate among scholars and media professionals alike. Politically biased media coverage, strictly defined, is the result of the political prejudices of news personnel or networks shaping (either consciously or unconsciously) the news coverage of political events or figures (Hofstetter, 1978). Political bias is often recognized by coverage that is either too liberal or too conservative coverage (Hofstetter, 1978). It seems logical to assume that political bias, were it to exist, would have an effect on viewers, and therefore voters. However, many claim that evidence for political bias in mass media coverage simply does not exist (Hofstetter, 1978). In study after study, researchers have failed to find evidence that this type of bias infiltrates American news culture. Regardless, claims of this political bias continue to be heard in outcries from the public and political figures—especially concerning cable news. However, the lack of empirical evidence for such bias suggests the need for further research about these claims and the potential effects of political bias on audiences.

The media frenzy surrounding Governor Sarah Palin during the 2008 presidential campaign provided an opportunity for investigation of political bias. The public and media fascination with Palin led to media coverage almost unprecedented for a vice-presidential candidate. In the weeks leading up to the vice-presidential debate, both CNN and Fox News produced and aired documentaries detailing Palin's life and political rise. Both programs were intended to inform the public about the relative unknown who had captured the fascination of the country. The research reported here was designed to compare the effects on audiences exposed either to the CNN or Fox News documentary.

Context of the 2008 Presidential Election

By the time the Democratic and Republican National Conventions arrived in late August and early September 2008, all eyes were on the presidential campaigns of Senators John McCain and Barack Obama. Of particular interest was speculation about the nomination of their running mates. Barack Obama made his announcement first, choosing Delaware Senator Joe Biden on August 22, 2008. The *New York Times* speculated that this choice was made in an effort to bring someone to the ticket who possessed foreign policy and national security experience (Nagourney & Zeleny, 2008).

On August 29, 2008, John McCain announced, to the surprise of many, that he had chosen Alaska Governor Sarah Palin as his running mate. Palin was the first Alaskan and second woman to run on a major party U.S. presidential ticket (CNN, 2008). Because she was so unknown, her personal life, policy positions, and political record drew intense media attention and scrutiny. With limited access to press conferences or face-to-face interviews, searches for information about Palin skyrocketed, and the media looked for any bit of news about her they could report (Rasmussen Reports, 2008).

In the weeks following the 2008 Republican National Convention, both the media's and the American public's need for all-things-Palin seemed endless. Palin was on the receiving end of many media attacks, and she was scrutinized on everything from her ideology to her clothing. When she finally granted a face-to-face interview with ABC News' Charlie Gibson, and then subsequently with Sean Hannity (Fox News) and Katie Couric (CBS), she was widely criticized as not being knowledgeable enough to be America's next vice president. Palin was also parodied throughout the campaign—most notably by Tina Fey on *Saturday Night Live*. It was in this context that both CNN and Fox News produced documentaries on Palin's life and political rise. The Fox documentary was the highest-rated program in the network's history with 2.7 million viewers (Associated Press, 2008).

Geraldine Ferraro, the first woman to appear on a major party's presidential ticket, faced many challenges from sexist media coverage (Stalnaker, 2008). However, according to an ongoing study at the University of Alabama called "the Palin Watch" (Stalnaker, 2008), American society is still divided over women's leadership roles and social responsibilities. The study also found that the American news media used similar news frames to describe both Palin and Ferraro (Stalnaker, 2008). Although these two women come from two different parties and ran for vice president nearly two and a half decades apart, "the Palin Watch" found that both of these female candidates have been centrally framed using three key factors: "1) their questionable experience, 2) their selection as a political stunt, and 3) their selection as a 'gamble'" (Stalnaker, 2008).

According to the Pew Center Project for Excellence in Journalism (2008), Sarah Palin experienced her best days in the media spotlight during her first few days as nominee, when relatively little was known about her. Coverage of Palin also peaked in the few days surrounding the vice-presidential debate on October 2, 2008. Over the course of the campaign, coverage of Palin followed a wavering trajectory, alternating between positive coverage one day and negative the next. Of her negative media coverage, much centered around her public record and policy experience, as well as her controversial encounters with the press.

Theory and Research on Partisan Media Bias

Journalists in a democratic society are charged with the responsibility of providing accurate, factual, reliable, and unbiased information to assist voters in the democratic process. Essentially, the facts should speak for themselves. Critics of the media claim that bias—particularly word choice or phrasing, and choice of visuals—occurs frequently and imparts an unbalanced or biased context to the story being reported. As Kuypers (2002) puts it:

> Americans look to the press to provide the information they need to make informed political choices. How well the press lives up to its responsibility to provide this information has a direct impact on Americans: how they think about and act upon the issues that confront them. (p. 197)

There is an assumption that in the absence of bias an issue or individual will receive similar coverage across news outlets. In general, media bias exists when a topic receives significantly more positive or negative coverage in comparison to the objective facts or to coverage by other reports (Hofstetter, 1976). Political, or partisan bias, of particular concern to the public and to this study, has been defined as media bias "caused by political views held by individual news personnel" (Hofstetter, 1976, p. 33). One of the primary questions in academic research of election coverage has been whether the news reflects a partisan or ideological bias. The concern is that one-sided or biased news reporting has the potential to influence voting decisions.

The discussion of media bias often centers around whether bias is real—due to a specific agenda viewpoint, or political leaning of the institution doing the reporting—or perceived by partisan audiences, suggesting that the problem lies with the viewers, readers, etc. who have their own biases while taking in reported information (Weatherly, Petros, Christopherson, & Haugen, 2007). Weatherly, et al. (2007) note that claims of media bias may lead to perception of bias even when no real bias exists. Alternatively, a person's own political inclinations may prevent the perception of bias even when bias does exist (Weatherly, et al., 2007). This type of effect is similar to the "hostile media bias" identified by researchers (Gunther &

Schmitt, 2004; Schmitt, Gunther, & Liebhart, 2004; Tsfati, & Cohen, 2005; Vallone, Ross, & Lepper, 1985). The hostile media effect bias suggests that partisans often perceive that media reports are biased against their own viewpoint, regardless of the objective nature of the media coverage.

Although numerous studies over the years have found little evidence of political bias in the media (see D'Alessio & Allen, 2000; Hofstetter, 1976; Niven, 2001), new research is surfacing, confirming what casual observers have argued for years: biased, although perhaps unintentional, reporting permeates the major U.S. news media. Groseclose and Milyo (2005) found that almost all sampled news media, with the exception of the *Washington Times* and Fox's *Special Report with Brit Hume*, presented coverage that was left of the ideology of the average Congress member, essentially confirming signs of liberal bias in the American news media. In presidential campaigns, some researchers have documented that many Democratic Party presidential candidates receive more positive treatment from the traditional news networks than do Republicans (Farnsworth & Lichter, 2007). Bill Clinton's advantage in election news coverage has also been independently validated by many media scholars (Farnsworth & Lichter, 2007; Just, et al., 1996; Kerbel, 1998, Lichter, Noyes, & Kaid, 1999).

Comparisons of CNN and Fox

Surprisingly few analyses have been performed directly comparing the content of CNN coverage to Fox News coverage. Conventional wisdom ascribes a liberal slant to CNN, while Fox is considered to lean in a more conservative direction. In the 1990s CNN was even labeled the "Clinton News Network" for its mostly favorable coverage of President Bill Clinton (Weatherly, et al., 2007, p. 91). On the other hand, Fox has been referred to as the "central hub of the conservative movement's well-oiled media machine" (Ackerman, 2001). Both networks claim no bias in their reporting styles and coverage—Fox even pushes the claim in its network slogan "Fair and Balanced"—although both networks also favor heavy usage of political pundits and opinion-based inquiry. It is important to note that "most claims of bias consist of anecdotal evidence and are forwarded by individuals with their own biases. Little in the way of systematic, scientific inquiries into bias has been conducted, especially using experimental methods" (Weatherly, et al., 2007, p. 92). Content analyses of presidential campaign coverage over the past two decades have shown that CNN has given Democratic presidential candidates more positive coverage than Republican candidates, and Fox sometimes provides more positive coverage for Republicans (Farnsworth & Lichter, 2008).

Weatherly, et al. (2007) studied public perceptions of media bias in headlines when the source (network) was unknown. Overall, participants "rated the headlines from CNN as significantly more liberal than those from Fox News" (p. 97). This study seems to not only show a difference between the two networks, but also presents a clear perception of liberal bias on the part of CNN. On the other hand, in a recent study of differences between CNN and Fox News in coverage of the Iraq war, Silcock (2008) focused on what he called a "pro-administration" bias in Fox's coverage. This finding could also be seen as a conservative bias, and would seem to follow the Weatherly, et al. (2007) finding if one keeps in mind that a Republican (George W. Bush) held the presidency during the study timeframe. Silcock (2008) showed evidence of Fox's "pro-administration" bias and CNN's differing coverage, through lead-story framing, time allotted to sound bites by U.S. cabinet and military officials, and the visual framing of Iraq war stories. The disparity in coverage, as Silcock (2008) notes, points to clear ideological news culture differences.

McClellan, Albiniak, and Higgins (2000) considered the perception that differences between CNN and Fox might have swayed the outcome of the 2000 U.S. presidential election. Before the end of election night, Fox called the election for George W. Bush, while CNN called it for Al Gore. The Republican complaint was that by prematurely calling a critical state like Florida for Gore, CNN may have unfairly influenced the election. On the other hand, Democrats criticized Fox after details emerged that the network's election desk manager was keeping Bush informed of results as they came in. Again, both networks claimed no bias and stated formally that differences in coverage were unintentional. Although limited, prior research suggests that differences between Fox and CNN coverage may lead to differences in audience perceptions, leading to our first hypotheses:

> H1: *Viewers will have more positive image evaluations of Sarah Palin after watching the Fox documentary on Palin than will participants watching the CNN documentary.*

> H2: *Political party affiliation will be significantly related to evaluations of Palin for participants of both the CNN and Fox documentaries.*

Political Learning

One function of political television programming about political candidates is to communicate information about the candidates' qualities and issue positions. Political advertising and debates have been shown to affect significantly viewers' knowledge of issues, policy stances, and candidate image attributes (Faber & Storey, 1984; Groenendyk & Valentino, 2002; Kaid, 2006; Kaid & Sanders, 1978).

Research on the effects of political documentaries in particular has provided evidence that such programming can affect emotional reactions as well as learning. Exposure to narrative documentary presentations of events or ideas can lead to increased political learning (Green, Brock, & Kaufman, 2004; Wirth, 2006). Political documentary (as well as reenactment) presentations of political events, particularly when accompanied by the generation of emotional responses, can have significant and measurable effects on knowledge gain (LaMarre & Landreville, 2009; Marcus, Neuman, & MacKuen, 2000). This research led to the following hypotheses and research questions:

> H3:   *Viewers of both documentaries will learn significantly more about the candidate's image qualities than about issues.*
>
> H4:   *Viewers of the Fox documentary will learn significantly more about the candidate's personal qualities than will viewers of CNN.*
>
> RQ1:   *Will there be a significant difference in the amount of learning about issues or candidate qualities after viewing the documentaries on Fox or CNN?*

Political Cynicism

While political cynicism is often defined in terms of voter mobilization, it essentially relates to the general distrust of and disdain for American politicians and the political system. Many studies have focused on the question of whether media-induced cynicism results from exposure to political messages, particularly negative political advertisements (Ansolabehere, Iyengar, Simon, & Valentino, 1994; Finkel & Geer, 1998; Kaid, Postelnicu, Landreville, Yun, & LeGrange, 2007). However, this proposition has attracted convincing evidence on the other side as well, suggesting that political advertising certainly does not evoke cynicism and may even stimulate engagement (Freedman & Goldstein, 1999; Goldstein & Freedman, 2002; Vavreck, 2000; Wattenberg & Brians, 1999).

Political documentaries, such as those produced by Fox and CNN on Sarah Palin, represent a different type of communication between a media source and voters than that seen in political ads or general news coverage. Documentaries such as these fall somewhere between entertainment television and informational programming. Perhaps the best-known examination of the evocation of political cynicism from political documentary viewing is Robinson's (1976) experimental study of the "Selling of the Pentagon" documentary, which found a strong relationship between viewing the documentary and political malaise or cynicism. Though few studies examine levels of political cynicism triggered by prime-time political documentaries, research correlating these two variables does exist.

Feldman and Sigelman (1985) claim that political documentaries are limited in their effects on individual levels of cynicism—". . . [I]t is simply too much to expect a television program to transform people's fundamental social and political values" (p. 559). Feldman and Sigelman (1985) also propose that documentary-type programs have extremely limited potential for changing attitudes of conviction when a political issue is discussed indirectly or in broad terms. However, when a program focuses on a narrow issue that is largely unfamiliar to viewers and about which viewers have not yet formulated concrete attitudes, change may be possible (Feldman and Sigelman, 1985). This reasoning may logically be applied to the Sarah Palin documentaries, as she was a stranger to most American voters at the time the programs were aired.

Additionally, de Vreese and Elenbaas (2008) cite several experimental studies (Cappella & Jamieson, 1997; Crigler, Just, & Belt, 2006; de Vreese, 2004) that have compellingly demonstrated that individuals exposed to strategically framed coverage of politics are significantly more cynical as a result of such exposure.

Given prior research and suppositions that demonstrate CNN may have a liberal leaning bias (and therefore produce a more negative portrayal of Palin), in conjunction with the above research demonstrating documentaries' ability to affect attitudes, the following hypothesis was proposed:

H5:   Viewers of the CNN documentary will exhibit higher levels of cynicism after viewing than will the viewers of the FNC documentary.

Political Information Efficacy

The theory of political information efficacy "focuses solely on the voter's confidence in his or her own political knowledge and its sufficiency to engage the political process" (Kaid, McKinney, & Tedesco, 2007, p. 1096). The theory argues that different levels of information processing occur from different sources of information, and thus, different sources will leave users with differing levels of confidence in their own political knowledge (Kaid, et al., 2007).

In a study of citizen engagement in 1996 and 2000, Kaid, McKinney, and Tedesco (2000) found that one of the principle reasons or justifications young voters give for their lack of participation in the political process is low levels of information about the candidates and issues. The authors, in attempting to understand this perceived obstruction to voting behavior, set out to describe the link between political efficacy and what they termed political information efficacy (Kaid, et al., 2007). Political efficacy involves an individual's faith and trust in government and the feeling that he can influence political affairs. Researchers have defined two levels of political efficacy: external and internal (Clarke & Acock, 1989; Delli Carpini, 2000; Finkel, 1985; Niemi, Craig, & Mattei, 1991). External political efficacy refers to a trust and belief that government will be responsive to the citizens' needs or demands (Delli Carpini, 2000). Internal political efficacy, on the other hand, refers to an individual's sense that participation in the political process will have an effect on government—will make a difference (Delli Carpini, 2000). The theory of political information efficacy is closely related to internal political efficacy but is directly related to one's confidence in his/her ability to vote based upon confidence in political knowledge (Kaid, et al., 2007).

Researchers have shown evidence that exposure to campaign messages such as political advertising, televised debates, even blogs can increase political information efficacy levels, giving citizens greater confidence in their ability to engage in the political process (Kaid & Postelnicu, 2005; Sweetser & Kaid, 2008). This research suggests that exposure to political documentaries might also create a greater knowledge base for young citizens, leading to the final hypothesis and research question:

> H6: Viewing the documentaries about Palin will result in an increase in political information efficacy.

> RQ2: Will there be any differences in political information efficacy based on partisan differences?

Method

Participants and Design

A pre-test—post-test experimental design was used to investigate the hypotheses and research questions. Participants were 133 undergraduate students at a large southeastern university. The experiments were conducted between October 2 and October 7, 2008. All together, 69 young citizens watched the CNN documentary on Palin, and 64 watched the Fox News program. The sample was composed of 55 percent male and 45 percent female respondents, with an average age of 20 years old. Forty-one percent of participants were Democrats, 32 percent Republicans, and 27 percent Independents or other.

Procedure and Materials

When assembled, each respondent filled out an "informed consent" document approved by the university's Institutional Review Board. Next, participants were asked to fill out a pre-test questionnaire. After completion of the pre-test questionnaire, participants were shown one of the documentaries produced and aired by either CNN (*Palin Revealed*) or

Fox (*An American Woman*). Following the viewing of one of the documentaries, participants were given a post-test questionnaire. Upon completion of the post-test questionnaire, participants were thanked, debriefed, and dismissed.

Dependent Variables

The pre-test and post-test questionnaires had the same measures for candidate evaluation, political cynicism, and information efficacy. A feeling thermometer ranging from 0 to 100 points was used to assess participants' evaluations of Sarah Palin and Democratic vice-presidential nominee Joe Biden, as well as Barack Obama and John McCain. Participants were asked to indicate how unfavorable (cold)/favorable (warm) they felt toward the candidates on a thermometer similar to the one used by the National Election Studies to measure attitudes toward the candidates (Rosenstone, Kinder, Miller, & the National Election Studies, 1997). A 12-item semantic differential scale[1] described by Kaid (2004) was also used to measure candidate evaluation. The 12 items were averaged into a single index which has provided high reliability scores in earlier research. When measuring evaluation of Palin, Cronbach's alpha was .94 in the pre-test and .96 in the post-test.

An eight-item scale measured political cynicism.[2] The values ranged from 1 (strongly disagree) to 5 (strongly agree). A composite cynicism score was computed with a Cronbach's alpha of .76 in both the pre-test and post-test. Information efficacy[3] was measured with a four-item scale with values from 1 (strongly disagree) to 5 (strongly agree). Cronbach's alpha levels for this measure were .83 in the pre-test and .87 in the post-test.

Results

Candidate Evaluation

First of all, as Table 11.1 shows, it is interesting to note that viewing both documentaries had a significant positive impact on participants' image evaluations of Sarah Palin. We measured image evaluation by summing the 12-item semantic differential scale for each candidate. Viewers of the CNN documentary rated Palin at 48.51 in the pre-test, $t = -2.387$, $df = 68$, $p = .02$. Viewers of the Fox version of the Palin documentary rated Palin at 47.67 in the pre-test and 56.39 in the post-test, $t = -8.719$, $df = 63$, $p = .001$. To test our first hypothesis we compared the amount of change between viewers of the two documentaries. There was no significant difference between the ratings of Palin in the pre-test for either the group that saw the Fox or the CNN documentary (see Table 11.1).

Table 11.1 Effect of Documentary Exposure on Image Evaluations and Learning
(N = 133)

Image evaluation	CNN (n = 69)		Fox News (n = 64)	
	Pre-test	Post-test	Pre-test	Post-test
Overall sample	48.51	50.62[b]	47.67	56.39[a,b]
Democrats (n = 55)	38.9[c]	40.9[c]	41.2[c]	48.9[b,c]
Republicans (n = 42)	62.7[d]	64.3[d]	59.8[d]	69.8[b,d]
Indep./other (n = 36)	47.1	50.2[b]	44.0	52.6[b]

a t-test shows difference between CNN and Fox News is significant at $p < .05$.
b t-test indicates difference between pre and post test ratings is significant at $p < .05$.
c ANOVA test indicates that the difference among party identification is significant at $p < .05$.
d Tukey's HSD test indicates that the difference between the Republicans and both Democrats and Independents is significant at $p < .05$.

However, confirming our hypothesis, those viewers who watched the Fox documentary exhibited significantly higher evaluations of Palin in the post-test (56.39) than the CNN viewers (50.62), $t = -1.842$, $df = 131$, $p = .04$.

Our second hypothesis predicted that partisan affiliation would affect the ratings of Palin for participants who watched the CNN and Fox documentaries. This hypothesis was confirmed with an ANOVA test. Table 11.1 shows that the distributions of Palin's ratings among partisan groups on the evaluation scale were significantly different in both the CNN and Fox versions on both the pre-test and post-test (pre-test, CNN: $F = 22.308$, $df = 2$, $p = .001$, Fox: $F = 12.369$, $df = 2$, $p = .001$; post-test, CNN: $F = 16.488$, $df = 2$, $p = .001$, Fox: $F = 9.792$, $df = 2$, $p = .001$). Tukey's HSD test indicates that the significant difference here is that the Republicans rated Palin significantly higher than either Democrats or Independents. Republicans, of course, rated Palin significantly higher both before and after viewing the documentaries. More surprising, Independents increased their evaluations of Palin after viewing both documentaries (CNN: $t = -2.983$, $df = 13$, $p = .01$; Fox: $t = -3.953$, $df = 21$, $p = .001$). Even more meaningful was the fact that all three partisan groups, even Democrats, increased their ratings of Palin significantly after viewing the Fox documentary.

Issue and Image Learning

Because neither documentary focused very much attention on policy issues,[4] we expected that our participants would learn more about Palin's personal qualities than about issues. Participants rated their amount of learning about both issues and candidate qualities on a scale from 1 (very little) to 7 (a great deal). This hypothesis (H3) was supported. Table 11.2 shows that participants who viewed the CNN documentary rated their

Table 11.2 Issue and Image Learning About Palin from Documentaries (N = 133)

	CNN (n = 69)	Fox (n = 64)
Learn about issues overall	3.52[a] (SD = 1.21)	3.19[a] (SD = 1.41)
Learn personal qualities	3.90[a] (SD = 1.06)	3.94[a] (SD = 1.11)

[a] t-test shows difference between issues and personal qualities is significant at $p < .01$.

issue learning at 3.52 and their candidate qualities learning significantly higher at 3.90, $t = -2.930$, $df = 68$, $p = .01$. Fox viewers also learned significantly more about candidate qualities (3.94) than about issues (3.19), $t = -4.172930$, $df = 63$, $p = .01$.

Our fourth hypothesis predicted that viewers of the Fox documentary would learn more about Palin's personal qualities than would CNN viewers. We expected this because Fox had a greater emphasis on human interest elements than did CNN.[5] This hypothesis was not confirmed. Table 11.2 shows that there was no significant difference between what CNN viewers and Fox viewers learned in terms of the amount of personal qualities of Palin.

Political Cynicism Effects of Documentary Viewing

Given the fact that the CNN documentary presented Palin more negatively,[6] our fifth hypothesis predicted that viewers of CNN's documentary would experience higher levels of political cynicism after viewing than would Fox viewers. Political cynicism was measured as a scale that summed eight items representing various elements of political cynicism as explained above. Table 11.3 shows that there was no significant difference in pre-test cynicism levels of CNN (23.74) or Fox (25.16) viewers. Similarly, there was no difference in cynicism levels on the post-test for CNN (24.22) or Fox (23.98). While these differences between documentaries were not significant, Table 11.3 also confirms that there was a significant decrease in cynicism levels between pre-test (25.16) and post-test (23.58) for Fox viewers, $t = -3.763$, $df = 63$, $p = .001$.

Political Information Efficacy and Documentary Viewing

Our last hypotheses related to expectations about the impact of viewing the documentaries on levels of political information efficacy (PIE). Considering all of our viewers together, the mean score for PIE before viewing was 14.42 (a summation of the four items used here to comprise the PIE measure), and this level increased significantly on the post-test to

Table 11.3 Effects of Documentary Exposure on Cynicism and Political Information Efficacy (N = 133)

	CNN (n = 69)		Fox News (n = 64)	
	Pre-test	Post-test	Pre-test	Post-test
Cynicism level	23.74	24.22	25.16	23.98[a]
Political information efficacy	14.38	14.72	14.47	14.86[a]
Democrats (n = 55)	14.06	14.63	15.13[b]	15.43[b]
Republicans (n = 42)	15.09	15.09	15.47	16.11
Indep./other (n = 36)	13.93	14.36	12.91[c]	13.18[c]

a   t-test shows difference between pre- and post-test is significant at $p < .05$.
b   Anova test indicates that the difference among party identification is significant at $p < .05$.
c   Tukey's HSD test indicates that the difference between the Independents and both Republicans and Democrats is significant at $p < .05$.

14.79, $t = -2.716$, $df = 132$, $p = .01$, confirming our hypothesis. However, Table 11.3 shows that this increase was primarily located within the viewers of the Fox version of the documentary. While CNN viewers experienced some increase in their PIE levels, the difference between pretest and post-test levels was not statistically significant. On the other hand, Fox viewers exhibited a PIE level of 14.47 before viewing the documentary, and these viewers were significantly more confident in their information about Palin in the post-test (14.86), $t = -2.569$, $df = 63$, $p = .01$.

Our last hypothesis predicted that female viewers would experience higher levels of PIE after viewing the documentaries than would males. Looking again at the entire sample together, this hypothesis is also confirmed. After viewing the documentaries, female viewers had a mean PIE score of 15.38, while male viewers had a significantly lower PIE score of 14.39, $t = 1.950$, $df = 132$, $p = .03$. The most interesting finding here is that females also had a higher level of PIE in the pre-test (15.05) than did male viewers (13.88), $t = 2.138$, $df = 132$, $p = .02$. It is interesting to note that these PIE levels were not differentiated by which version (CNN or Fox) of the documentary was viewed.

Our final research question queried whether there was any difference in PIE based on partisan affiliation of the viewers. An ANOVA comparison indicated there were differences in PIE levels among partisan groups in before viewing (Democrats, 14.51; Republicans, 15.26; Independents, 13.30), $F = 3.908$, $df = 2$, $p = .02$; and after viewing (Democrats, 14.96; Republicans, 15.55; Independents, 13.64), $F = 3.694$, $df = 2$, $p = .02$. Tukey's HSD test indicated that in both before and after viewing analyses the major difference lies in the fact that Independents have lower levels of PIE than Republicans (in both cases, $p = .02$). A deeper analysis of partisan effects indicates that these differences are primarily the Fox viewing group, which Table 11.3 shows had specific partisan differences among Republicans, Democrats, and Independents on both the pre-test

($F = 4.436$, $df = 2$, $p = .02$) and post-test ($F = 5.405$, $df = 2$, $p = .01$). In both cases (pre and post), Tukey's HSD test shows that the significant difference is in the levels of PIE for Independents. Independents have significantly less confidence in their information about Palin in the pre-test (12.91) compared to Republicans (15.47), $p = .02$, and Democrats (15.13), $p = .02$. This difference for FNC viewers in the post-test remained significant, with Independents exhibiting slightly higher, but not significantly so, levels of PIE. This PIE level for Independents (13.18) in the post-test remained significantly lower than either Republicans (16.11, HSD, $p = .03$) or Democrats (15.43, HSD, $p = .05$).

Discussion

As enthusiastic media consumers in American partisan society, it is natural for individuals to select media sources that reinforce their viewpoints and ideologies. Claims of cable news bias have resulted in a fair amount of name-calling and finger-pointing, while the networks repeatedly contest claims of biased reporting. Regardless, viewers and journalists seem to recognize the partisanship views held among the two cable news giants in America: Fox News and CNN. Fox is consistently viewed as having a conservative bias. On the other hand, Rassmussen Reports (2007) reported in 2007 that a full third of American adults believe that CNN has a liberal bias. Up until now claims of partisan bias in the media have primarily been based upon similar opinion polling and conventional wisdom. This study seeks to lend empirical support to those claims and act as a launching point for future studies.

While both documentaries had a positive influence on participants' image evaluations of Palin, viewers of the Fox documentary exhibited significantly higher image evaluations of Palin than viewers of the CNN documentary. Had the two documentaries reported the facts about Palin in a similar fashion, one could reasonably expect that post-test measures of Palin's image would be comparable. But this was simply not the case. The significant differences in the post-test evaluations of the two experimental groups imply that the documentaries produced by Fox and CNN were dramatically different, and that Fox's documentary clearly portrayed Palin more positively than did CNN's documentary.

Partisanship also presented as an interesting element in this experiment. It is not surprising that Republicans rated Palin significantly higher than either Democrats or Independents in the experiment. However, it is quite intriguing that Democrats increased in their image evaluations of Palin after viewing the Fox documentary, and Independents' evaluations rose significantly in both groups. It seems evident that Fox's more positive presentation was able to overcome prior negative feelings, and that in the case of Independents, a simple gain of knowledge made these voters more open to the vice-presidential candidate.

We predicted that viewers would learn more about Palin's personal qualities than about campaign issues, and that Fox viewers would take away more about the Governor's personal life than viewers of the CNN documentary. This first expectation was confirmed, revealing both documentaries' heavy reliance on personal background and characteristics to paint a picture of Palin. This is interesting when one considers that these documentaries were intended to inform the public before a highly promoted vice-presidential debate. Contrary to the researchers' predictions, there were no significant differences between the Fox and CNN groups in learning about Palin's personal qualities. Again, this reveals that both documentaries focused primarily on personal qualities of Palin—one of the biggest similarities between the two programs.

Results were unexpected when looking at cynicism levels following the viewing of these documentaries. It is possible that these results may simply be attributable to the fact that, at the time of viewing, most Americans had very little information about Sarah Palin. In this case, being provided any information—regardless of the tone or content—could have the tendency to limit cynicism. It is interesting to note, however, that Fox viewers (who viewed a more positive presentation) experienced a significant decrease in cynicism, pointing to the somewhat logical idea that reporting that is not specifically negative can have positive effects on how voters feel about the political system.

In combining the two groups we found a significant increase in levels of PIE after viewing the documentaries. However, it is important to note that the majority of this increase occurred in the group watching the Fox documentary. This finding leads us to question whether Fox's more positive presentation caused viewers to feel more confident in their own political knowledge, or if the differences in content (rather than tone) between the two documentaries caused the disparity. Interestingly, female participants showed increased levels of PIE across the board, and showed higher levels of PIE than male participants in both viewings. We speculate that this phenomenon may be due to the subject of these documentaries being a woman. It is possible that women paid more attention to details about Palin from the outset, and were more confident in their political information and the ability to put it to use after having viewed information about a female politician. Also interestingly, levels of PIE in Independents decreased after viewing the documentaries. Independents, and their ability to decide the vote, are often the targets of political campaigns. This study shows that for this particular group of voters, information based mostly on personal attributes rather than political issues does not lend itself to raising personal confidence political information. These lower levels of PIE can in turn affect the vote—with individuals either lacking enough confidence to vote at all, or going with the candidate for whom they feel the most confident about the information they have.

Overall, this study presents dramatically the ways in which differences in coverage can affect voters. Such findings certainly suggest that differences in news coverage patterns may be more important than previously thought. Future research should consider other ways in which coverage differences may be manifest and in what areas of political information and attitudes these differences may arise. Further, researchers may be able to learn more about gender differences in politics from expansion of studies like this one, considering differences in reactions of male and female voters to male and female political candidates.

Notes

1. The 12 bipolar adjective pairs, rated on a 1–7 scale, were qualified–unqualified, sophisticated–unsophisticated, honest–dishonest, believable–unbelievable, successful–unsuccessful, attractive–unattractive, friendly–unfriendly, sincere–insincere, calm–excitable, aggressive–unaggressive, strong–weak, active–inactive.
2. The eight-item political cynicism index was composed of the following measures: (a) Whether I vote or not has no influence on what politicians do, (b) One never knows what politicians really think, (c) People like me don't have any say about what the government does, (d) Sometimes politics and government seem so complicated that a person like me can't really understand what's going on, (e) One can be confident that politicians will always do the right thing (reverse scored), (f) Politicians often quickly forget their election promises after a political campaign is over, (g) Politicians are more interested in power than in what the people think, and (h) One cannot always trust what politicians say.
3. The four-item political information efficacy index was composed of the following measures: (a) I consider myself well qualified to participate in politics, (b) I think that I am better informed about politics and government than most people, (c) I feel that I have a pretty good understanding of the important political issues facing our country, and (d) If a friend asked me about the presidential election, I feel I would have enough information to help my friend figure out who to vote for.
4. An independent content analysis indicated that issues received very little attention in either the FNC or the CNN documentary (see Miles, Sharp, Del Castillo, Maple, & Kaid, 2009).
5. A content analysis indicated that the human interest frame was reflected more often on the FNC documentary than in the CNN documentary (see Miles, Sharp, Del Castillo, Maple, & Kaid, 2009).
6. A content analysis showed that significantly more CNN segments had a negative tone about Palin than was true for segments in the FNC documentary (see Miles, Sharp, Del Castillo, Maple, & Kaid, 2009).

References

Ackerman, S. (2001). *The most biased name in news: Fox news channel's extraordinary right-wing tilt.* Retrieved June 30, 2010, from: www.fair.org/index.php?page=1067.

Ansolabehere, S., Iyengar, S., Simon, A., & Valentino, N. (1994). Does attack advertising demobilize the electorate? *American Political Science Review, 88*(4), 829–839.

Associated Press (2008, September 10). *ABC plans prime time Palin special*. Retrieved June 30, 2010, from www.foxnews.com/wires/2008Sep10/0,4670,TVABCPalin, 00.html.

Cappella, J. N., & Jamieson, K. H. (1997). *Spiral of cynicism: The press and the public good*. New York: Oxford University Press.

Clarke, H. D., & Acock, A. C. (1989). National elections and political attitudes: The case of political efficacy. *British Journal of Political Science, 19*(4), 551–562.

CNN (2008, August 29). *McCain taps Alaska Gov. Palin as vice president pick*. Retrieved June 30, 2010, from www.cnn.com/2008/POLITICS/08/29/palin. republican.vp.candidate/index.html.

Crigler, A., Just, M. & Belt, T. (2006). The three faces of negative campaigning: The democratic implications of attack ads, cynical news and fear arousing messages. In Redlawsk, D. P. (Ed.), *Feeling politics: Affect and emotion in political information processing*. New York: Palgrave/Macmillan.

D'Alessio, D., & Allen, M. (2000). Media bias in presidential elections: A meta-analysis. *Journal of Communication. 50*(4), 133–157.

de Vreese, C. H. (2004). The effects of strategic news on political cynicism, issue evaluations and policy support: A two-wave experiment. *Mass Communication & Society, 7*(2), 191–215.

de Vreese, C. H. & Elenbaas, M. (2008). Media in the game of politics: Effects of strategic metacoverage on political cynicism. *The International Journal of Press/Politics, 13*, 285–309.

Delli Carpini, M. X. (2000). Gen.com: Youth, civic engagement, and the new information environment. *Political Communication, 17*(4), 341–349.

Faber, R. J., & Storey, M. C. (1984). Recall of information from political advertising. *Journal of Advertising, 13*(3), 39–44.

Farnsworth, S. J., & Lichter, S. R. (2007). *The nightly news nightmare: Television's coverage of U.S. presidential elections, 1988–2004* (2nd. Ed.). Lanham, MD: Rowman & Littlefield.

Farnsworth, S. J., & Lichter, S. R. (2008). Trends in television network news coverage of U.S. elections. In J. Strömbäck & L. L. Kaid (Eds.), *The handbook of election news coverage around the world*. New York: Routledge, pp. 41–57.

Feldman, S., & Sigelman, L. (1985). The political impact of prime-time television: "The Day After." *The Journal of Politics, 47*(2), 556–578.

Finkel, S. E., & Geer, J. G. (1998). A spot check: Casting doubt on the demobilizing effect of attack advertising. *American Journal of Political Science, 42*(2), 573–595.

Freedman, P., & Goldstein, K. (1999). Measuring media exposure and the effects of negative campaign ads. *American Journal of Political Science, 43*(4), 1189–1208.

Goldstein, K., & Freedman, P. (2002). Campaign advertising and voter turnout: New evidence for a stimulation effect. *Journal of Politics, 64*, 721–740.

Green, M. C., Brock, T. C., & Kaufman, G. F. (2004) Understanding media enjoyment: The role of narrative engagement into narrative worlds. *Communication Theory, 14*(4), 311–327.

Groenendyk, E. W., & Valentino, N. A. (2002). Of dark clouds and silver linings: Effects of exposure to issue versus candidate advertising on persuasion, information retention, and issue salience. *Communication Research, 29*(3), 295–319.

Groseclose, T., & Milyo, J. (2005). A measure of media bias. *The Quarterly Journal of Economics. 70*(4), 1191–1237.

Gunther, A. C., & Schmitt, K. M. (2004). Mapping boundaries of the hostile media effect. *Journal of Communication. 54*, 55–70.

Hofstetter, C. R. (1976). *Bias in the news: Network television coverage of the 1972 election campaign.* Columbus, OH: Ohio State University Press.

Hofstetter, C. R. (1978). *News bias in the 1972 campaign: A cross-media comparison.* Minneapolis, MN: AEJ Publications Manager.

Just, M. R., Crigler, A. E., Alger, D. E., Cook, T. E., Kern, M., & West, D. M. (1996). *Crosstalk: Citizens, candidates, and the media in a presidential campaign.* Chicago: University of Chicago Press.

Kaid, L. L. (2004). Measuring candidate images with semantic differentials. In K. L. Hacker (Ed.), *Presidential candidate images.* Westport, CT: Praeger, pp. 231–236.

Kaid, L. L. (2006). Political advertising in the United States. In L. L. Kaid, & C. Holtz-Bacha (Eds.). *The Sage handbook of political advertising.* Thousand Oaks, CA: Sage, pp. 83–208.

Kaid, L. L., & Postelnicu, M. (2005). Political advertising in the 2004 election: Comparison of traditional television and Internet messages. *American Behavioral Scientist, 49*(2), 265–278.

Kaid, L. L. & Sanders, K. R. (1978). Political television commercials: An experimental study of type and length. *Communication Research, 5*(1), 57–70.

Kaid, L. L., McKinney, M. S., & Tedesco, J. C. (2000). *Civic dialogue in the 1996 presidential campaign: Candidate, media, and public voices.* Cresskill, NJ: Hampton.

Kaid, L. L., McKinney, M. S., & Tedesco, J. C. (2007). Political information efficacy and young voters. *American Behavioral Scientist, 50*(9), 1093–1111.

Kaid, L. L., Postelnicu, M., Landreville, K., Yun, H. J. & LeGrange, A. G. (2007). The effects of political advertising on young voters. *American Behavioral Scientist, 50*(9), 1137–1151.

Kerbel, M. R. (1998). *Edited for television: CNN, ABC and American presidential elections* (2nd Ed.). Boulder, CO: Westview.

Kuypers, J. A. (2002). *Press bias and politics: How the media frame controversial issues.* Westport, CT: Praeger.

LaMarre, H. L., & Landreville, K. (2009). When is fiction as good as fact? Comparing the influence of documentary and historical reenactment films on engagement, affect, issue interest, and learning. *Mass Communication & Society, 12*(4), 537–555.

Lichter, S. R., Noyes, R. E., & Kaid, L. L. (1999). No news or negative news: How the networks nixed the '96 campaign. In L. L. Kaid, & D. G. Bystrom, (Eds.), *The electronic election: Perspectives on the 1996 campaign communication.* Mahwah, NJ: Lawrence Erlbaum, pp. 3–13.

Marcus, G. E., Neuman, W. R., & MacKuen, M. (2000). *Affective intelligence and political judgment.* Chicago: University of Chicago Press.

McClellan, S., Albiniak, P., & Higgins, J. M. (2000, November 20). Networks on the defensive. *Broadcasting & Cable, 130*(48), 8–9.

McCombs, M. E., Shaw, D. L., & Weaver, D. L. (1997). *Communication and democracy: Exploring the intellectual frontiers in agenda-setting theory.* Mahwah, NJ: Lawrence Erlbaum.

Miles, M., Sharp, K., Del Castillo, E., Maple, T., & Kaid, L. L. (2009). *Two different Sarah Palins: Comparing presentations of CNN and Fox documentaries.* Unpublished paper, University of Florida.

Nagourney, A., & Zeleny, J. (2008, August 23). Obama chooses Biden as running mate. *The New York Times.* Retrieved June 30, 2010, from www.nytimes.com/2008/08/24/us/politics/24biden.html?_r=1.

Niemi, R. G., Craig, S. C., & Mattei, F. (1991). Measuring internal political efficacy in the 1988 National Election Study. *The American Political Science Review, 85*(4),1407–1413.

Niven, D. (2001). Bias in the news: Partisanship and negativity in media coverage of presidents George Bush and Bill Clinton. *The Harvard International Journal of Press/Politics. 6*(3), 31–46.

Pew Research Center Project for Excellence in Journalism (2008). *Winning the media campaign.* Retrieved June 30, 2010, from http://journalism.org/node/13310.

Rasmussen Reports. (2008). *Palin power: fresh face now more popular than Obama, McCain.* Retrieved June 30, 2010, from: www.rasmussenreports.com/public_content/politics/elections/election_2008/2008_presidential_election/palin_power_fresh_face_now_more_popular_than_obama_mccain.

Robinson, M. J. (1976). Public affairs television and the growth of political malaise: The case of the "Selling of the Pentagon." *American Political Science Review, 70,* 409–432.

Rosenstone, S. J., Kinder, D. R., Miller, W. E., & the National Election Studies. (1997). *American national election study 1996: Pre- and post-election survey* [Computer file]. Ann Arbor, MI: University of Michigan, Center for Political Studies (Producer) and Inter-university Consortium for Political and Social Research (Distributor).

Schmitt, K. M., Gunther, A. C., & Liebhart, J. L. (2004). Why partisans see mass media as biased. *Communication Research, 31*(6), 623–641.

Silcock, B. W. (2008). The battle of ideological images: CNN vs. FOX in the visual framing of the invasion of Iraq. *Electronic News, 2*(3), 153–176.

Stalnaker, D. (2008, October 23). *Similarities found in media coverage of Palin and Ferraro, according to study by UA communication students.* Retrieved June 30, 2010, from: http://uanews.ua.edu/anews2008/oct08/media102308.htm.

Sweetser, K. D., & Kaid, L. L. (2008). Stealth soapboxes: Political information efficacy, cynicism, and uses of celebrity Weblogs among readers. *New Media & Society, 10*(1), 73–98.

Tsfati, Y., & Cohen, J. (2005). Democratic consequences of hostile media perceptions: The case of Gaza settlers. *Harvard International Journal of Press/Politics, 10*(4), 28–51.

Vallone, R. P., Ross, L., & Lepper, M. R. (1985). The hostile media phenomenon: Biased perception and perceptions of media bias in coverage of the Beirut massacre. *Journal of Personality and Social Psychology, 49*(3), 577–585.

Vavreck. L. (2000). How does it all "turnout"? Exposure to attack advertising, campaign interest, and participation in American presidential elections. In L. M. Bartels & L. Vavreck (Eds.), *Campaign reform: Insights and evidence.* Ann Arbor, MI: University of Michigan Press, pp. 79–105.

Wattenberg, M. P., & Brians, C. L. (1999). Negative campaign advertising: Demobilizer or mobilizer? *American Political Science Review, 93,* 891–899.

Weatherly, J. N., Petros, T. V., Christopherson, K. M., & Haugen, E. N. (2007). Perceptions of political bias in the headlines of two major news organizations. *The Harvard International Journal of Press/Politics. 12*(2), 91–104.

Wirth, W. (2006). Involvement. In J. Bryant, & P. Vorderer (Eds.), *Psychology of entertainment.* Mahwah, NJ: Erlbaum, pp. 199–214.

Chapter 12

International Coverage of the U.S. Presidential Campaign

Obamamania Around the World

David L. Painter, Eisa Al Nashmi, Jesper Strömbäck, Juliana Fernandes, Zheng Xiang, and Ji Young Kim

Spurred by the development and diffusion of communication technologies, the 2008 U.S. presidential campaign sparked enormous interest not only in the United States, but also around the world (Grove, 2008; Pew Research Center, 2008a, 2008b). In response to this unprecedented demand for information about U.S. politics, foreign news organizations were involved in the campaign in numbers and from countries heretofore unseen (AFP, 2008). Indeed, a chorus of international voices was added to the context of the campaign, and many heralded Democrat Barack Obama's election as the 44th president of the United States as well. For example, Pew Research Center (2008b) noted after the election: "Across much of the world, newspapers welcomed Obama's victory. To many, the election showcased what they like about the United States—the vitality of its democracy and the notion of America as a land of opportunity."

Although the United States has long been the most frequently mentioned country in foreign press coverage of international news (Katzenstein & Keohane, 2007; Wu, 2004), the intensity of this worldwide attention reached extraordinary heights with the 2008 presidential campaign. Specifically, the focus on Barack Obama was so great it lent credence to Republican John McCain's attack ad labeling him "the biggest celebrity in the world." As an African-American with a multi-cultural heritage, Obama's nomination by the Democratic Party captured the imagination of many abroad, but his relative lack of experience and unconventional upbringing caused many at home to take pause.

Regardless of whether people welcomed the election outcome or not, their opinions and attitudes are generally informed by the news media. The fact that most people rely on the media for information about politics and society (Bennett & Entman, 2001; Nimmo & Combs, 1983) is even more evident with respect to international affairs. This influential role invites examination of how the international media covered the 2008 U.S. presidential election. Specifically, the goal is to see whether the coverage and the framing was biased in favor of Obama over McCain; and to analyze some of the systemic influences on international press coverage of U.S. politics. Examining international press coverage of the 2008 U.S. presidential campaign may also facilitate the development of frameworks for the analysis of media sources from around the world.

Against this background, this chapter investigates how the print media in a diverse set of countries covered the 2008 U.S. presidential election. This study includes Brazil, China, Egypt, Saudi Arabia, South Korea and the United Kingdom, representing a wide geographic dispersion of countries with different levels of political and media systemic freedoms.

The Pictures in Our Heads

As theorized by Lippmann (1997), what people think they know about the world beyond their everyday experience is largely based on information transmitted by the media. This reliance on media coverage is particularly evident when focusing on international affairs, where direct experiences are rare. Knowledge of modern politics can thus be described as mediated, where perceptions of reality are oftentimes more important than reality per se (Nimmo & Combs, 1983).

How the media cover domestic and international affairs is of immense import. As noted by Shanahan and Nisbet (2007, p. 8), "public opinion is a synthesis of information and predisposition." Because news media provide the information, opinion formation cannot be understood without taking mediated information into consideration. Additionally, while predispositions may exert influence on public opinion, there is also evidence that information effects may counterbalance such biases in a significant manner, especially in terms of international relations (Holsti, 2008).

Considering the importance of the media's coverage for opinion formation, it is only natural that research on how the media cover political events and processes, especially election campaigns, has a long history. Although there is a great deal of research on national media coverage of national elections (Strömbäck & Kaid, 2008a), there is virtually no research on the media coverage of elections in other countries (but see Golan & Wanta, 2003). The main exception is research on how European and U.S. media cover elections to the European Parliament (de Vreese, Banducci, Semetko, & Boomgaarden, 2006; Holtz-Bacha, 2005; Kaid, 2008; Maier & Maier, 2008).

Improving our understanding of international media coverage of U.S. presidential elections is important to inform both communication studies and public diplomacy (Entman, 2008; Shanahan & Nisbet, 2007). Such research may also cast new light on the interaction between the tone toward presidential candidates and news framing. Further, research in this area could improve our understanding of the extent to which levels of political and media systemic freedoms influence international media coverage. Thus, development of a framework for analysis of international media coverage of U.S. politics may be advanced.

As there is virtually no research on international media coverage of U.S. presidential elections, there is no established framework that can be readily applied to such analysis. Nevertheless, research on national media coverage of national elections suggests that, in general, election news is shaped by an interaction between political systems, media systems, journalistic norms and values, electoral procedures, and how people orient themselves toward media and politics (Esser, 2008; Strömbäck & Kaid, 2008b; Zaller, 2001). Some of these factors can be assumed to be of less importance with respect to how international media cover U.S. presidential elections, whereas other factors can be assumed to be more significant. The latter include, for example, factors associated with foreign news reporting in general (van Ginneken, 1998); attitudes toward the U.S. (Shanahan & Nisbet, 2007); and how newsworthy events involving the U.S. are perceived around the world (Wu, 2004). With these considerations in mind, the next sections will outline the variables used in this study, suggest a framework for investigating international media coverage of U.S. presidential elections, and present our hypotheses and research questions.

Tone and Framing: How Did International Media Cover the Election?

The first question in this study is related to how international media covered the 2008 U.S. presidential election. While descriptive in nature, questions about how international media covered this election are both interesting in themselves and important for subsequent analyses of factors shaping such news coverage.

In this study, the main focus was on the tone and the framing of the coverage of the 2008 U.S. presidential election. With respect to tone, a distinction can be made between the overall tone toward the 2008 campaign and each of the presidential candidates, John McCain and Barack Obama. In all three cases, a distinction can be made between a positive, negative and neutral tone. Based on this level of analysis, the first research question is:

> RQ1:   What was the international media's tone toward the 2008 U.S. presidential election and the candidates John McCain and Barack Obama?

This analysis provided information on whether the international media coverage indeed was characterized by "Obamamania," as suggested by responses from many newspapers and people around the world (Pew Research Center, 2008a, 2008b).

Another important aspect of political news is how the media frame politics and political processes, events, and actors. Although framing still constitutes a somewhat "fractured paradigm" (Entman 1993; D'Angelo 2002), at its core, framing is concerned with how events, issues or social actors are organized in communicative messages and individuals' conceptualizations (de Vreese, 2003; Tankard, 2001).

One of the most common lines of framing analysis with respect to political and election news is contrasting the use of issue versus game or strategy frames (de Vreese & Semetko, 2002; Patterson, 1993; Strömbäck & Dimitrova, 2006). Not only has such research shown that the media in many countries display a strong tendency to frame politics as a strategic game or a horse race rather than as issue disputes or policy choices (Strömbäck & Kaid, 2008a), but also that exposure to news that frame politics as a strategic game can activate and increase political cynicism (Cappella & Jamieson, 1997; De Vreese & Elenbaas, 2008; Valentino, Beckmann & Buhr, 2001).

More important in this context is that the extent to which international media applied an issue frame or a strategic game frame when covering the presidential election can provide insights into whether people around the world were largely exposed to information about the issues at stake in the election or about the game, the horse race or the strategies used by the candidates. This question is also important because the frames used by the media might have impacted and therefore mediated the tone of the coverage. Thus, the second research question is:

RQ2:   How often was an issue frame as opposed to a strategic game frame dominant in international media coverage of the 2008 U.S. presidential election?

Toward a Framework for Analyzing International Media Coverage

The interaction and interdependencies of media coverage, media framing, systemic factors, and public opinion are complex and fluid (Entman, 2004; Hallin, 1986; McCombs, 2004). Most scholars agree, however, that both political and media systems are important for understanding how the media cover issues, events and processes—including, but not restricted to, domestic elections (Blumler & Gurevitch, 1995; Esser, 2008; Hallin & Mancini, 2004). Siebert, Peterson and Schramm (1956) focused on the levels of systemic freedom within a country in their seminal categorization of the worldwide press into four theoretical models: authoritarian, libertarian, social responsibility, and Soviet-totalitarian. While research on the media coverage of domestic elections has focused on systemic features such as level of media commercialism, electoral systems, political communication or political news cultures (Blumler & Gurevitch, 1995; Gurevitch & Blumler, 2004; Esser, 2008; Pfetsch, 2001, 2004; Strömbäck & Kaid, 2008b), when covering foreign news, other systemic factors might be more important.

Not least important might be the levels of media freedom and political freedom. Countries where political and media freedoms are strong may have a closer affinity with the U.S., but research has also shown the media in free countries tend to focus on the negative rather than the positive side of news because negativity and conflict are viewed as prominent criteria of newsworthiness. Moreover, the current trend toward more interpretive news might further increase the amount of negativity in media coverage from free countries (Farnsworth & Lichter, 2007; O'Neill & Harcup, 2009; McNair, 2000; Patterson, 1993). This would suggest that the overall tone toward the U.S. presidential campaign, as well as toward the candidates, would be more negative in countries where political and press freedoms are strong than in countries where these freedoms are weak.

In either case, the level of political and media freedom could also have an impact on the degree to which the coverage of the U.S. presidential campaign and of McCain and Obama was neutral. In countries where political and media freedoms are restricted, the media usually follow the political line of the regime, whereas in democratic countries, the media are free to choose how they cover current events. Thus, in the former case, the media might tend to cover the election and the candidates in a neutral manner so that their coverage does not interfere with the political and diplomatic relationships between the U.S. and the countries at hand, while in the latter case, the media do not have to consider the political and diplomatic implications of their coverage. Combined with the notion of increasing media negativity and the rise of interpretive journalism, this would suggest that there is an inverse relationship between the degree to which the countries are characterized by political and media freedom, and the degree to which the media in these countries covered the U.S. presidential campaign and the candidates in a neutral manner.

Due to the lack of research on factors shaping the news coverage of elections in other countries, and the counteracting tendencies suggesting different directions between the degree of political and media freedom on the one hand and the share of neutral stories and tone of the coverage of the 2008 U.S. presidential election on the other, asking research questions are deemed more appropriate than posing hypotheses. In this context, the third research question asks:

RQ3:   What are the differences in the coverage of the 2008 U.S. presidential election between countries with different levels of political and media freedom?

Further, it might also be the case that the frames used by international media when covering the election affected the tone of the coverage. This is particularly true with respect to the tone toward the candidates. More specifically, if the results show that the tone was more positive toward Obama than McCain, but only in stories where a strategic game frame as opposed to an issue frame was dominant, this would suggest that the coverage and its tone was driven more by the electoral horse race than by candidate or policy preferences. If, on the other hand, the results suggest that the tone was more positive toward Obama than McCain regardless of which frame was dominant, the tone may have been driven by a preference for Obama over McCain and their respective policies. Thus, it is important to control for the dominant frame of the news stories before drawing conclusions about the tone of the media's coverage.

Considering that Obama won the election and was ahead in the polls through most of the campaign, it can be expected that the tone toward Obama was more positive and toward McCain more negative in stories where a strategic game frame was dominant. Hence, two hypotheses are asserted for testing:

> H1:   *The tone toward Obama will be more positive in stories where a strategic game frame as opposed to an issue frame was dominant.*

> H2:   *The tone toward McCain will be more negative in stories where a strategic game frame as opposed to an issue frame was dominant.*

Methodology and Data

To test the above hypotheses and answer the research questions, this study used a quantitative content analysis of two newspapers in each of the selected countries. To enable an analysis of the influence of political and media freedoms on coverage of U.S. politics, a diverse set of six countries from around the world was selected—Brazil, China, Egypt, Saudi Arabia, South Korea, and the United Kingdom. Using classifications from Freedom House (2008), these countries were grouped according to levels of political and media freedom as shown in Table 12.1.

In order to capture coverage unique to each country, native language stories from the selected newspapers were gathered. The first criterion for newspaper selection was circulation, and the second criterion was searchable archives through Lexis/Nexis, Factiva, Newsbank, or the individual paper's Web site. All stories were retrieved through online media and were designated as appearing in the print copy as well. The newspapers and number of stories from each is shown in Table 12.1.

The content analysis covers the period from the start of the Democratic convention (August 25) to Election Day (November 4). Within this time span, two constructed weeks were randomly selected.[1] The keywords used

Table 12.1 Countries, Political System, Media System, and Newspapers Analyzed

Country	Political system	Media system	Newspaper name	n
Brazil	Free	Partly free	O Estado de S. Paulo	51
			Folha de S. Paulo	46
China	Not free	Not free	People's Daily	20
			Guangming Ribao	30
Egypt	Not free	Partly free	Alahram	44
			Algomhuria	11
Saudi Arabia	Not free	Not free	Alriyadh	24
			Al-Jazira	23
South Korea	Free	Free	Chosun Ilbo	42
			Joongang Ilbo	33
U.K.	Free	Free	The Telegraph	39
			The Guardian	44
Total				407

in the search process were the names of the main candidates (Obama, McCain, Biden, and Palin). As the two constructed weeks yielded less than 20 stories from the Chinese papers, it was determined that all stories appearing within the time span of the study would be used. A test showed that there were no significant differences between the coverage during the constructed weeks and the entire sample of stories from the Chinese press. The unit of analysis was each individual news article, which was coded for dominant frame, overall tone toward the 2008 U.S. presidential election, and tone toward the candidates.

With respect to the framing of the election, drawing upon earlier research (Kaid, 2004; Strömbäck & Dimitrova, 2006), all news articles were coded for the dominance of the following frames: issue/policy, game/horse race, scandal, media, human interest, conflict, and personalization frames. In this chapter we will, however, only make use of those articles where either an issue frame or a strategic game frame was dominant. An issue frame would be an article organized around an existing or possible policy or issue proposed for consideration. A strategic game frame is an article organized around discussions of polls, campaign tactics, winning or losing, fundraising efforts, campaign plans, or analysis and interpretations of locations in which candidates are devoting resources.

Regarding the tone, the stories were coded for the overall tone toward the 2008 U.S. presidential election as well as toward the candidates. The tone toward the election as such was coded as positive when the manifest content was presented in an overwhelmingly favorable manner. If a story criticized an electoral issue or the election itself in an overwhelmingly negative manner, the story was coded as negative. If there was no specific point of view in terms of favorable or unfavorable, a balanced point of view, or any difficulty in making a determination, the tone was coded as neutral. Particular attention was paid to the headline and quoted material within the story. The same coding principles were followed when coding the tone toward Obama and McCain.

The units of analysis were coded by the six researchers. Intercoder reliability was determined by randomly selecting 20 stories from *The Guardian*, which were coded by all coders. There were no significant disagreement on any specific categories, and intercoder reliability using Holsti's formula (North, Holsti, Zaninovich, & Zinnes, 1963) was 89 percent.

Results: Obamamania Around the World?

Our first research question inquired about: (a) the overall tone of the news stories toward the 2008 U.S. presidential election and (b) the tone toward the two major presidential candidates. As Table 12.2 shows, the international media's coverage of the 2008 U.S. presidential election was overwhelmingly neutral across countries. Sixty-six percent of the stories were neutral, 18 percent were positive, and 16 percent had an overall negative tone. Although the overall tone toward the U.S. election was largely neutral, significant differences were observed across countries ($\chi^2 = 65.17$, $df = 10$, $p < .001$). Among all six countries, the U.K. (24 percent), South Korea (23 percent) and Brazil (20 percent) had the greatest share of negative stories, whereas China (34 percent) had the greatest share of positive stories, followed by South Korea (29 percent) and Brazil (24 percent).

Similarly, more than half of the stories mentioning Obama and McCain also had a neutral slant across countries. However, there were some distinct differences between the two candidates with respect to the distribution of positive and negative stories. As Table 12.2 shows, of the stories mentioning Obama, 39 percent were positive; while for McCain, only 7 percent of all stories were positive. Conversely, 37 percent of the stories mentioning McCain were negative; while for Obama, only 10 percent were negative. Thus, overall Obama received much more positive coverage than McCain in the foreign press.

However, there were some differences across countries in regard to tone toward the candidates. As Figure 12.1 shows, Saudi Arabia (49 percent), Egypt (45 percent), and South Korea (43 percent) presented the most positive coverage of Obama, while the coverage of Obama in the U.K. (64 percent), China (62 percent) and Brazil (49 percent) was mostly neutral. Regarding the coverage of McCain, the tone was more negative in Saudi Arabia (49 percent), South Korea (48 percent), and Egypt (45 percent) than in China (35 percent), the U.K. (28 percent), and Brazil (27 percent).

Table 12.2 Overall Tone Toward the 2008 U.S. Presidential Election and the Candidates (%*)

Tone	Saudi Arabia (n = 47)	Egypt (n = 55)	China (n =50)	Brazil (n = 97)	U.K. (n = 83)	South Korea (n = 75)	All (n = 407)	χ^2	df	p
Positive	2	0	34	24	12	29	18	65.17	10	.001
Neutral	94	93	60	57	64	48	66			
Negative	4	7	6	20	24	23	16			

Tone	Saudi Arabia (n = 39)	Egypt (n = 42)	China (n =37)	Brazil (n = 71)	U.K. (n = 50)	South Korea (n = 42)	All** (n = 281)	χ^2	df	p
Barack Obama								19.81	10	.031
Positive	49	45	25	37	30	43	39			
Neutral	49	48	62	49	64	36	51			
Negative	3	7	3	14	6	21	10			

Tone	Saudi Arabia (n = 39)	Egypt (n = 42)	China (n =37)	Brazil (n = 71)	U.K. (n = 50)	South Korea (n = 42)	All** (n = 281)	χ^2	df	p
John McCain								20.41	10	.026
Positive	5	2	5	14	2	12	7			
Neutral	46	52	59	59	70	40	55			
Negative	49	45	35	27	28	48	37			

Notes: *Percentages were rounded off to the nearest integer to facilitate illustration. **Sample size is based only on positive, neutral, and negative. N/A was excluded from the analysis.

Panel A

Tone toward candidate Barack Obama (%)

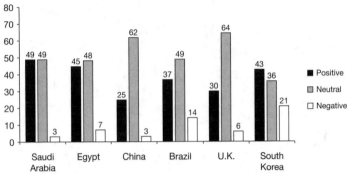

Panel B

Tone toward candidate John McCain (%)

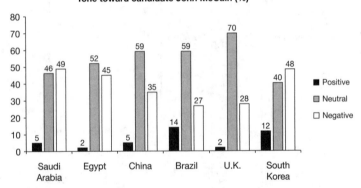

Figure 12.1 Coverage tone toward candidates Barack Obama and John McCain (%*).
Note: *Percentages were rounded off to the nearest integer to facilitate illustration.

Our second research question asked how often an issue frame was dominant compared to a strategic game frame. As shown in Table 12.3, the strategic game frame was dominant in 67 percent of the stories across countries while the issue frame was dominant in 32 percent of the stories. The results also show that there were significant differences in the distribution of dominant frames across countries ($\chi^2 = 38.01$, $df = 5$, $p < .001$).

Our third research question focused on the differences in coverage between the countries based on levels of political and media freedom. First, in regard to the importance of political freedom, Table 12.4 shows that

Table 12.3 Dominant Frame of 2008 U.S. Presidential Election by International Media (%*)

Frame	Saudi Arabia (n = 23)	Egypt (n = 55)	China (n =50)	Brazil (n = 97)	U.K. (n = 83)	South Korea (n = 75)	All (n = 246)	χ^2	df	p
Game	48	46	46	68	86	89	67	38.01	5	.000
Issue	52	54	54	32	13	11	32			

Note: *Percentages were rounded off to the nearest integer to facilitate illustration.

Table 12.4 Dominant Frame and Tone by Political System (%*)

Dominant Frame	Free[a] (n = 149)	Not free[b] (n = 97)	All** (n = 246)	χ^2 32.45	df 1	p .001
Game	81	46	67			
Issue	19	57	32			
Overall Tone	Free[a] (n = 255)	Not free[b] (n = 152)	All (n = 407)	χ^2 29.93	df 2	p .001
Positive	22	12	18			
Neutral	56	82	66			
Negative	22	6	16			
Tone Barack Obama	Free[a] (n = 163)	Not free[b] (n = 118)	All*** (n = 281)	χ^2 7.03	df 2	p .030
Positive	36	43	39			
Neutral	50	52	51			
Negative	13	4	10			
Tone John McCain	Free[a] (n = 163)	Not free[b] (n = 118)	All*** (n = 281)	χ^2 5.29	df 2	p .071
Positive	10	4	7			
Neutral	58	52	55			
Negative	32	43	37			

Notes: *Percentages were rounded off to the nearest integer to facilitate illustration. **Sample size is based only on the top two dominant frames. ***Sample size is based only on positive, neutral, and negative. N/A was excluded from the analysis.

a Free countries include U.K., South Korea, and Brazil. b Not free countries include China, Saudi Arabia, and Egypt.

there were significant differences between politically free and not free countries in the overall tone toward the 2008 U.S. presidential election. Eighty-two percent of the stories in politically not free countries were neutral, compared to 56 percent in free countries. The amount of positive and negative stories in politically free countries was quite balanced: 22 percent were positive and 22 percent were negative. In politically not free countries, only 6 percent of the news stories had a negative slant whereas 12 percent had a positive slant.

Table 12.4 also shows that the tone toward Obama was more positive (politically free: 36 percent; not free: 43 percent) whereas the tone toward McCain was more negative in both groups of countries (politically free: 32 percent; not free: 43 percent). Although the tone was more positive toward Obama and negative toward McCain, the majority of stories in both politically free and not free countries were neutral (51 percent and 55 percent).

With respect to the dominance of an issue versus strategic game frame, the results show that there were significant differences between politically free and not free countries (χ^2 = 29.93, df = 2, p < .001). As Table 12.4 shows, among politically free countries, the strategic game frame was dominant in 81 percent of the stories; while in countries not free politically, it was dominant in 46 percent of the stories. In contrast, the issue frame was dominant in 19 percent of the stories in politically free countries, while 54 percent of the stories in politically not free countries focused on issues or policy alternatives.

Overall, these results suggest that the level of political freedom had an impact on the coverage of the 2008 U.S. presidential election. The next step was to investigate whether the same held true with respect to levels of media freedom.

When the countries under study were grouped according to levels of media freedom, a significant difference was observed in the overall tone toward the election (χ^2 = 17.92, df = 4, p < .001). As Table 12.5 shows, although the coverage was mostly neutral across the three groups, there were distinct differences between countries with free, partly free, and not free media systems. In countries with free media, 20 percent of the stories were positive and 23 percent were negative; in countries with partly free media, 15 percent of the stories were positive and 15 percent were negative. This finding suggests free and partly free countries were quite balanced regarding the tone toward the election. However, in countries with a not free media, 19 percent of the stories were positive and 5 percent were negative.

As for the tone toward the individual candidates, no significant differences were found across countries with free, partly free, and not free media systems (see Table 12.5). The tone toward Obama and McCain, respectively, was very similar across all three groups of countries.

Table 12.5 Dominant Frame and Tone by Media System (%*)

Dominant frame	Free[a] (n = 102)	Partly free[b] (n = 82)	Not free[c] (n = 62)	All** (n = 246)	χ^2	df	p
Game	87	58	47	67	33.27	2	.001
Issue	13	41	32	32			
Overall tone	Free[a] (n = 158)	Partly free[b] (n = 152)	Not free[b] (n = 97)	All (n = 407)	χ^2 17.92	df 4	p .001
Positive	20	15	19	18			
Neutral	56	70	76	66			
Negative	23	15	5	16			
Tone Barack Obama	Free[a] (n = 92)	Partly free[b] (n = 113)	Not free[b] (n = 76)	All*** (n = 281)	χ^2 6.22	df 4	p .183
Positive	36	40	42	39			
Neutral	51	49	55	51			
Negative	13	11	3	10			
Tone John McCain	Free[a] (n = 92)	Partly free[b] (n = 113)	Not free[b] (n = 76)	All*** (n = 281)	χ^2 2.42	df 4	p .659
Positive	7	10	5	7			
Neutral	56	57	53	55			
Negative	37	34	42	37			

Notes: *Percentages were rounded off to the nearest integer to facilitate illustration. **Sample size is based only on the top two dominant frames. ***Sample size is based only on positive, neutral, and negative. N/A was excluded from the analysis.

a Free press includes the U.K. and South Korea. b Partly free press includes Brazil and Egypt. c Not free press includes China and Saudi Arabia.

However, the results also show that in all three groups, the tone toward Obama was more positive and toward McCain more negative. Regardless of the level of media freedom, the foreign press had a more positive and less negative tone toward Obama and a less positive, but more negative tone toward McCain. In this respect, the results suggest Obamamania was clearly evident in the press from around the world. Interestingly, the tone toward Obama was the most positive and the tone toward McCain was the most negative in countries with media systems classified as not free.

The level of media freedom also had an impact on the framing of the U.S. presidential election (χ^2 = 33.27, df = 2, p < .001). In countries with free media, the strategic game frame was dominant in 87 percent of the stories, while the issue frame was dominant in only 13 percent. Countries with partly free or not free media presented coverage that was more balanced between the strategic game and issue frames. In partly free countries, the strategic game frame was dominant in 58 percent of the stories, while 41 percent were organized around issues. In not free countries, the strategic game frame was dominant in 47 percent of the stories, while the issue frame was dominant in 53 percent of the coverage. Thus, increasing media freedom appears to be associated with increasing use of a strategic game frame as opposed to an issue frame by the foreign press.

In addition to levels of political and media systemic freedoms affecting the tone of press coverage, this investigation also inquired into whether the framing of the election stories had an impact on the tone toward Obama and McCain. To investigate this question, we proposed two hypotheses. The first hypothesis predicted the tone toward Obama would be more positive in strategic game framed stories than in issue framed stories. As shown in Table 12.6, this hypothesis is supported (χ^2 = 17.828, df = 2, p < .001). Whereas 54 percent of the stories in which a strategic game frame dominated had a positive tone toward Obama, less than half of that amount, or 23 percent of the stories in which an issue frame was dominant, had a positive tone. About 66 percent of news stories where an issue frame was dominant were neutral toward Obama, in contrast to about 39 percent of the stories where a game frame was dominant.

Conversely, the second hypothesis predicted the tone toward McCain would be more negative in stories where a strategic game frame was dominant than in stories where an issue frame was dominant. Results in Table 12.6 show that the tone toward McCain was significantly more negative in stories where a strategic game frame (48 percent) was dominant than in stories where an issue frame was dominant (31 percent). About 64 percent of issue framed news stories were neutral toward McCain, as compared with 44 percent in the stories where a strategic game frame was dominant (see Table 12.6). Hence, the second hypothesis is also supported (χ^2 = 7.096, df = 2, p < .05).

Table 12.6 Tone Toward Candidates in Dominantly Issue- vs. Game-Framed
Stories (%*)

	Issue frame	Game frame	χ^2	df	p
Tone** Barack Obama					
Positive	23	54			
Neutral	66	39	17.828	2	.000
Negative	11	7			
Tone** John McCain					
Positive	4	8			
Neutral	64	44	7.096	2	.029
Negative	31	48			

Notes: *Percentages were rounded off to the nearest integer to facilitate illustration. **Sample size is based only on positive, neutral, and negative. N/A was excluded from the analysis.

Discussion and Conclusion

Although story framing as well as levels of political and media systemic freedoms did have a significant influence on international media's coverage of the 2008 U.S. presidential election, the consistently more positive tone in stories about Obama relative to McCain cannot be overstated. The graphic representation of this coverage presented in Figure 12.1 also dramatically illustrates the phenomenon of Obamamania around the world. Just one week before the November 4 U.S. election, for example, the headline of a Gallup report proclaimed that "World Citizens Prefer Obama to McCain by More Than 3-to-1" (Gallup, 2008). These international opinion polls, conducted in 70 countries from May to September 2008, revealed that with respect to public opinion, Obamamania appeared to be prevalent around the world.

The results of this study show that not only public opinion, but also the press coverage, around the world was both more positive and less negative toward Obama than the tone toward McCain. This finding holds true for all six countries included in this study: Brazil, China, Egypt, Saudi Arabia, South Korea, and the U.K. Thus, it also holds true regardless of the degree of political freedom or media freedom. Although there were other differences across media from the different countries, on a general level, Obama certainly received more favorable coverage in the press from free as well as partly free and not free countries.

While Obamamania appears to have been prevalent around the world, it should also be noted that the majority of news stories in most countries had a neutral tone toward both candidates as well as the U.S. election as such. Overall, 66 percent of the stories had a neutral tone toward the U.S. election, 51 percent toward Obama, and 55 percent toward McCain.

Interestingly, the tone toward the U.S. election was more neutral in countries without free political and media systems than in countries with free political and media systems. With respect to the tone toward the candidates, there were no significant differences in the share of neutral stories depending on levels of political and media freedom.

While the positive tone toward Obama and the negative tone toward McCain suggest the international media were affected by (and contributed to) Obamamania, and by a desire for change from the policies associated with the Bush presidency and the Republican Party, there is more to the story.

With respect to the framing of the 2008 U.S. presidential election, the results show that a strategic game frame was dominant in 67 percent and an issue frame in 32 percent of the stories. Thus, the coverage of elections in other countries appear to be as influenced by the tendency to frame politics as a strategic game as the coverage of domestic elections (Strömbäck & Kaid, 2008b; Patterson, 1993; Cappella & Jamieson, 1997). What is equally important, however, is that this contributed to the positive tone toward Obama and negative tone toward McCain. For example, whereas the tone toward Obama was positive in 23 percent of the issue framed stories, it was positive in twice as many, or 54 percent, of the stories in which a strategic game frame was dominant.

These results suggest that the positive tone toward Obama and negative tone toward McCain to a significant degree was driven by the media's focus on the electoral horse race and the campaigns strategies. As Obama was ahead in the polls for most of the time during the campaign, it is only natural that the tone toward him was more positive in stories that focused on the electoral horse race and the way the campaigns were run. From this perspective it was not policy or candidate preferences that spurred the positive tone in the coverage of Obama and the negative tone toward McCain, but rather the media's great appetite for stories about the electoral horse race—which, in turn, is spurred by media commercialism (Patterson, 2000).

Interestingly, the results also show that the media in countries with free media systems used the strategic game frame significantly more often (87 percent) than the media in countries with partly (58 percent) or not free (47 percent) media systems, and in countries with free (81 percent) as opposed to not free (46 percent) political systems. Thus, while "game is the name of the frame" (Nord & Strömbäck, 2006) for the media in democratic countries, the media in authoritarian systems provided more coverage of policy issues. They were also more neutral in terms of overall tone.

Thus, from a normative perspective, a case could actually be made that the countries with the least freedoms in some respects provided a better, in terms of more issue-oriented and neutral, coverage of the 2008 U.S.

presidential election than countries with more political and media freedoms. When focusing on the tone and framing of the coverage, the less free the country, the more likely were the media to provide coverage of the issues beyond campaign strategies and poll results. Conversely, the media from freer countries were less neutral and more negative overall in their stories about this election.

Normative considerations notwithstanding, the results show that political and media systems—or, more specifically, degrees of political and media freedom—do matter (Hallin & Mancini, 2004) for the media's framing of politics and the tone of the coverage. These results fit nicely with research on political news coverage in democratic countries, with the important qualification that the systemic characteristics investigated here differ from those in research on political news coverage in democratic countries (Strömbäck & Kaid, 2008a). These results also suggest the importance of expanding comparative research on the framing of election news to include countries beyond established democracies.

Not surprising, however, was the finding that the tone of foreign media coverage was more positive toward Obama and more negative toward McCain. When considered in the context of rising anti-Americanism, spurred by negativity toward the Bush administration and U.S. involvement in Iraq, evaluations of Republican candidates—perhaps especially those with a military background—would intuitively be negative.

Moreover, the symbolic significance of an African-American becoming the leader of the free world could also reasonably be predicted to dominate most any other influences. From such a perspective, the symbolic significance of Obama's candidacy and strong prospects of winning the election both eclipsed traditional news values and transcended other systemic or policy-related values. It was a story simply too good not to tell for media that are always searching for good stories that can capture people's attention and imagination, and that do not want to challenge and risk alienating public opinion.

Note

1. The dates selected were: August 25; September 4, 7, 12, 19, 21, 29, and 30; October 9, 15, 18, 25, and 29; and November 4, 2008.

References

AFP (2008, November 3). Army of global journalists descends on US for election. Agence Presse—France. Retrieved June 30, 2010, from: http://afp.google.com/article/AleqM5hi-dGU5SsaQHPKYmwOBEL9wXpAWQ.

Bennett, W. L., & Entman, R. (Eds.) (2001). *Mediated politics: Communication in the future of democracy*. Cambridge: Cambridge University Press.

Blumler, J. G., & Gurevitch, M. (1995). *The crisis of public communication.* London: Routledge.

Cappella, J. N., & Jamieson, K. H. (1997). *Spiral of cynicism: The press and the public good.* New York: Oxford University Press.

D'Angelo, P. (2002). News framing as a multiparadigmatic research program: A response to Entman. *Journal of Communication, 52*(4), 870–888.

de Vreese, C. H. (2003). *Framing Europe. Television news and European integration.* Amsterdam: Aksant.

de Vreese, C. H., & Elenbaas, M. (2008). Media in the game of politics: Effects of strategic metacoverage on political cynicism. *International Journal of Press/Politics, 13*(3), 285–309.

de Vreese, C. H., & Semetko, H. A. (2002). Cynical and engaged. Strategic campaign coverage, public opinion, and mobilization in a referendum. *Communication Research, 29*(6), 615–641.

de Vreese, C. H., Banducci, S. A., Semetko, H. A., & Boomgaarden, H. G. (2006). The news coverage of the 2004 European parliamentary election campaign in 25 countries. *European Union Politics, 7*(4), 477–504.

Entman, R. M. (1993). Framing: Toward clarification of a fractured paradigm. *Journal of Communication, 43*(4), 51–58.

Entman, R. M. (2004). *Projections of power. Framing news, public opinion, and U.S. foreign policy.* Chicago: University of Chicago Press.

Entman, R. M. (2008). Theorizing mediated public diplomacy: The U.S. case. *The International Journal of Press/Politics, 13*(2), 87–102.

Esser, F. (2008). Dimensions of political news cultures: Sound bite and image bite news in France, Germany, Great Britain, and the United States. *The International Journal of Press/Politics, 13*(4), 401–428.

Farnsworth, S. J., & Lichter, S. R. (2007). *The nightly news nightmare. Television's coverage of U.S. presidential elections, 1988–2004.* Lanham, MD: Rowman & Littlefield.

Freedom House (2008). *Freedom in the world & freedom of the press.* Retrieved April 20, 2009 from: www.freedomhouse.org/template.cfm?page=15

Gallup Report (2008). *World citizens prefer Obama to McCain by more than 3-to-1.* Retrieved April 20, 2008 from: www.gallup.com/poll/111253/World-Citizens-Prefer-Obama-McCain-More-Than-3to1.aspx.

Golan, G., & Wanta, W. (2003). International elections on US network news. An examination of factors affecting newsworthiness. *Gazette: The International Journal for Communication Studies, 65*(1), 25–39.

Grove (2008). *YouTube: The flattening of politics. Nieman Reports.* Retrieved June 16, 2008 from: www.nieman.harvard.edu/reportsitem.aspx?id=100019.

Gurevitch, M., & Blumler, J. G. (2004). State of the art of comparative political communication research: Poised for maturity? In F. Esser & B. Pfetsch (Eds.), *Comparing political communication: Theories, cases, challenges.* New York: Cambridge University Press, pp. 325–344.

Hallin, D. C. (1986). *The "Uncensored War"—the media and Vietnam.* Berkeley, CA: University of California Press.

Hallin, D. C., & Mancini, P. (2004). *Comparing media systems. Three models of media and politics.* New York: Cambridge University Press.

Holsti (2008). *To see ourselves as others see us: How publics abroad view the United States after 9/11*. Ann Arbor, MI: The University of Michigan Press.

Holtz-Bacha, C. (Ed.) (2005). *Europawahl 2004: Massenmedien im Europawahlkampf* (European vote 2004: The mass media in the European election campaign). Wiesbaden, Germany: VS-Verlag, pp. 228–251.

Kaid, L. L. (2004). *2004 TV news code book*. Gainsville, FL: College of Journalism and Communications, University of Florida.

Kaid, L. L. (Ed.) (2008). *The EU expansion. communicating shared sovereignty in the parliamentary elections*. New York: Peter Lang.

Katzenstein, P. J., Keohane, R. O. (2007). *Anti-Americanisms in world politics*. Ithaca, NY: Cornell University Press.

Lippmann, W. (1997). *Public opinion*. New York: Free Press.

Maier, M., & Maier, J. (2008). News coverage of EU parliamentary elections. In J. Strömbäck & L. L. Kaid (Eds.), *Handbook of election news coverage around the world*. New York: Routledge, pp. 403–420.

McCombs, M. (2004). *Setting the agenda: The mass media and public opinion*. Cambridge, UK: Polity Press.

McNair, B. (2000). *Journalism and democracy. An evaluation of the political public sphere*. London: Routledge.

Nimmo, D., & Combs, J. E. (1983). *Mediated political realities*. New York: Longman.

Nord, L. W., & Strömbäck, J. (2006). Game is the name of the frame: European parliamentary elections in Swedish media 1996–2004. In M. Maier & J. Tenscher (Eds.), *Campaigning in Europe—Campaigning for Europe*. Berlin: LIT Verlag, pp. 191–205.

North, R. C., Holsti, O., Zaninovich, M. G., & Zinnes, D. A. (1963). *Content analysis: A handbook with applications for the study of international crisis*. Evanston, IL: Northwestern University Press.

O'Neill, D., & Harcup, T. (2009). News values and selectivity. In K. Wahl-Jorgensen & T. Hanitzsch (Eds), *Handbook of journalism studies*. New York: Routledge, pp. 161–174.

Patterson, T. E. (1993). *Out of order*. New York: Vintage.

Patterson, T. E. (2000). The United States: News in a free-market society. In R. Gunther & A. Mughan (Eds.), *Democracy and the media. A comparative perspective*. New York: Cambridge University Press, pp. 241–265.

Pew Research Center (2008a). *Election weekend news interest hits 20-year high. Top events of campaign 2008*. Retrieved March 25, 2009 from http://pewresearch.org/pubs/1025/election-news-interest.

Pew Research Center (2008b). *Global media celebrate Obama victory—but cautious too. A changed view of American democracy*. Retrieved March 25, 2009 from http://pewresearch.org/pubs/1033/global-media-celebrate-obama-victory-but-cautious-too.

Pfetsch, B. (2001). Political communication culture in the United States and Germany. *The Harvard International Journal of Press/Politics*, 6(1), 46–67.

Pfetsch, B. (2004). From political culture to political communications culture: A theoretical approach to comparative analysis. In F. Esser & B. Pfetsch (Eds.), *Comparing political communication. Cases, theories, challenges*. New York: Cambridge University Press, pp. 344–366.

Shanahan, J., & Nisbet, E. (2007). *The communication of anti-Americanism: Media influence and anti-American sentiment.* Report Presented to the United States Institute for Peace. Retrieved March 31, 2009 from www.comm.cornell.edu/msrg/USIPreport.pdf.

Siebert, F., Peterson, T., & Schramm, W. (1956). *Four theories of the press.* Urbana, IL: University of Illinois Press.

Strömbäck, J., & Dimitrova, D. V. (2006). Political and media systems matter. A comparison of election news coverage in Sweden and the United States. *The Harvard International Journal of Press/Politics, 11*(4), 131–147.

Strömbäck, J., & Kaid, L. L. (Eds.) (2008a). *The handbook of election news coverage around the world.* New York: Routledge.

Strömbäck, J., & Kaid, L. L. (2008b). A framework for comparing election news coverage around the world. In J. Strömbäck & L. L. Kaid (Eds.), *Handbook of election news coverage around the world.* New York: Routledge, pp. 1–18.

Tankard, J. W. Jr. (2001). The empirical approach to the study of media framing. In S. D. Reese, O. H. Gandy Jr., & A. E. Grant (Eds.), *Framing public life. Perspectives on media and our understanding of the social world.* Mahwah, NJ: Lawrence Erlbaum Associates, pp. 95–106.

Valentino, N. A., Beckmann, M. N., & Buhr, T. A. (2001). A spiral of cynicism for some: The contingent effects of campaign news frames on participation and confidence in government. *Political Communication 18*(4), 347–367.

Van Ginneken, J. (1998). *Understanding global news. A critical introduction.* London: Sage.

Wu, H. D. (2004). The world's window to the world: An overview of 44 nations' international news coverage. In C. Patterson & A. Sreberny (Eds.), *International news in the twenty-first century.* New Barnet, UK: John Libbey Publishing, pp. 95–108.

Zaller, J. R. (2001). The rule of product substitution in presidential campaign news. In E. Katz & Y. Warshel (Eds.), *Election studies. What's their use?* Boulder, CO: Westview Press, pp. 247–269.

Index